A
NATIONAL
ACOUSTICS

A NATIONAL ACOUSTICS

MUSIC AND MASS PUBLICITY IN WEIMAR AND NAZI GERMANY

BRIAN CURRID

University of Minnesota Press
Minneapolis • London

Portions of chapter 2 were previously published as "'A Song Goes Round the World': The German *Schlager* as an Organ of Experience," *Popular Music* 19 (2000): 147–80. Reprinted with permission.

Published by the University of Minnesota Press
111 Third Avenue South, Suite 290
Minneapolis, MN 55401-2520
http://www.upress.umn.edu

Library of Congress Cataloging-in-Publication Data

Currid, Brian.
 A national acoustics : music and mass publicity in Weimar and Nazi Germany / Brian Currid.
  p. cm.
 Includes bibliographical references (p.) and index.
 ISBN-13: 978-0-8166-4041-6 (hc)
 ISBN-10: 0-8166-4041-6 (hc : alk. paper)
 ISBN-13: 978-0-8166-4042-3 (pb)
 ISBN-10: 0-8166-4042-4 (pb : alk. paper)
 1. Music and state—Germany—History—20th century. 2. National socialism and music—Germany—Weimar (Thuringia). 3. Mass media and public opinion—Germany. I. Title.
 ML3917.G3C87 2006
 780.943'09043—dc22
                                        2006001059

The University of Minnesota is an equal-opportunity educator and employer.

Für Wilhelm

Der Augenblick der Wahrheit, wenn im
Spiegel das Feindbild auftaucht.

The moment of truth: when the face of
the enemy appears in the mirror.

—Heiner Müller

Contents

Acknowledgments

This book has been a long time in the making. Needless to say, many have helped bring it to completion.

I would like to thank the following for financial support during the research and completion of this project: German Academic Exchange Service, Chicago Humanities Institute (Franke Institute), the Department of Music and the Division of the Humanities at the University of Chicago, the Social Sciences Research Council (Berlin Program), and the Deutsche Forschungsgemeinschaft.

Many audiences and colleagues have been subjected to parts of this book at various stages. I thank them all for patient listening and insights. Thanks to Romana Swallisch in Berlin and Mary Carbine, along with the staff of the University of Chicago Film Studies Center, for help with video stills. I am grateful to the archives and archivists that played a role in this project, in particular Herr Tau at the Freie Universität Berlin and the Berliner Philharmoniker Archives.

My appreciation goes especially to Richard Morrison at the University of Minnesota Press, for his interest in this project and for his patience.

Finally, I thank my friends in Berlin and Chicago and my family in the United States and in Germany for productive distraction and input.

Introduction

---•---

German Sounds, Sounding German, and the Acoustics of Publicity

M any of us have a distinct impression of the *sound* of Nazi Germany. This is not surprising: Germans and non-Germans alike repeatedly encounter "remixes" of a very particular German sound imagined to be typical of the period. This is particularly evident in the constant flow of mass cultural products, ranging from blockbusters distributed for cinematic release to made-for-TV fiction films and popular documentaries, which in ever-increasing numbers re-narrativize and re-stage some version of "the Nazi years." These overlapping genres of media hyperproduction guarantee and require not only the continuing circulation of certain now well-known or easily imagined visual aspects of the period—most prominently the image of marching blonde youths or hysterical mass rallies. Despite perhaps subtle changes in accent and volume over the last half-century, these remixes have provided a fairly consistent and distinct impression of the acoustic culture of Germany of the 1930s and '40s, featuring the roar of a crowd, the echo of a goose step, the sound of march music, and the resonant voice of Adolf Hitler.

Not only do certain traces of this acoustic culture circulate very widely, they also remain astonishingly resonant. This is in part because these sonic traces never stand alone; as part of the sound track of "The Twentieth Century," they are situated in a specific acoustic that amplifies their volume, simplifying the meaning of history by mapping the history of acoustic culture onto political history in a system

1

of direct correspondences. In this structure, the sound of Nazi Germany is contrasted to another set of acoustic metonyms, which together resonate as "The Weimar Years"—Adolf Hitler and march music on the one hand, Marlene Dietrich (or more likely, Liza Minnelli) and jazzy, decadent chansons on the other.[1] Still other sounds also frame the Nazi period: postwar swing and rock and roll. The sound of liberation is the sound of American popular music, a sound that, for these well-trained ears, is absolutely distinct from sounds that might have come before—while the "sound" of the Nazi period serves to metonymize mass evil, the sound of American popular music serves as a stand-in for a culture of thrillingly liberated, but doomed decadence. Finally, the *telos* of acoustic liberation sounds the beginning of Germany's arrival in "the West," the final departure from the *Sonderweg* to join the triumphant establishment of liberal capitalist democracy.

Now it should come as no surprise that scholarly work on Nazi popular culture, not to mention the immense historiography of the political realities of the Nazi period, has repeatedly called various aspects of this picture into question. Although the vast literature on the period can scarcely be summarized in this introduction, a few cursory comments can help to give a sense of general landscape. On the political level, so-called "functionalist" approaches to the operation of the Nazi state allowed for a far more differentiated picture of political effectivity to emerge, even if "intentionalist" accounts—or worse still, studies of German national character—continue to attract a large amount of public attention.[2] While "functionalist" accounts have placed both the Weimar Republic and Nazi Germany firmly within the context of European industrial society, intentionalist accounts tend to focus on individual or party agency. While both schools of research have made their contributions to the field, it seems clear that the functionalist literature offers richer forms of explanation, in that it not only refuses ahistorical generalization, but also develops a sophisticated image of the complexities and contradictions that characterized the period.

In terms of popular culture, particularly in the area of film studies, but also in wider realms of consumer culture and everyday life, many scholars have repeatedly engaged in dislodging elements of a mythified, Hollywood notion of life in Nazi Germany. At least since the 1980s, social and cultural historians like Detlev Peukert and in particular the students of *Alltagsgeschichte* have focused on the development of consumer culture and "modernization" in Germany of the

1930s, and have painted a highly differentiated picture of the continuing practice and formation of mass consumption under the Nazi regime.[3] Finally, film scholars like Stephen Lowry, Eric Rentschler, and Karsten Witte have also done a great deal to dismantle the postwar stereotypical notion of Nazi film, which focused intensely on "propaganda films" to the neglect of the large body of cinematic production in the period (Lowry 1991; Rentschler 1996; Witte 1995).[4] In particular, Linda Schulte-Sasse (1996), whose own work also begins with a critical reading of Hollywood's version of Nazism, has done a great deal to reframe the debate by refocusing the discussion of "ideology." Many of these authors have even questioned the standard periodization itself, which implicitly insists on the automatic validity of 1933 as a historiographical marker of dramatic social and cultural change. Instead, they have shifted the focus towards longer-term transformations which, although certainly not unaffected by the "political" in a narrow sense, are not completely assimilated to its realm of effectivity.[5]

In the arena of music as well, long-held paradigms for understanding the history of the period have been in flux in recent years. Not only Pamela Potter's (1998) recent excellent study of musicology in the Third Reich, but also Michael Kater's (1997, 1992) work on both musical life in general and jazz in particular have challenged clichéd notions of music's role in the Weimar and Nazi periods. However, despite these concerted efforts to complicate and refine our understanding of music's role in this historical period in particular and in the social more generally, in the area of popular music simplistic narratives tend to quickly reemerge, and the popular narrative is implicitly reinvoked in a more subtle way. Even the mythical *"Jazzverbot,"* which many scholars have pointed out never actually took place in a nationwide sense, continues to be reinvoked in current debate. Somehow, popular music after 1933 is cast as more provincial, less sexy, and generally more boring.[6] Even works that powerfully disrupt clichéd notions of popular culture in this period tend to lose their critical edge when music enters the picture. Schulte-Sasse's insightful study provides a particularly instructive example in her aforementioned reading of one of the worst recent examples of Hollywood's Nazi industry, *Swing Kids*. She persuasively argues: "Such Hollywood representations, which have become a form of memory as we collectively imagine 'Nazi Germany,' do more than just deprive the era of its contradictions and heterogeneity; they rob it of the one thing even the most murderous state cannot live without; its normalcy" (1996, 4). But when she moves from the level of narrative and visual analysis, Schulte-Sasse's very subtle reading of the narrative and visual similarities between *Swing Kids* and various films of the Nazi period is marred by the following symptomatic footnote: "*Swing Kids* does have one redeeming feature: its focus on unharnessed music (the 'racially suspect' jazz that Nazism objected to) and sensual, frenetic dance as a form of bodily liberation from the lockstep synchronized by the Nazi drill machine" (2). Read in contrast to Schulte-Sasse's finessed interpretations of the pleasures of the visual, this statement is surprising indeed, and suggests the dominance of certain profoundly ideological conceptions of pleasure and embodiment in theorizing the role of musical practice. This book will suggest that the notion that jazz, swing, or indeed any other form of popular musical practice should or could be "unharnessed" is precisely what needs to be critiqued.

This is by no means only a problem in discussing music and the Nazi period: indeed, the highly stubborn ahistorical linkage of particular forms of musical practice to "freedom" evidenced here turns out to be a central problem in cultural studies in general. As the often misread and not seldom misquoted jazz essays of Adorno suggest, it is precisely the association of freedom with mass cultural products that is the center of the problem; the strangely circular allergic reactions to Adorno's admittedly somewhat uninformed reading of jazz, readings with which we are all too familiar, miss the point entirely: the insistence on the inherently "liberatory" quality of jazz is precisely the domestication of a supposed wildness that Adorno refers to. That "jazz"—itself a notoriously vague term—in certain contexts might be mobilized in an oppositional sense is one issue; there were indeed moments of opposition that formed around an articulation to musical practice during the Nazi period. But at the same time, as this book will show, any number of musical films from the period quite clearly suggest that this dialect of musical "expression" was in some ways just as at home in fascist mass culture as it is (or was) in "our own." Musical mass culture in fascism, similar to that in other capitalist countries, will prove not to be a zone of repression in any simple sense, but instead a locus of the configuration and reconfiguration of different audiences, subjectivities, and modes of production and consumption that are articulated in quite specific ways to ideologies of collectivity

1

---•---

Radio, Mass Publicity, and National Fantasy

Radio in Germany began as an hour-long, multimedia, multisite event on the evening of October 29, 1923. Made up of a series of instrumental solos and vocal numbers, this "radio concert" mixed recordings and moments of live performance. Not only did this performance, broadcast from the Vox House at Postdamer Platz, mix musical and technological media, it also was a truly crossover event in terms of musical style. Primarily made up of short pieces from the so-called classical tradition, including chamber music, chamber arrangements of symphonic works, and operatic arias, the hour also included one "gypsy song," and ended with a recording of a military band playing the German national anthem.[1]

While we should not over-interpret this event as somehow automatically indicative of the later course of broadcasting in Germany, it does illustrate the central place of music in the history of German broadcasting even in its infancy. At the same time, the shifts during this hour among genres and musical media—and the concomitant shifts in radio's musical address that these entailed—encapsulate the complexity of radio music as a not always harmonious ensemble of social practices. The multiple practices of reception with which this radio concert was in fact heard signal the indeterminacy of the radio audience in its early years. We can only speculate here, but it seems likely that not only the select audience equipped by the radio station could receive this broadcast, but that the large, scattered population of radio amateurs was also certainly to some extent in tune with the happenings in Berlin. This indeterminacy was further complicated by the multiple forms of sociomusical address engaged by the repertoire featured in this first radio broadcast. Shifting between multiple registers of musical publicity and intimacy, from the operatic aria to the chamber duet, this first moment of radio broadcasting exemplifies the issues that confronted radio broadcasting in its early years, particularly when the broadcast was dedicated to some form of musical practice. Any facile reference to this event as a concert can only be considered more than misleading.

In the following years, musical broadcasting would continue to dominate radio programming; throughout the 1920s, despite some regional variation, purely musical broadcasting would make up around 50 percent of broadcast time at most German radio stations.[2] As time went on, the percentage of musical broadcasting would in general be characterized by a steady rise, so that during World War II, music took up more than 70 percent of airtime (Pohle 1955, 327; Drechsler 1988, 33). But despite the centrality of musical broadcasting, German radio history has tended to focus on other aspects of radio programming, attempting to explain the seeming special relationship between the course of German history in this period and the structure and practice of German radio broadcasting.[3] Considering its emergence at the beginning of what Detlev Peukert has termed the period of "deceptive stability" (1989, 193ff.), it is not surprising that radio broadcasting in the 1920s and '30s has primarily been discussed in relation to both the failure of the Weimar political system and the rise of the Nazi dictatorship. Radio, in this historiography, not only failed to establish the conditions for a more democratic mass public in the Weimar period; it also played a key role in leading the masses in ways that would later be directly mobilized by the Nazis in their rise to power. The history of Weimar radio thus becomes a lesson in "what went wrong." Indeed, the postwar history of West German broadcasting, in particular the way the relationship between the state, commercial interests, and political power has been negotiated, has had everything to do with various diagnoses of the nature of this process.

In this kind of history, the narrative of radio's entanglement with the political climaxes after 1933—after the so-called *Gleichschaltung*, or consolidation, of the radio—the power of the Nazis to manipulate public opinion had reached unimaginable heights seemingly overnight. Ansgar Diller's account of radio's importance in this period of German history, part of a five-volume standard work on the history of German radio, encapsulates the logic of this narrative at the very beginning of his book.

> Among the mass media press, film, and radio, the "eighth power" of the twentieth century [radio] let itself with the most ease be incorporated by the Nazis for their goals. Through radio the masses could be directly led and could receive National Socialist propaganda . . . [T]he techniques of these means of control . . . included hour long speeches of National Socialist party and state leaders, reports from *Reich* and *Gauparteitage*, state acts and exhibition openings. (1980, 9–10)[4]

While admitting that "concessions to distraction and relaxation" were also required, Diller's narrative focuses on the manifestly propagandistic, "political" nature of radio broadcasting in the early Nazi period, and takes as axiomatic radio's power to produce the desired effects in the minds of the German masses. This leads to the use of odd sources: it was indeed Goebbels who called the radio the "eighth power" of the modern world, echoing Napoleon's words on the press.[5] The fact that this radio history begins with this observation gives a sense of the extent to which this kind of account takes Goebbels's own "theory" of the medium and its effectivity in a very literal way as a starting point. This is symptomatic of a general trend in media studies on the Nazi period to take Nazi claims about the media and the use of the media as a point of departure.[6] In particular, this dominant narrative of radio's relationship to German politics in the 1930s—especially as influenced by the theory of totalitarianism—continues to cast the *Volksempfänger*, or People's Receiver, in a starring role.[7] This series of relatively inexpensive receivers was first introduced in 1934, at the height of the Nazis' *Gleichschaltung*, or consolidation of German radio. Like lesser known models such as the *Deutsche Kleinempfänger DKE* (The German Small Receiver), first on the market in 1938, these radios were manufactured without shortwave capacity and were somewhat weak in their receiving capabilities, making, it would seem, the reception of foreign stations difficult, if not impossible. The technical limitations of these models, combined with their relative affordability are usually described as the guarantors of a hypernational radio public during the Third Reich, which in turn is understood as a form of mass manipulation unique in modern history (Diller 1980, 304; Dahl 1978, 114–15).[8]

Of course, it is true that Weimar radio did not enable the establishment of any kind of democratic mass publicity. It is equally true that the National Socialists—not unlike other political agents in the West during the 1930s—soon learned to master the use of the radio for various forms of acoustic spectacle. All the same, as a historical mass account, these two observations and the broader historical narrative they underwrite are quite limited. This view of radio neglects to consider in historical or theoretical terms the question of radio's *mediacy:* its forms of address and its structures of publicity. As a result, radio appears as a transparent mode of communication which, due to its technological power, can fulfill many of communication's quasi-omnihistorical requirements, and thus allows for its easy manipulation.[9] It is perhaps a consequence of this blindness that the role of music, indeed the role of all "nonpolitical" or only marginally political broadcasting, has more or less been taken for granted, interpreted as a mere addition to the matters of true historical relevance. When the role of music in the radio of this period is approached at all, it is understood as simply another aspect of the well-oiled machinery of Nazi propaganda, only increasing the seeming automatic effectiveness of broadcasting as a means of mass control. Nanny Drechsler, for example, offers an account of radio music in the Third Reich typical of this approach to the subject.

> The entertainment function of the radio was fully exploited . . .
> by the national socialist government, especially by Goebbels, as a
> propaganda measure of the first degree; the preference of broad
> levels of listeners for folk and modern dance music was always
> respected . . . It was of the utmost importance to satisfy the need of
> the masses for entertainment and distraction from the everyday
> world of work, and later war. (1988, 124)

While Dreschler's approach is useful for its focus on the political nature of entertainment, her interpretation begins and ends with Goebbels and his attempts to mobilize entertainment for the purposes of ideological obfuscation and distraction. The "needs" of the masses for entertainment and distraction that were in turn satisfied by Goebbels's propaganda apparatus are taken for granted, and lack any sense of history or specificity. Drechsler claims, for example, that the radio allowed "indoctrination and entertainment to be extended into the private sphere without difficulty" (1988, 12) and continues in her study to link all aspects of radio in the Nazi period to form a "virtually closed system of communication" (47). We should at least be wary of the scope of these claims. Considering the way research in other areas of everyday life and state organization has shown the omnipresence of contradiction and contestation throughout the Nazi period, it seems most unlikely that such sweeping claims could hold true for a phenomenon as complex as radio, and in particular musical broadcasting.[10]

Admittedly, the Nazis' own representation of their media policies went a long way to support this transparent conception of radiophonic mediacy in the national scene: the *Volksempfänger* was a central icon in national fantasies of presence and temporality during the fascist period.[11] The central image of the advertising campaign for the VE 301, often reproduced in postwar accounts of the history of German radio, is emblazoned with the words: "All of Germany listens to the Führer with the *Volksempfänger!*" [*"Ganz Deutschland hört den Führer mit dem Volksempfänger!"*] (Figure 1). A mass of tiny people, extending infinitely in all four directions, surrounds a huge model of the radio.

The infinitude of national number (and the concomitant threat of the mass) is here organized by the centrality of the radio. This is a mass, in other words, with form, with direction: a *Volk*. This kind of icon of a sublime acoustics of national publicity was in turn mobilized quite effectively in various kinds of national narrative production, and was particularly effective in explicitly cross-media productions like the 1940 musical film *Wunschkonzert*. The title of this film refers to the Request Concert for the Armed Forces, a radio show that began broadcasting soon after the start of the war.[12] The "Request Concerts" in German radio had a longer history, beginning in 1936 as the "Request Concert for the *Winterhilfswerk*." This weekly program revolved (officially at least) around musical requests from listeners, from both the front and those left at home. In the film, the radio broadcast is used as a narrative device to structure the various tragic, romantic, and comic plot lines, suturing private experience to national event.

The penultimate scene of this very successful film is part of a longer depiction of a climactic broadcast, in which each of the various subplots ultimately finds its resolution. When seen in the context of this film's tremendous popularity, this scene seems at first glance to confirm the historiography's account of radio's special effectivity during the Nazi period and its focus on the special power of the *Volksempfänger*.[13]

Figure 1. "All of Germany Listens to the Führer with the People's Receiver."

Stuffed with icons of a particular German national symbolic, the cluster of social technologies that produces and polices national fantasy (see Figure 2),[14] the shots in this scene present the spectator with a series. Beginning at the site of the broadcast, we witness first the actual announcer of the *Request Concert*, Heinz Goedecke, miming maternal pathos as he recounts a song request from the mother of a fallen soldier. Then the conductor is shown fulfilling the mother's wish, followed by Wilhelm Strienze, . . . who sings the song in his smooth tenor voice.

Good night, Mother, good night.
You thought about me every hour.
You worried yourself and tortured yourself about your boy.

Every evening you sang a lullaby.
Good night, Mother, good night.
I caused you worry and grief.
You forgave me, you watched over me.
Good night, Mother, good night.[15]

In the attempt to orchestrate a set of spaces as simultaneously national and maternal, the next shot is an image familiar to the spectator from earlier in the film—the back of Hitler's head positioned in the center of the balcony. The subsequent shot of a radio in the mother's home establishes a syntactic link that mediates in a national register between the site of broadcast and the scene of reception. The rest of the scene extends the series of national icons deeper into the home: a Beethoven bust, the piano, the picture of the son as soldier, some flowers, and finally the mother. Articulating the link between the public and the private or, as Heinz Goedecke and Wilhelm Krug phrased it in the book accompanying the radio show:

> The mother sat at her radio receiver—there the announcer told the story . . . everything was quiet, at the radio station and everywhere

Figure 2. Wunschkonzert (1940), "Gute Nacht, Mutter" sequence.

where the announcer's story reached, now the mother knew: that
[her son] not only died *[gefallen]* for you, but for all.
"Good Night, Mother," the loudspeaker sang. (1941)

Scholars like Eric Rentschler and Linda Schulte-Sasse have increasingly focused on the complex nature of the role of the cinema during
the Nazi period, offering more nuanced readings of cinematic products
and interpretations of cinematic culture. As I suggested in the introduction, this represents a breakthrough not only in thinking about Nazi
cinema, but also in thinking of this period's media history more generally. But when we look at the prevalent readings of a film like *Wunschkonzert*, we still tend to find that even a "revisionist" approach to the
film history of the period does not carry over into a more critical account of the history of other forms of publicity.[16] Even Linda Schulte-
Sasse's interpretation, by far the most theoretically nuanced, is not free
of this kind of understandable shortcircuit, when she argues that in this
film, "art-kitsch-death-sacrifice-memory fuse with each other . . . to
nostalgically culminate in a vague notion of unity" (1996, 297). In the
same vein, Marc Silberman has commented "here, visual and narrational
conventions eliminate any possible contradiction in order to monopolize the mass public's imagination and to channel escapism into an explicitly ideological project" (1995, 67). And David Bathrick's (1997)
reading of the film, while admirably one of the very few descriptions
of the film that actually attempts to engage with the history of radio
and place the film in that context, is ultimately limited in that it seems
to rely on the almost total success of both the *Wunschkonzert* and Nazi
radio in the production of coherent, congruent, and effective forms of
acoustic fantasy. In other words, these readings of the film *Wunschkonzert* parallel the standard account of radio history in the Nazi period
by conceptualizing radio and the fictional, cinematic representation of
radio as unproblematically securing both character and spectator in
the fascist national scene. When turning to the acoustic side of Nazi
mass culture, it seems that the tendency to oversimplify remains strong,
even for scholars who carefully attempt to disengage the facile standard accounts of other areas of mass culture in the Nazi period.[17]

To be sure, these accounts of both the film and the broader history
of radio do partially illuminate how radio participated in what Walter
Benjamin saw as the fascist attempt to aestheticize the political (1977b,
169). During the transition from the Weimar Republic to Nazi rule,

the period between 1931 and 1933, the right-wing nationalist parties exhibited a remarkable interest in the radio and exerted a great deal of influence on radio practice.[18] In particular, the Nazi party was adept at manipulating the rules and regulations of radio broadcasting from the Weimar period (during which "political" broadcasting was forbidden) to use for its own ends.[19] During the Nazi period itself, the propaganda apparatus of the state certainly did focus its efforts on the radio as a powerful mode of implanting a collective fantasy of a sublime acoustics of the nation. When it came to radio, Nazi public relations insisted that its resonance across a nationally dispersed public was identical with a full, properly national collective affect. At the same time, Nazi officials did see the radio as central in their media plans: Especially during the early days of the Nazi regime, the party and the state regarded the rapid takeover of the radio as essential to the project of *Gleichschaltung*. Many of the representatives of the so-called *Systemrundfunk*, the Nazi term for the "liberal, Marxist, capitalist, Jewish" radio of the *Systemzeit*, i.e., the Weimar period, were quickly removed from their positions and arrested after the Nazis came to power.[20]

It is, however, one thing to recognize the Nazi *attempt* to produce and control the ideological, material conditions of the sonic experience of national belonging, or the acoustics of a nationalized publicity. It is quite another to believe the Nazis' own claims about the total success of their acoustic engineering, to accept the claim of the *Volksempfänger* advertisement that "all of Germany listened to the *Führer*." To return to the *Volksempfänger* itself, this centerpiece of National Socialist radio policy was subject to simple forms of technical failure. While it might seem banal to focus on these "merely" technical problems of radio practice, the dominant trend in historiography relies on a healthy foundation of technological determinism to justify its claims about the kind of national publicity radio represented. The overpowering commonplace assertion of the omnipresence of the radio and Hitler's voice in the Nazi period in fact reflects more Hollywood's imagination of what Nazi Germany was like than the reality of 1930s life. Even *The Reports from the Empire*, the enormous body of information collected by the Security Service (*Sicherheitsdienst*, or *SD*) and distributed among various parts of the Nazi bureaucracy, document that the entire class of small receivers often failed to pick up German stations. Even more damaging, this 1940 report points out that many foreign stations were readily available on these receivers.

> It is said that for a long while, one has hardly been able to receive
> any German stations with the small radio receivers; at the same time,
> one can hear foreign radio stations on German airwaves uninterrupted
> and somewhat loudly. It is often noted, that after the close of the 10
> o'clock news, many foreign radio stations break through on the
> German airwaves. (Boberach 1984, 1692)[21]

But even if the fantasy of a plugged-in nation was in many ways tech-
nically unfeasible, the difficulties of the technological determinism that
underwrites the centrality of the *Volksempfänger* in accounts of Nazi
propaganda's success lie elsewhere. Not only do we need to interrogate the technical feasibility of the *Volksempfänger* claim: Did all of
Germany really listen to the Führer? Could all of Germany listen? We
also need to consider what and how this kind of claim signified in the
historical context of early radio practice in Germany. In what sense
was "all of Germany" an available mode of address for a radio practice? How was radio understood to produce this address, and how might
we analyze the history of its development? In other words, what did
listening in the context of radio as a new mode of mass publicity en-
tail? The various phenomena involved in the complex of practices
which we label "radio" are indeed given coherence in this kind of narrative through a lens of technological determinism; here, the power
of the medium—its use seemingly self-evident—is guaranteed by the
power of the technology. This kind of argument ignores the fact that the
social does not merely structure a medium at the level of use, deciding
whether it is "on" or "off," but rather determines its function as a set
of contingent social arrangements. Radio is no more simple a cultural
practice than the cinema, and needs to be understood as a complex
apparatus dependent on multiple psychic, social, and technological elements for its operation. In order to begin to untangle some of these
problems, we need to investigate the relationship between those historically new forms of social practice and experience engaged by the technology of radio and forms of imagining national belonging in Germany.
 In order to rethink this history, I will focus on the very aspect of
German radio that the standard account takes for granted: the constitution of the radio public, particularly in the various forms of acoustic
culture which adhered to the radio, and in particular, musical broadcasting. My discussion will be organized in a loose sense chronologically,
looking first at the ways these issues played out during the Weimar

Republic, and then looking at the ways these issues continued to plague the constitution of a national radio audience even during the "Third Reich." Ending my discussion of this period of radio history with a return to my analysis of *Wunschkonzert*, I will illustrate how even in those modes of national fantasy that seem most coherently structured and tightly articulated, the tensions within the radio as a national form and the forms of incongruence and incommensurability that inhered between radio's new form of mass publicity and German national fantasy continued to haunt the production of a national acoustics. I will reexamine these problems by focusing on two inseparable aspects of the nature of the radio audience: this chapter will attempt to relocate the empirical manifestation of the audience in social practice,[22] while at the same time examining the function of the radio audience as a site of ideological production. Indeed, the shifting tensions between the empirical and normative aspects of the radio audience—and mass cultural audiences more generally—will dominate this investigation as a whole.

"And who was everybody?": Radio Public(s), National Public in the Weimar Years

In its early years, radio was plagued by a fundamental crisis in intelligibility. Bertolt Brecht already remarked on this problem in 1932, writing in his well-known essay on "Radio as an Apparatus of Communication" that "the public did not wait for the radio, but rather the radio waited for the public" (1967). Brecht continued to specify this problem as one of address: "Suddenly it was possible to tell everybody everything, but one had, if one thought about it, nothing to say. And who was everybody?" Although Brecht's remark is routinely cited in almost all histories of radio broadcasting in Germany, the implications of his observation have not truly been explored to a sufficient extent. The problem Brecht described manifested itself in a number of different ways. First, the empirical nature of the radio audience, its content and form, presented a puzzle both to radio commentators and to administrators. Second, the question of the public function of radio in relation both to the state as understood in the liberal capitalist framework and the culture industries—affirmative, critical, or somehow independent—was seen as an unresolved area of confusion and struggle. Radio's relationship to its public(s) was therefore at least as complicated and contingent as film scholars have argued the relationship of the cinema to modes of spectatorship (Hansen 1991, 23). Radio began with a definitional conflict that encompassed both the nature of radio's address and the place of the listener. Who would be able to broadcast? Who was responsible for broadcasting? What would be broadcast and to whom? What *is* broadcasting? Each of these questions was the subject of conflict and/or debate.[23]

Indeed, it is instructive to remember the potential multiple-directionality of radio as a technology of sound mediation. While Brecht called in 1932 for the democratization of access to radio technology as promising utopic possibilities for social transformation, the years between 1918 and 1924 were more or less anarchic in terms of the use of the technology. At the very beginning of radio broadcasting, *Bastlerei* (radio hamming) was one of the primary modes of using the new technology. Amateur radio hams (in the familial stereotype of the period, fathers and sons) who explored the airwaves on simple receivers they had built themselves, formed a subculture that stood outside the officially sanctioned mode of listening that would soon find favor. In 1923, there were tens of thousands of so-called *Funkbastler* in Germany, who for the most part had learned to build their own receivers as radio technicians in World War I; at the time there were only 1,300 state-sanctioned receivers (Pohle 1955, 25). The radio operators saw the reception of radio programs as a sport and demanded the introduction of the so-called American model of radio: the legal recognition of a relatively unregulated system of private reception and broadcasting of radio (26). The supposed passivity of the radio audience was thus far from a given. Unlike film and television, "passive" participation only slowly replaced the originally large group of so-called radio athletes *(Funksportler)* (Lerg 1965, 270).[24]

The active subculture of radio-amateurs soon was seen as a threat to the security of the state and the public order. Not only could these unlicensed receivers pick up "private" radio signals, there was also no simple regulatory mechanism that could be used to control the kinds of news that such a network might disperse. Already in the political turbulence of the postwar years, radio played an important part: during the revolution of 1918, private radio broadcasting played a key role in linking workers' and soldiers' councils (Räte) across the republic. The state had not forgotten the power of radio to organize alternative publics: Erich Zweigert, an interior ministry official, described the problem in the following terms.

The number of secret radio devices *[Funkanlagen]* is constantly increasing. The existence of such devices seriously endangers the security of the state and the public order, since they offer state-subverting circles *[staatsumstürzlerische Kreise]* the possibility to achieve a comprehensive secret news network *[Nachrichtennetz]*, that in dangerous cases could seriously endanger the implementation of measures of the constitutional government. (cited in Lerg 1965, 166)[25]

The more or less anarchic early phase of radio broadcasting came to an end when the legal status of radio broadcasting and reception was settled by a series of governmental decrees. These decrees were not only intended to secure the state's monopoly over broadcasting rights and put an end to uncontrolled broadcasting, they also sought to regulate the formation of listening publics across the airwaves. In part this was done to guarantee a financial basis for broadcasting: radio fees were introduced, and the perceived chaos of radio's culture of consumption began to transform into one of regulated, licensed listening.[26] Radio fees were instituted already before the first day of regular broadcasting, costing twenty-five Reichsmark.[27] But it was also intended to limit the kinds of potentially politicized radio publics that might form around the new technology: In July 1923, the government announced regulations concerning the type of radio receivers that could be manufactured and operated. Approved devices were stamped with the letters "RTV," standing for the *Reichstelegraphen-Verwaltung*, or Imperial Telegraph Administration, and were only to be capable of reception in the range between 250 and 700 MHz (Pohle 1955, 45). At the same time, the government required the users of these devices to acquire, for a fee, permission from the *Reichspost* to use the radio, the so-called loan *(Verleihung)* to the private user of the state's sole right over the airwaves *(Funkhoheit)* (45). By the time of the "Emergency Decree on Radio" *(Funknotverordnung)* of 1924, a basic framework for radio broadcasting and receiving had begun to take shape, a framework that arguably would continue to determine the formal structure of radio broadcasting well into the postwar period in Germany.[28] This emergency decree took effect on April 4, 1924, and stipulated not only the new fee of two Reichsmark per month for "radio-participants," but also allowed state officials broad powers to investigate the licensing of radio receivers. This decree went so far as to grant police and inspectors from the post office permission to search homes and other private spaces without a warrant in order to establish whether or not radio receivers were properly stamped and licensed.[29]

Although the attempt to control the subculture of radio amateurs by enforcing a transition from *Bastler* to listener was met with some passionate opposition,[30] it was ultimately successful in displacing the earlier model of radio sport and enforcing a "proper" distinction between public and private use of the airwaves. But this does not mean that the radio audience was easily assimilated into the state's production of a listening population of radio participants. Indeed, multiple apparatuses were involved in the production of various radio populations, and there was no guarantee for the dominance of any one form of address, nor was there any assurance that the audience would comply with regulations. This makes itself abundantly clear in the discursive production that circulated around the radio during the Weimar Republic. If the concerns of the very early days of radio broadcasting were focused largely on maintaining the state's control over broadcasting and reception, the problem that most concerned commentators as time went on was the nature of the growing mass of licensed (or unlicensed) listeners.[31] This concern was exacerbated by the fact that radio, in this early period, was listened to primarily with headphones (Halefeldt 1990, 52).[32] Seeming to collide with both literary and theatrical models of publicity, the mass of solitary radio listeners presented a puzzle: how was this new zone of social experience to be understood?

In 1927, the novelist Arnold Zweig wrote about the seemingly new mode of sociality introduced by the radio. Trying to grasp the nature of the audience, Zweig remarks that the aesthetics of radio are molded by a "web of laws which makes the audience a unity, that holds sway over every listener, and which creates a productive new kind of dissemination of aesthetic impressions as an intellectual *[geistig]* counterpart to the receiver." But while this first description seems to emphasize the determining aspects of radio technology for the construction of the audience, the certainty of this description quickly comes undone. In moving from an abstract aesthetics of the radio to a phenomenology of radio listening, the tone seems to become unnerved, as Zweig attempts to describe this new form of public by way of a comparison to older forms of public and different media contexts. "The radio audience has an almost ghostlike quality." Interesting here is the fact that the spectral figure is associated not so much with broadcasting itself, but the form of the radio audience.[33] Zweig sees the growth of radio as a form of disassociation from more familiar forms of public sphere, and the more "traditional" apparatuses of embodiment and disembodiment of their constitutive media structures.[34] The radio upsets that balance.

> It is . . . a huge number, but a huge number of entirely separate individuals or small groups. It lacks entirely the experience *(Erlebnis)* of the mass that gives the audience of the theater, concert, or public gathering their characteristic emotion element *[Gefühlsfaktor]*. (1927)

For Zweig, the combination of the never-before-imaginable sheer numbers of the mass audience, combined with isolated, individuated listening gives rise to number without coherence, without *"Gefühlsfaktor."* But his description continues to falter, mobilizing one final media comparison to make his point somewhat more intelligible.

> Of all the types of audience, the radio listeners amount to the greatest number, but they do not gain anything from this. [They remain] In agreement or rejection of the production broadcast to them as alone as the reader before his book, or like a group to whom something is read. The radio produced the paradox of the soundless listener . . . [T]he audience is a mass of the alone. (1927)[35]

This passage is in some ways representative of a more general concern about the quality of the mass inhabiting new forms of public culture in the Weimar period.[36] But Zweig's attempt to decipher *radio's* mass public in particular allows us to grasp some of the issues at stake in imagining this special "mass of the alone." The nervousness of this passage, evidenced by the excessive media metaphors he uses to make his point, makes clear that the imagined coherence of the radio was not only insecure; the new form of public that the radio required and produced is for Zweig something of an unfathomable contradiction. Characterized by both its unprecedented scale and its equally unprecedented dispersion, the audience is not an unproblematic unity that can be inserted easily into more traditional modes of imagining and structuring national space and time. Instead, radio is uncanny: it has a "ghostlike quality," and as such remains difficult for the author to describe.[37] Zweig's radio is corrosive of the intelligibility, meaning, and order of *both* public and private realms, and thus requires a fully new language to grasp its social effectivity.

This corrosive effect was not only due to the strange, individual quality of the headphoned mass; even after the use of headphones declined as the primary mode of radio reception, the status of radio as a form of publicity remained unclear. To make things worse, once particular solutions had been established on the basic questions of how radio listening was to be organized, the rapid expansion of the radio audience constantly required new strategies of discipline and incorporation to transform the mass of consumers into a collectivity of radio participants. Hans Flesch, a key figure in the development of Weimar radio and the first artistic director of the *Südwestdeutscher Rundfunkdienst* (Southwest German Radio, the Frankfurt radio station), commented early in the history of Weimar radio: "The explosive spread of the radio makes it difficult for the radio administrator, who sits on the point of observation, to grasp his audience" (Anonymous 1924, 84).[38]

> But when the great masses realized that for just a little money and the help of a small detector apparatus radio could provide them with excitement and joy, the make up of the audience changed entirely, and soon the workers and small employees made up the main portion of the listeners. But other classes (*Schichten*) also took part, and thus it soon seemed difficult to bring this huge mass under one hat in terms of taste. (Anonymous 1924, 85)[39]

This uneasy relationship between the expanding market of individuated listeners and the formation of an audience, a public, can also be traced in the symbolic strategies used to ameliorate this problem by envisioning the radio audience in the visual culture of the Weimar period. Figure 3 illustrates an attempt to standardize and serialize the "huge number" of the "unfathomable audience." Using iconic representations of personhood, it articulates the growth in radio listenership to a claim about the infinitude of *national* number. It is a graphic representation of the growth in *Rundfunkteilnehmer*, i.e. juridically sanctioned radio listeners ("participants") who paid their radio dues to the *Reichspost*.

Figure 3, from 1929, represents its listeners with ever-larger photographed faces of women wearing headphones. The female images focus our attention on the production of an unmediated pleasure as registered in the face: less a concentrated than a distracted subject, the women in these images are thoroughly evocative of the mass.[40] The women's faces appear without bodies, offering a new form of emphatically modern personhood not located in any specific geographic locale other than the abstractly public national frame. The image visualizes an audience automatically plugged in to the pleasurable conflation of collectivity and individuality, and thereby celebrating the modern moment of radio. In contrast, other images of the period inserted radio into a more traditional form of reception, where the acoustics of publicity were adapted to more established notions of privacy.[41]

Indeed, the now seemingly obvious notion of a radio audience was far from stable. In particular, radio's status as a technology of publicity was called into question by its similarity to other services of the modern age: in what sense, for example, was there a distinction between radio and other new or increasingly prevalent consumer technologies of the period? If it is absurd to imagine the domestic consumers of electricity or water as an "audience," what was it about radio and the other sound technologies that made them constitutively different?[42] This problem of radio's function—as a type of publicity or a private consumer good—can be seen in a different way if we consider the legal question of the rights of the radio-participant to publicly play his or her radio, documented in an interesting way by an article published in the *Juristische Wochenschrift* in 1931. The author, Alexander Elster, attempts to adjudicate the question of radio's publicity at the site of reception in order to solve the question of radio dues.

> Whether the receiver of the broadcast is allowed the reproduction of that which is broadcast to a third person through loudspeakers,

Figure 3. "Five Years of German Listener Numbers."

because the original broadcast permit includes this, and that it is just as if the doors in a concert hall were opened, is a controversial question. (1866)[43]

Elster here attempts to settle whether or not the public playing of a radio program constitutes a second reproduction (*Wiedergabe*) ontologically independent and thus juridically distinct from the primary act of broadcasting. Elster saw the issue as revolving around the difference between the public and the private sphere, a distinction that he found not difficult to make. But of course, the entire legal apparatus that Elster brings to bear on this question indicates precisely how difficult it is to uphold this fundamental legal distinction between the public and the private in the context of radio. The strain of the analogy that Elster brings to bear on this legal question returns us directly to Zweig's concerns: Elster attempts to take the acoustics of traditional publicity (the resonant concert hall and its open or closed door) and force them onto the practice of radio broadcasting and listening. If Elster's often-convoluted legal prose shows us anything, it is that this comparison—in many ways indicative of an increasingly hegemonic model of radio broadcasting and listening—was by no means a secure one.

In order to distinguish the radio's "audience of the alone" from other consumer collectives, the radio audience had to be given recognizable contours, not only for radio commentators, but for users of the technology as well. Advertising would play a key role in this process, offering images of private/public participation in the radio audience which would transform radio broadcasting into a set of modes of interpellation. Various attempts to insert the radio into familiar mediations between publicity and privacy are depicted in Figures 4, 5, and 6. These images stage particular modes of listening: like the male image of radio participants, they seek to reintegrate the subject engendered by radio's new kind of mass publicity into familiar domestic or otherwise private surroundings. The first two of these images are advertisements for radio devices that appeared in the *Funkalmanach [Radio Almanac]*, the official catalogue for the annual national radio exhibition—in many ways the central ideological factory for producing the radio nation.[44]

We see first high society around the radio speaker, and second a domestic scene of three generations gathered in front of the home radio. In both images, the radio itself seems to become an active *participant* in the social scene. The first (Figure 4) seems to stage a sort of

Figure 4. Advertisement in Funkalmanach *for Grawo loudspeakers, sold at a Berlin radio store, 1924.*

Figure 5. Advertisement for *Siemens and Halske* radios in Funkalmanach, 1924.

conversation between the radio and the elegantly dressed high-society couple standing before the speaker. The second (Figure 5) also seems to stage a sort of cathexis toward technology, this time through the medium of childhood, as the little girl seems to present her doll as tribute to the much smaller loudspeaker.

The domestic scene of the second image, reinforced by the slippers on the feet of the centrally placed patriarch, makes radio a new form of family life within customary parameters. The first image, on the other hand, with its image of dancing couples in the background, seems to claim a new possibility for urban entertainment, while at the same time reinforcing standard class-models of high-bourgeois leisure.

The third image (Figure 6), an advertisement for a radio program guide, articulates the individuated modes of listening familiar from the graphic presentations of national number to particular moments of everyday life.

Here, the unimaginability of the mass is ameliorated by taking recourse to standardized forms of costume and masquerade, in which the radio headphones become, as it were, part and parcel of the forms of personality exhibited, a central feature in the overall physiognomy of the listener. Utilizing the symbolic codes of clothing, typeface, and bodily expression, each of the images presents a different way of experiencing the pleasures of radio, and in so doing intends to deflect attention from the standardization of the technology itself by celebrating the potential for individual choice in radio programming. From stock reports to fairy tales, each kind of radio broadcasting is here pictured to address a different kind of national subject—child, housewife, businessman, sports fan—with varying relationships to the economic, familial, and political apparatuses that constitute everyday life as the realm in which these subjects operate.

In attempting to provide an ideological scaffold for the construction of a radio audience, the national imaginary always played a key role. This is made abundantly clear not only in graphic representations of "German radio participants," but more importantly in the development of broadcast practice in Germany itself. National broadcasting was an early goal of the federal government in Berlin. As early as 1926, it was possible to mobilize a national audience by linking up the various German radio stations in a *"Reichssendung."* These hookups were used primarily for events of great national symbolic value, as in the case of the "liberation ceremonies" for Cologne, the first live,

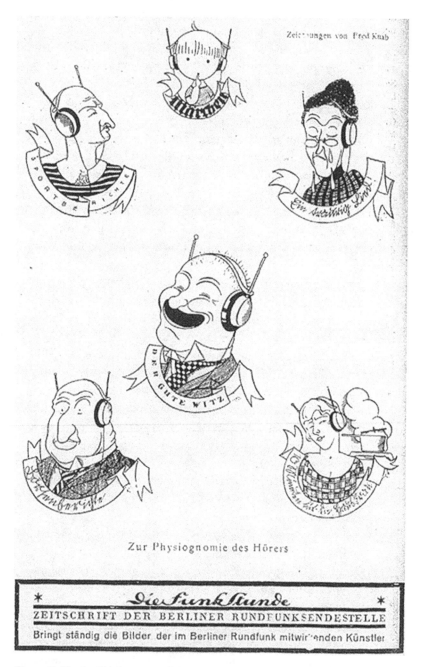

Figure 6. "On the Physiognomy of the Listener," advertisement for Die Funkstunde, 1925.

national broadcast in German radio history (Anonymous 1933)—meaning that the event was transmitted by all then-existing radio stations in Germany. But the ideological work reflected in the attempt to ideologically conceptualize and represent the radio audience in the early period of German radio was matched by disagreements within the state apparatus about how radio in Germany should be organized along national lines. First of all, the early period of radio was marked by bitter turf battles between different bureaucracies in the Reich administration, primarily between the Interior Ministry and the *Reichspost*. The differences between these two authorities resulted from a legal conflict of authority. Since the "Telegraphy Act" of 1892, the post office had been solely responsible for the exercise of the Reich's *Funkhoheit*, which in turn had been guaranteed to the Reich by the 1870 Constitution (Pohle 1955, 29). Seeing its role as a "neutral" administrator of this power, the post office came into direct conflict with the Interior Ministry, which saw radio as a matter not only of internal security, but more importantly as a kind of propaganda tool for the Reich (27).[45] These two claims, while primarily used to make political moves within the cabinet, also indicated two very different conceptions of radio: the Postal Service saw itself as responsible for governing the airwaves and distributing licenses to private corporations for broadcasting. The Interior Ministry, on the other hand, found this kind of use of the airwaves a danger to the security of the Weimar state, and wanted to use the airwaves for their own program. Additionally, the history of radio in Weimar was structured by a long-lasting struggle between the authorities in Berlin and those of the *Länder*.[46] While the Weimar constitution guaranteed the federal government control over the airwaves, it also delegated all cultural and police authority to the states. Since radio programming in particular seemed to combine aspects of each of these areas, it remained unclear how authority over this activity should be delegated. When, in 1925, for example, the federal government began to attempt to coordinate the radio stations in Germany under a system of what Hans Bredow, the government official most responsible for organizing radio broadcasts in Germany, termed "centralized decentralization," state governments complained that the reforms suggested by the federal government were only a means for Berlin to exploit what should merely be a technical monopoly in order to secure influence over the populations in each of the individual states in general political and cultural matters (Halefeldt 1997, 110–11). Like the conflict between the Reich authorities, these disagreements also indicate how difficult it was to achieve a national consensus of any kind on the nature of radio. At stake here was nothing other than the role of radio in the national symbolic and the *kind of national fantasy* that the radio was to implant.[47]

But national fantasy's claim on the new form of publicity that radio represented was not only disrupted by the politics of the state proper, it also emerged as a site for more local kinds of political consciousness and struggle. Radio, as an ideological sphere of social praxis, thus became a key battleground in very real and concrete battles for hegemony, both within and beyond the limits of the national form. Class, for example, which had long enjoyed a strong position as an alternate suture to the nation in the German context, continued beyond the early years of the Workers' Radio Movement to serve as one way in which the radio audience was intelligible and effective as a historical subject.[48] But these alternate sutures do not take place on the mere level of ideology, but in the material organization of radio listening as a practice of everyday life. This was evident not only in the writings of the Workers' Radio Movement, but can also be heard in the attempts of more bourgeois journalists in mainstream, left-liberal radio journals to negotiate the problem of class in their treatment of the radio audience. In 1927, Klaus Pringsheim, a conductor, critic, and composer, took issue with the musical program of the *Berliner Funk-Stunde*, the local radio in Berlin, in an article he wrote for *Rundfunk-Rundschau*.[49]

> More consideration—for the worker-listeners—consideration in the planning of the music program . . . Afternoons entertainment music, evenings serious music . . . thus roughly is the program format of the Berlin Radio Hour. It is the typical schedule of the leisured contemporary who always *has* time, always is rested; it is the daily musical dose for so-called "high society." "One" goes for tea in the afternoon, in the evening to the theater or to a concert, and at night there is dancing. Those who don't want to "go out" receive their musical five o'clock tea delivered to their home; at the usual night hour he has his dance band in the speaker . . . The [hours from 8 until 10 pm] must belong to the worker. That doesn't mean that at this time "worker's music" should be played, we don't expect any "proletarian solemnities *[Feierstunden]*" from the Radio Hour, but only that music should be played which is also suitable for the worker. (1927)[50]

Pringsheim sees the radio as not only delivering a certain good, but also providing a daily time frame for the routines of everyday life.[51] Unlike Zweig's more general concerns about the disintegration of communal life, Pringsheim attempts to describe the class specificities of the radio audience, in terms of both temporality and desire. In other words, Pringsheim sees the radio as potentially formative of new kinds of public, while simultaneously failing to properly provide the kinds of publicity that the "workers" (as opposed to the "proletariat") need. For our purposes, his concerns index a different kind of recurring disruption in the acoustics of national publicity. He attempts to mobilize radio in a reformist project of redistribution adequate to the organization of time intrinsic to the Fordist division of labor. One subset of the national collective is, in this logic, left at a temporal disadvantage when it comes to participation in the new technology. His account thereby seeks to obscure the direct connection between the excess of time enjoyed by the first listener and the lack of time suffered by the "worker-listener." Furthermore, the organization of the workday, an increasingly intimate regime of ideological discipline, is explicitly linked to an apparatus of cultural consumption, whereby leisure is to be "programmed."

Pringsheim obviously does not envision the radio as part of a constitutively antagonistic social arrangement—such an analysis would in fact have been unintelligible, if not syntactically impossible, in this discursive framework—but rather as a utopian possibility for a distributive *ethics* of publicity. While earlier utopian fantasies of an ideal "speech situation" through the double nature of radio technologies no longer find an echo here, Pringsheim sees radio's form of publicity in less participatory, and more distributive terms. Pringsheim's commentary can be seen as participating in the Weimar Republic's welfare-state.[52] This represents a kind of discourse petitioning to the welfare-state: radio's services are being improperly distributed and redistribution of its resources is required. The need for this kind of petition points out that radio—not unlike the state in more general terms—was the scene of contestation, although contestation limited by the terms of political consciousness that constituted and were constituted by the shifting forms of publicity in the Weimar Republic.

At the same time, despite Pringsheim's attempt to subsume class into a nonantagonistic collective, his text nevertheless betrays the ways class would continue to disrupt radio's national moment when he nervously rejects the possibility of so-called "proletarian solemnities," which (we are lead to believe) lie beyond the pale of acceptable modes of sociability. But an emphasis on social antagonism should not let us lose sight of the fact that multiple hegemonic strategies were in fact successful in organizing the ensemble of social practices known as radio and blocking out the intrusion of social antagonism.

The national address of the radio was the central way to ameliorate the continuing presence of social antagonism around and in broadcasting and reception. By the final year of the Weimar Republic in 1932, the struggle over radio took concrete political form in its reorganization. The "reform" of 1932 basically nationalized German radio, in the authoritarian climate of the Hindenburg's presidential "democracy" (established in 1931). The hegemonization of radio publics in national terms was not only secured by this "reform," but was also supported by the ideological apparatuses surrounding the acoustic staging of national unity. Furthermore, listening practice had, by the early 1930s, begun to sediment, allowing radio to become more easily linked to specifically national forms of address. If we consider for a moment President Hindenburg's role in the late Weimar Republic as a very specific icon of national publicity, this was eminently produced in the sphere of radio listening. The presence of his voice in national radio was but one element in the increasing mobilization of a media symbolic for mobilizing national fantasy. But here as well, the construction of a national hegemony around the figure of Hindenburg—or even Hindenburg's voice—was always overdetermined by multiple registers of antagonism, registers that would continue to emerge in new forms after 1933. While Brecht's 1932 question, "Who was everybody?" had by now found a number of hegemonic answers, these answers would continue to shift in the years ahead.

"I like to listen to fun music": Radio Publics in the Nazi Period

Hitler's radio debut came surprisingly late. Reading a "Call to the German People" from a microphone in front of the Berlin chancellery, his speech marked the opening of the election that would ultimately bring him to power in January 1933. While Goebbels would later in his published diaries praise the speech as "very effective and wonderful in its arguments," other opinions made themselves heard while they still could. Diller offers an interesting account of this in his history of Nazi radio policies:

> The social democratic radio magazine, *Volksfunk [People's Radio]* had an entirely different opinion. They called the speech low in content, and said that Hitler's voice sounded like it came from a barracks *[kasernenhofartig]*, was unpleasant, and didn't sound at all German. They reported that a telegram came from somewhere in Austria saying that even his own countrymen couldn't understand him. (1980, 61–62)[53]

Hitler's premiere might at first glance be read as a merely personal failure on his part to adapt to the national stage, to adjust the style and content of his voice and speech to an already established national acoustics. The claim that "even his own countrymen" could not understand him is revealing, not only for the confused place of Austrianness in relation to this national fantasy of the German People, but also because of the way this (mis)recognition revolves around the sound of a German voice. Presumably, the commentator here is pointing out the unintelligibility of Hitler's accent mediated through the radio. The eruption of radical difference and nonidentity in the guise of incomprehension not only in the space of the broader nation, but projected back technologically into the space of the *Heimat*, points toward the kinds of ruptures we should look for in the staging of national fantasy in National Socialist radio. In other words, this fragmentary evidence indicates not Hitler's personal failure or any simple lack in the quality of technology, but rather represents a moment when the disturbances and "dead spots" in the national acoustics reveal themselves.

For the historian looking back at this period, it is essential to allow for the possibility that this moment was less the exception and more the rule. The dominant trend in the historiography, as I have suggested, has tended to do the very opposite; but considering the prehistory of radio in Weimar, there is no reason we should imagine that the radio became magically hypereffective overnight in 1933. The use of radio in the Nazi period to produce a national acoustics was, like radio in Weimar, not by any means an unending success story of ever-increasing control and fluency in producing and directing the desires of an always already existing national audience. The issues that "tortured" the broadcasters at the beginning of radio were in many ways even more striking during the Nazi period. Indeed, the nationalization of radio in 1932 and the radicalization of radio policy in 1933 had exacerbated the problem of national address. In 1934, one "theoretical" periodical about radio, *Rufer und Hörer (Callers and Listeners)*, published the results of a survey, "500 Berlin Schoolchildren Talk about Radio."[54] The children confess their dislike for forms of broadcasting that attempt to achieve *"Volksbildung"* through music, be it *"Volksmusik"* or *"ernste Musik"* (serious music). One child supposedly answered in ways that seem strikingly similar to Pringsheim's criticism seven years before.

> I like to listen to fun music. But the music is usually scheduled for 11 o'clock at night; I always have to go to bed then and can't listen to the radio. That is always a shame. If the people in our house had to write this essay, they'd say that their husbands come home in the evening tired from work, and they can't wait at night until 11 o'clock for fun music that could distract them . . . I would like fun music after school from 2 'til 7. (Wulff 1934, 124)[55]

Here again, class disrupts the fantasy of national presence-to-itself, and its spatial and temporal requirements. The organization of leisure and distraction that the radio was supposed to provide emerges here as a continuous site of struggle between the pedagogical and performative lives of the nation (Bhabha 1990). While on the one hand, the increasingly explicitly national address of radio requires listeners, and therefore "fun" music that does not scare off the exhausted worker-listeners, the "new order" of post-1933 Germany sought to use the radio as a tool of national formation, an explicitly pedagogical tool. But this boy's comment suggests that class remained a zone of contestation in this attempted project: retaining the vocabulary of Weimar welfare-state appeals, his comment illustrates the very real failure of the early "revolutionary" trends in Nazi radio policy to disengage the political potential of the working class milieu. At the same time, it also seems to point toward the ways the "new order" at least needed to attempt to adapt to these conditions.[56]

Thus, class, by which I refer less as an ahistorical sociological description and more in a historically specific sense than one of the primary potential forms of hegemonization for the Weimar Republic, remained a primary zone of radio's incongruent relationship to the national in the Nazi period. But class was further complicated by the equally divisive issue of regionality and locality. This was in part a result of the structures left in place from the Weimar period. In the early years of the Nazi period, the Berlin leadership found itself in a struggle with authorities in the *Länder* over control over radio. The first struggle on the political level would in the end be concluded in favor of Berlin, and federalist organizational principles were eliminated in principle, replaced by the *Führerprinzip* as a model for radio organization.[57] But in terms of broadcast decisions and audience demands, the relationship between the local and the national remained a thorny issue throughout the Nazi years. Goebbels would attempt a further step towards centralization in 1938, dividing the German radio stations into three regional groups, and thereby rationalizing radio programming across the nation. But this move met with fierce opposition (Diller, 1980, 169ff.). This was not only a practical problem: these issues also entailed a deeper, ideological history of the coding of place in the German context. As Celia Applegate has pointed out, the relationship of German nationalism to regionality was tense and complex, particularly in the Nazi period.

While radio had to negotiate between local and national horizons of mass experience in order to secure its intelligibility, it was also continually disturbed by the potential supranational publics which radio seemed almost designed to address.[58] Discourse on radio had always simultaneously imagined the new medium as both a tool of national address *and* international understanding. As the technology improved, making its ability to transcend the national-domestic scene through the reception of foreign stations more available to a wider audience, a newer threat to radio's national status became more clear. This did not decrease, but instead increased after 1933, when advances in radio technology facilitated the reception of foreign stations.[59] Even if the reality of radio meant that the reception of foreign stations remained far less than ideal—not to speak of the problems of domestic reception—the "world" and fantasies of contact with that "world" were central in the medium's cultural imaginary.

One indicator of this is advertising for radio receivers: in a typical advertisement for high-end receivers dating from late in 1938 (Figure 7), Blaupunkt offers an image of a happy German couple at the radio, and the following text:

> As if it came from next door . . . so does the song sound, so does the word sound—and travels indeed many thousands of miles from foreign countries into our rooms . . . world travel within your own four walls. Listen with Blaupunkt to what the world broadcasts.

Figure 7. "As if it came from next door": advertisement for Blaupunkt radios from Berliner Illustrirte Zeitung, 1938.

This exoticization of the distant might be seen as having been limited by the price of the more expensive radios capable of shortwave reception. But radio in general promised to provide all listeners with access to a new world of sonic travel.

> The world has become small . . . but nonetheless, somewhere behind the mountains, in the wide spaces of the east German plains, in a lonely fishing village on the Frisian coast, sits a person, for whom the world has remained—even still today—exactly as big, exactly as endless as it was for his fathers. He does his work, and suffers from the ancient sickness of all Germans: the yearning for the far-away *[Fernweh.]* . . . One day, a small, unimpressive radio *[Apparat]* stands in the apartment of this individual pining for the far away *[Fernwehkranke]*, and on the roof of his house is an antenna. The loner flips a switch, turns on a dial—and stops, breathless: out of the device comes the voice of a man, clear and full-sounding, who speaks of distant parts of the earth, of foreign people, of adventurous trips and wild experiences . . . The world may be infinitely big, unreachable and distant for us. The microphone of the radio station brought it close to us, and suddenly we too are in the middle of events, listening in, experiencing together *[miterlebend]*. (wher. 1938, 3–5)[60]

This passage comes from an article in the radio journal *Die Sendung [The Broadcast]* and deals with one radio show in particular, "Experienced, Told" *["Erlebt, erzählt"]*, in which the pleasures of the big city— "even the voices have hairdos" (4)—were brought to the small town through the magic of radio. The description mobilizes a kind of affect difficult to assimilate to the properly national: in order to manage this problem, the text claims that the desire for extraterritorial experience is itself a trait of German national character: "that age-old German sickness, the yearning for the far-away." What is being glamorized here is not a hypernational experience of place, centralized in Berlin, but more a general "German" need for travel in the broad sense. The key referent here is "the world": radio, in this account, is ultimately cosmopolitan in its pleasures, even for the little man in the German hinterlands.

In the following year, at the beginning of the war in September 1939, listening to foreign radio became a capital offense. But, as the *Reports from the Reich* repeatedly make clear, listening to foreign stations continued. A yearly report about radio from 1939 remarks that since the beginning of the war, "in almost all German listening circles German language news and programs from foreign stations are being listened to, now as much as then" (Boberach 1984, 278).[61] In an anecdote reported from the Austrian province of Styria in 1942, a family is informed that their son has died in battle, and orders a memorial mass. At home, they hear on British radio in German their son's name on a list of survivors. Realizing the punishment for listening to foreign stations, the family goes through with the planned memorial mass for their now still-living son as if nothing had happened—but arriving at the church, find it empty of all mourners. The author of the SD report containing this story comments that the listening to foreign stations is seen as a petty crime, and "that the population in part is not aware of the danger of listening to foreign station and the intentions and goals of the prohibition" (Boberach 1984, 1119). That empty church gives us some idea of the fragility of the national radio audience. Its missing complement, the implied collective of well-informed nonmourners and radio listeners, is at least indicative of the regime's perception of the popularity of foreign radio listening, and certainly points to the possible existence of quite developed modes of alternative forms of local and transnational publicity constituted around the radio.

While the tensions between shifting radio publics in terms of class collectivities, national address, and international allure required repeated fine-tuning in order to secure the specific national hegemony established under National Socialism, even the installation of the radio in the modern home was not yet secure: the habitus of the listener and his or her place in or outside the radiophonic collective remained an area of "theoretical" difficulty. In a 1935 article in *Rufer und Hörer* entitled "Are You Listening Correctly?: On the Art of True Radio Reception," the duties of the national listener are spelled out. "The listener as well has duties . . . mental sacrifice and the mental attitude . . . [of] making oneself ready, holding oneself ready for the true pleasure of reception offered by the broadcast" (Blanke 1935). If the author of this article saw the need for an explicit national pedagogy of radio habitus, the "how" of radio listening became even more problematic with the spread of so-called "community reception" *[Gemeinschaftsempfang]*, a model of radio listening that was at odds with the "standard" domestic arrangement. From the very first days of broadcasting, "community reception," then known as *Saalfunk* [Hall Radio], presented an alternative model. Radios would be placed in public spaces (like theaters and cinemas), and a fee would be charged to guests of the "performance." A failure in the early days of radio due to the poor quality of sound amplification, by the latter half of the 1920s public radio listening came into its own. The Nazis placed an enormous weight on the idea of "community reception," placing speakers in all sorts of public and semi-public environments (from the public squares—occupied by so called *Reichslautsprechersäulen* [Imperial Louspeaker Columns]—to the factory) to encourage listening in public for special radio events.[62]

Commentators of the period attempted to negotiate the uneasy relationship between domestic and "community" reception. Suggesting that while the officially sanctioned innovations of *Gemeinschaftsempfang*, "on public squares and in streets" (Koeppen 1934, 103) certainly represented an emphatically national public acoustics, one of these writers[63] sought to integrate the private sphere of radio listening, the "original form" of radio reception, into the Nazi national moment, by redefining the private as a new kind of public:

> But beyond nurturing communal reception, domestic reception, the original form and the one mode of reception proper to radio, must nevertheless not be neglected. Especially domestic reception is of the utmost importance for the new, National Socialist radio, and needs to be reformed to fit the National Socialist model . . . Domestic reception too is in almost all cases community reception. And further, it is the natural, iron-clad community of the family, that here completes an act of listening and is constantly supported by the spiritual radio . . . Unlike a record, [with the radio] a voice, a tone, a sound, penetrates from outside and fills the room with immediate life . . . the home suddenly becomes the place of a great event, the narrowest living space *[Wohnraum]* becomes the broadest shared space *[Mitraum]* . . . The greatest palace and the poorest hut approach

each other on a communal plane of space *[gemeinsame Raumebene]* and finally come together in an experience that is not an illusion as in film, but rather has a real basis. (103–4)[64]

Here, as in the Weimar examples, we witness two quite different approaches to the acoustics of radio's mass publicity and their relationship to national fantasy. In the first, the radio's national moment is to be guaranteed by extending or multiplying everyday, local structures of private life to the national level; in the second, radio is celebrated for offering the possibility of an entirely new form of listening subject or collective. By arguing that the Nazi use of the radio should ultimately return to the private sphere of the family, this text attempts resolution; but, as we shall see, the domestic and the national-collective scenes of radio publicity could only *approach* congruence as "communal planes of space," and remained at odds with one another throughout the period of Nazi rule.

The ideological management of these problems took a number of forms. One technique was the anthropomorphic representation of radio technology. In *Es lebe die Liebe [Long Live Love]* (Engels 1944), Johannes Heesters, a Dutch star of musical film in Germany in the 1940s and '50s and the main heartthrob of late fascist mass culture, sings *"Mein Herz müßte ein Rundfunksender sein,"* or "If Only My Heart Were a Radio Station." Karsten Witte writes about this scene:

Heesters makes clear in singing by what media the exchange of feelings is directed. "If only my heart were a radio station, then you could hear something." The reverse shot shows a remarkably young, mostly female audience, in which the spectators of 1944 could catch a glimpse of themselves. In this revue scene, "The World Belongs to Me," the girls no longer dance on the piano keys, but on the radio buttons, while the pulled-back curtain reveals that musicians are sitting in the radio tubes. A naive translation work of the otherwise unfathomable technology of the mass medium radio, funny if necessary: but also appealing to the yearning of the Nazis to change art in all those places where it seems decadent back into [God-] created nature. From the musicians in the radio tubes, it is only a step to the church window built from sunshine, to the house built from the German woods . . . Art, in whatever medium it is thematized by the revue film, is always subject to a metamorphosis into the origin myth. (1995, 237–38)[65]

What is interesting about this scene and this song in the context of this discussion is the way in which the radio seems to want to account for its failures through spectacularizing the desire of its national (female) subjects (Figure 8). But ironically, the mode of musical production that emerges from the radio tubes in this case operates in no one code of proper national taste.

Indeed, the pleasures of this song (and by extension, of radio) depend as much on the feeling of national simultaneity as they do the dispersion of that moment: the acoustics of the radio nation, in other words, can only operate by producing simultaneously "unisonality"[66] and the dissonance of local "choice." Heesters sings:

> I am unfortunately oh so shy, and speaking is hard for me.
> What I say sounds so serious, as if I were cold and heartless.
> But in fact I am so romantic and a secret poet,
> who, filled with colorful dreams, goes through life unrecognized.
> Which right now saddens me so,
> since I am so in love with you.
>
> If only my heart were a radio station,
> then you could hear something.
> It would sound into the whole wide world,
> "I love you alone, oh please tune me in."
> Then I could, from early until midnight,
> swear to you my faithfulness.
> And I would have dared to put out a program for you
> thought out with love, that would be fabulous.
> As a symphony,
> as dance music,
> My song of happiness would sound.
> "I love you when will you be finally mine."[67]

Attempting to make explicit an erotics of listening, this song imagines the radio as a tool of an otherwise impossible "true" personal expression, even to the point that the lyrics transform the self-promotion of the medium in its broadcasts ("tune in") into a statement of erotic attachment ("tune me in"). But musically, this utopia of affect contributes one final example of the ways that the radio in Nazi Germany failed to remain limited to the properly national fantasy that it was used primarily to implant. The person to whom this song is addressed is not only presented as a world listener, but also as the consumer

Figure 8. From the "Radio Station" number in Es lebe die Liebe (Engel 1944).
From Belach (1979, 173).

of multiple musical forms. In the song, love would sound at first as a symphony, then as dance music. These different modes of affect are literalized in a unique way in the song, when after the word "symphony," a bar of mock orchestral music is inserted, and after the word "dance music," a moment of swing. The fullness of affect here is sounded as more an imitative collage of consumer "choice" than a synthesized acoustics of presence: the focus of interest in these breaks are precisely the extreme points of the national palette of musical taste, imagined as contrasting points on the radio band. In other words, Heesters's song is unable to limit its resonances to the imagined space that the acoustics of national publicity are supposed to make manifest and illustrates how radio remained a zone of ideological dissonance and excess up until the last years of Nazi rule.

The forms of ideological management engaged during the Nazi period thus need to be read not as supporting the claims Nazi radio made about itself, but instead interpreted for the ways they illustrate the faults and fissures of fascist domination, and in so doing illuminate the historical specificity of the relation between "the political" and radio in the 1930s and '40s. If we now return to the film discussed at the beginning of this chapter, another highly interesting attempt at ideological management, how might the historicization of the relationship between German mass publicity and national fantasy change our interpretation of this film? And what does a reading of the film add to our understanding of this problem?

Wunschkonzert

As I pointed out at the beginning of this chapter, recent accounts of this film have tended to accept the successful operation of the ideological "system" of *Wunschkonzert*. They remain bound within the narrative logic of the film itself, and accept in an odd way the truth claim of its conclusion. This film certainly seems to illustrate the ways radio was all-successful in the production of national simultaneity and national affect through mobilizing event and erotics, going out of its way to claim for radio the happy serendipity of the national scene. But if we step outside its narrative logic and try to explore the gaps in its operation, we might be able to produce a reading of the film that goes beyond its own propaganda about itself, and in so doing use the film to reconstruct a more complex image of the fascist public sphere as a tense field structured by various forms of social antagonism.

Consider the following contemporary plot summary:

> A voice floats across the airwaves. "Here is the Greater German Radio! We begin the Request Concert for the Armed Forces." A magical tie unites front and *Heimat*. In the foxhole in France, on the submarine on a mission, at the air base on the coast, in the silent room of a mother, in thousands, hundreds of thousands of homes, everywhere the stream of words, song, and music sounds and floats. "Calling Captain Herbert Koch, . . ." speaks the trusted voice of Heinz Goedecke from the speaker at the home of the Wagners, ". . . he wishes to hear the Olympic Fanfare in remembrance of the Olympic Games in Berlin." A joyous shock flashes across Inge's face. Her eyes become teary. A sign of life from Herbert—now everything will turn out well. She in fact succeeds in getting Herbert's address. A hurried, happy exchange of letters sets the date for a meeting in Hamburg.
>
> And again, the Request Concert unites all Germans. The suffering and joy of the lone individual, the unknown, and the nameless becomes the suffering and joy of the entire nation. All hearts beat in the same rhythm of emotion.[68]

This passage is taken from a plot summary of *Wunschkonzert* printed in the *Illustrierte Filmkurier* which accompanied the film. The national pathos here is of course far from subtle: not only does this passage invoke the nation as a unified sonic phenomenon, "everywhere the stream of words, song, and music sounds and floats *[klingt und schwingt]*," this national everywhere, specified and localized in a serialized somewhere, represents not simply a list but an ordering: from the foxhole through the "silent room of a mother" to "thousands, hundreds of thousands of homes *[Wohnungen]*." This passage sounds like a cinematic voice-over, evocative of the epistemological certainty of weekly newsreels, and claims to model the way individual national subjects are interpellated erotically as part of a national spectacle.[69] Using the radio to sonically reminisce about the time of their first meeting at the 1936 Berlin Olympic Games, Inge and Herbert are able to reconstruct an erotic contact on the national stage which had been disrupted by the requirements of the national. The state's proprietary claims on Captain Herbert Koch, an air force pilot, were in fact the reason for the couple's original separation.

But considered in light of the difficulties and tensions involved in radio's hegemonic claim, it is precisely this description of a seemingly neatly sutured national moment that indicates rupture: the multiplicity that characterizes the not-so-everyday national scene in some sense *needs* to be ordered by this would-be voice-over. This passage indexes as well the ways this ordering is implicated in forms of paradoxically productive national violation. The radio becomes an instrument of expropriation: the affect of the "lone individual, the unknown, the nameless," her joy or suffering, is *nationalized* by the voice of Heinz Goedecke. In return, the listener is provided with a public prosthesis: the synchronous, disembodied beating of a depersonalized "heart" provides the listener with a form of prophylaxis against the discordance that inheres within the national apparatus and the experience of her own nonnational affect (Warner 1992; Berlant 1993). The doubleness of this passage and the history of the uneasy relationship between radio's mass publicity and national fantasy more generally indicate the ways these national acoustics were marked by disturbance and policing of that disturbance.

Consider again the staging of radio listening in the mother's room: Looking at this scene before the backdrop of radio history, this abundance of national symbolism is haunted by the specter of contradiction, throwing the very claim that the scene is trying to make into relief as just that, a claim, a moment of national pedagogy. In addition, the scene articulates with an earlier moment in the film, when radio played a quite different role in the acoustics of national publicity. This earlier scene, soon after the film's beginning, produces the *Heimat* as a coherent topography by depicting various banal activities of small-town life, only after the call of the radio announcing the declaration of war and the national imperative it implies has already disrupted that coherence. This scene also stages motherhood and nationhood in the domestic sphere, using a different kind of acoustic mediation: we witness the son, dressed in his army uniform, playing the Adagio from Beethoven's *Pathétique* Sonata (labeled indeed three times as "Beethoven"), only to hear his playing disrupted by the sound of soldiers singing from outside on the street. Although this new sound will serve to carry the spectator of the film through the space of *Heimat* to a new narrative situation, this functional explanation of narrational strategy does not erase the way the national needs to produce itself both as disruptive event and timeless interiority.[70]

In that the film uses "Gute Nacht, Mutter," an already popular song from the year before, to "express" the love of and for a mother, the two temporalities that give the national public its tense reemerge: the nation as a series of popular events, and the nation as an ahistorical, classic paradigm. Motherhood and radio here claim to be both of these, but the very seriality of the shots undermines this pretense. The pathos of both the song's lyrics and its music (with its wistful major seventh and its use of both the major and minor thirds) is reinforced by the way the camera traces out the emptiness of the room. The last two lines of the song correspond with the concluding of the camera movement on the figure of the lone woman at the window, and the mother almost rhythmically wipes a tear from her eyes.

But the way this scene wants to argue that radio somehow consoles with the sentiment of last year's popular song is incongruous to the earlier depiction of the classic domestic scene and its accessories of *Bildungsbürgertum*, accessories (bust, piano) that are now emphatically drafted into national service by the series of the shots and the slow, deliberate camera movement. While one might argue that the film seeks simply to equate various forms of national music, both popular and "serious," the plot denies this logic. It remains difficult to imagine the now-dead son, who begins the film by playing *Beethoven* and whose death we witness as he plays Reger on an organ during battle, as ever having expressed filial love in the sentiment of the pop song. Indeed, the intensity of the earlier scene's Beethoven cult excludes this possibility.

The film's need to finally articulate this plot line with the popular thus points more than anything to a gap between national and popular in the way they stage and "sound" domestic personhood. This scene attempts to map quite different acoustic arrangements of the national on to one another isomorphically, and in so doing produces a cognition of the incongruent results of these articulations. If the *Hausmusik* scene produces the familial space as the locus of a national sound (Beethoven) caressing and interpellating the subject in his familial persona, only to be disrupted by the nation's diachronicity as represented by the sounds of military mobilization, the latter scene attempts to erase the difference between the nation as historical event—here evoked in the popular song—and the nostalgia of the domestic as it adheres to the maternal body. Attempting to piece together this national acoustics in the room of the mother, this moment wants to allow a properly national-popular musical affect to resonate in the space of the cinema, where the spectator, like the mother, is caressed by the comforting tones of Strienze's voice. But both the mother and the spectator are not only placed at the radio, they are also placed at the piano. The attempt to mobilize a now-silent piano as a marker in a national-domestic space *sounded* by the radio unwillingly recalls the very diachronicity that disrupted the national-domestic scene in the first place. Three incompatible national acoustics compete with each other here: classical, military, and maternal, and the film unwittingly shows the work expended in the attempt to banish the disturbing cognition of this incompatibility.

This incompatibility is reinforced by an odd piece of extra-filmic evidence. The song's very popularity became a problem in securing its attachment to the apparatus of national affect that the film attempts to make operative, in that the form of the popular song refuses to remain attached to the superficially successful workings of the film's plot. The following Security Service report registers this problem:

> In "Music to Quitting-Time," broadcast by Imperial Broadcaster Leipzig on February 3, the song *"Gute Nacht, Mutter"* was played as a dance song. It has been remarked that this song, even if it was already played and obviously also recorded beforehand, doesn't lend itself in terms of its content to being a dance song . . . since, because of the film *Wunschkonzert*, it is seen in a particularly tragic situation by many national comrades *[Volksgenossen]*. (Boberach 1984, 2035)

Not only is the film's attempt to overcome the opposition between a "popular" experience of nationalized motherly affect and *Bildung* clumsy, but here, the very popularity of the song surfaces outside the film as yet another indicator of rupture in the way radio attempts to construct a national fantasy of acoustic presence. *Request Concert* thus ironically exhibits the contradictions inherent in fascist mass culture, particularly in its supernational and pseudocosmopolitan forms. Even in its most extreme formulations, the attempt to produce a coherent acoustics of national publicity fails on multiple levels to erase the specter of contradiction, indeed indexes the nature of this contradiction as constitutive of the national.

The Totalitarian Allegory

Since its beginnings in the Weimar Republic, radio continued to represent an arena of publicity and a technology of collective fantasy subject to various forms of insufficiency and failure. Even during the Nazi period, radio was not a simple medium for delivering "propaganda" to the people, but rather a tense, contradictory social field alternatively shaped by various forms of mass publicity and hegemonizing and hegemonic modes of national fantasy. As we have seen, these processes of hegemonization in, through, and around (the) radio were by no means limited to the structuring of the political in a simple sense, but produced national subjects in practice by crafting of everyday life by means of multiple registers of social normativization. While the acoustic element, and particular the musical sphere, played a crucial role in the assembly, disintegration, and reassembly of the various hegemonic structures that organized the relationship of "the radio listener(s)" to the nation, it also was inevitably engaged by other developments that were or were not so easily assimilable to national fantasy: the establishment of modern forms of consumer culture, fantasies of international and local presence, and the organization of the modern domestic sphere. By considering radio listening as part of the historical production of situated forms of audiovisual culture, we can begin to enter a richer world of social inquiry, whereby multiple moments of practice, coordinated and articulated to one another by larger social dynamics, come together in the deceptively simple act of turning on the radio, or, as we shall see later, playing a record or watching and listening to a film. By no means merely a top-down dynamic, the history of radio in this period should be seen as the recurrent attempt to reestablish hegemonic relations on multiple social levels by synchronizing contradictory moments within different ideological state apparatuses in the multiple practices of radio broadcasting and radio listening.

Although I have been suggesting empirical ways in which various aspects of what I have abbreviated as the standard account of radio in the "Third Reich" fail to convince, the crucial issue here is not merely empirical, but theoretical and profoundly political, and hinges on the question of whether or not a historical look at the development of fascism should function critically or affirmatively in the present tense of its writing. The account of the centrality of radio as the ultimate instrument of propaganda rests on two related claims about the nature of fascism, the Nazi takeover, and the constitution of a national audience. The first claim deals with the nature of the popularity of the Nazis, the second with the related question of mass agency, whereby the rise of fascism is attributable to some sort of excess of democracy, or as Bracher (1984) has phrased it, "the problems of the democratic idea," exacerbated by the distorting role of technology;[71] the second relies on the operation of radio as a simple conduit for "propaganda," mass manipulation through the modern mass media in a simple and profoundly *unmediated* sense. These claims rest not only on shaky ground as far as "evidence" and current trends in the historiography of fascism are concerned, but additionally and more importantly, have a very particular kind of political valence. These two unspoken assumptions, the first regarding the nature and form of the national audience and the second about mass culture's direct and automatic effectivity on a self-evident national scale make up the unarticulated theoretical basis of this body of historiography.[72] Implicitly placing the bulk of the blame on both a small minority of media manipulators—Goebbels and company—and the supposed stupidity of the masses, the capitalist elites who actually supported the system seem almost to come off scott-free.

Any narrative of the coming to power of the Nazi party that accepts the production of a national plebiscite as in a simple sense *real*, a pathological moment of the conflation of a radically "other" desire and perverse interest, tends to see the coming of National Socialism as more a product of mass-distributed delusion (Bracher's "ideology"), false consciousness, or hypnosis unique in the history of mass culture than a subtle series of events by which given power relations operated within existing modes of governmentality and publicity in a specific political and economic conjuncture to produce a new kind of state apparatus.[73] To be clear: at issue here is not whether the Nazi government was "popular," but rather exactly what "popularity" meant in the Nazi period. Consent is manufactured in a number of different ways, not all of which require *conviction*. It is one thing to recognize and describe the ways in which Nazism's rise had everything to do with a certain style of mass politics and publicity, but it is quite another thing to conflate the Nazis' own imagination of the self-evidence of their mass basis with any attempt at critical historical description of the operation of the "mass" in the public sphere of Weimar and Nazi Germany.

Although they may pretend not to offer a *theory* of fascism, these by-and-large empirical studies of radio administration and broadcasting are intelligible only within a quite limiting and politically invested theory of fascism's historical moment: the "theory" of totalitarianism. Developed in the 1950s in the context of the Cold War, the classical account of totalitarianism was based on establishing links between fascist and communist domination. The classic text here is Hannah Arendt's *The Origins of Totalitarianism*, published in both (West) Germany and the United States immediately after World War II, and surely the foundational text in postwar totalitarianism "theory." Conveniently excluding capitalism, Arendt's study, despite its rhetorical brilliance and clarity, is useless to grasp the history of 1920s and '30s Germany in any kind of ultimately critical way, marred by a thoroughly affirmative relation to liberal democracy. The recent popularity of totalitarianism in a post–Cold War world is more than disturbing. As Slavoj Žižek has recently argued,

> Throughout its entire career, "totalitarianism" was an ideological notion that sustained the complex operation of "taming free radicals," of guaranteeing the liberal-democratic hegemony, dismissing the Leftist critique of liberal democracy as the obverse, the "twin," of the Rightist Fascist dictatorship . . . the moment one accepts the notion of "totalitarianism," one is firmly located within the liberal democratic horizon . . . [T]he notion of "totalitarianism," far from being an effective theoretical concept, is a kind of stopgap: instead of enabling us to think, forcing us to acquire a new insight into the historical reality it describes, it relieves us of the duty to think, or even actively prevents us from thinking. (2001, 3)

This stopgap takes the form of an allegory: the allegory of totalitarianism does seek to explain domination, but by locating domination only in a seemingly radically other form of the political. In this "other form," the vectors of effectivity in the social are fundamentally different to liberal democracy. The politics of this historiography and its totalitarian allegory are complicated, and in some sense, ironic: the rise of Nazism is in this narrative the fault of a broadly undifferentiated social group, the masses, which was easily manipulated by radio. This inherently conservative, anti-republican tendency is accompanied by liberalism's own version of conspiracy theory, which focuses attention on the manipulation of the masses by a relatively small group of party activists who successfully mobilized radio for their own political goals.[74] Common to both of these modes of explanation is the attempt to find something uniquely pathological about mass culture's development within the Germany of the 1920s and 1930s, and to displace the more general problematic of hegemony and "the state" and their relationship to the institutions and practices of mass culture onto some form of social formation imagined to be absolutely other to the "proper" modes of political behavior characteristic of liberal capitalism.[75] The totalitarian allegory stages the production of domination in a scene of absolute, invasive control of the private realm by an implicitly anthropomorphic state or animalistic mass; while it would be an error to deny the persuasiveness of this just-so story, the structure of this allegory can only ultimately affirm the form of domination particular to liberal democracy.[76]

The political force of the totalitarian allegory is particularly clear in the postwar radio historiography of the Federal Republic. In this kind of work, postwar West German radio broadcasting is implicitly, if not explicitly, redeemed as either banally malign or even proper to a genuine democratic political culture. The allegory of totalitarianism implicitly produces the postfascist period in the West as postideological. What counts in this kind of historiography as "political" and "ideological" is especially troubling. If one clear lack in the Weimar public sphere was precisely *political* radio, the ban on which was manipulated primarily by the national(ist) parties, the description of fascist broadcasting as somehow "more" political and ideological than either what came before or after should certainly be questioned. The pretense that moments of national consolidation in the patriotic mode—like the broadcast of "liberation ceremonies" from "freed" Rhineland cities or even the everyday production of national normativity—are somehow not political is in fact one of the primary ways in which this mode of radio broadcasting was intelligible as not interested, but national, in its desire and effects. Indeed, although the accusation of 'political' broadcasting was also mobilized against the National Socialists' attempt to insinuate themselves into radio in the early 1930s, this accusation was primarily directed not against the Right in the late Weimar period, but against the Left.[77] There is then something cynical about the "centrist" reading of radio's "politicization" after 1933, when it is clear that the conditions of publicity were already thoroughly politicized during the late Weimar years.[78]

Even the use of the term "propaganda" to describe fascist radio policies and practices, although of course descriptive in terms of intention and faithful to the ways the Nazis themselves imagined their own radio policies, also operates implicitly within a theory of totalitarianism, and is subject to the same kinds of problems that characterizes such discourse about the fascist "body-politic" and its implantation into the German public sphere. This discourse presumes that mass culture in fascism operated in ways that were somehow *obviously* more ideological[79] than mass culture in liberal democracy, a claim that should at least be reexamined if not reconsidered entirely.[80]

The intent of this kind of "revisionist" approach is of course not to somehow redeem or normalize fascism, but to suggest that the need to imagine fascism as a dystopic space entirely external to our own social world tells us more about the conditions for the reproduction of the attendant political forms of capitalism (liberal democracy) than it does about the historically specific operation of fascism. At issue is not the normalization of fascism, but an attempt to de-normalize recent and current forms of the social. A historiography of fascism that seeks on the one hand to truly grasp fascism in its historical specificity, while on the other hand retaining its critical potential in the present tense of its writing needs to theorize fascism in ways that make it precisely comparable to other forms of domination[81] and link it to other forms of the production of hegemony. This is not to say that liberal democracy is fascist, but it is to say that liberal democracy is also about domination. More to the point, modes of repression and national production characteristic of fascism are not entirely foreign to other social formations, even liberal democracy, particularly in the current climate. I can only speak generally here, but the production of figures of abjection in U.S. discourse like the "welfare mother" (in the early vocabulary, *Asoziale*), the "three times you're out career criminal" (in Nazi language, *Berufsverbrecher*), and most importantly, the "terrorist," in many ways repeat key aspects of fascist discourse and are used in strikingly similar ways to produce new forms of hegemony. If we are committed to thinking as much about these phenomena as we are to analyzing fascism, then it is certainly important to clarify how these modes of representation and domination are similar in kind if not in scale to those so clearly presented to us in the historic moment of fascism, and not to insist on the epistemologically banal historical "singularity" of either Nazi hegemony or the crimes that it allowed.

In order to get at this political and theoretical problem, the historicity of the "mass," and more particularly, of the German national public qua "mass," need to be investigated. As I have suggested in this chapter, one crucial way to interrogate the historicity of "the mass" is to see mass culture itself as the site of shifting practices that continuously (re)produce and (re)structure different forms of hegemony. As we shall see, even in its fantastical incarnations, this mass was by no means merely part of a teleological development towards a *Volks-gemeinschaft* under totalitarian control, where "all of Germany listened to the *Führer*," but a deeply contradictory site. These contradictions are the subject of the following chapters. Integral to this conception of mass culture is the central role of antagonism in the production of both "society" and subjectivity.[82] In other words, the forms of acoustic publicity that adhered to the radio were just as characterized as other forms of publicity by what Negt and Kluge describe as the "rifts [and] marginal cases" (1972, 7) that represent the possibilities of alternative modes of publicity in history. Rather than presupposing a plugged-in, easily manipulated German people as the nonagents of German history, a politically invested history of fascism must take these spaces of incongruence within the acoustics of national publicity as its starting point. The issue of fascist publicity is precisely the question of how these forms of public sphere were repeatedly hegemonized to support the status quo: this is a problematic which inhabits all eras of modern acoustic culture. Instead of providing "Germany" with a media alibi, a critical media history needs to remember the constant contingency of media audiences. A balanced perspective on the role of mass culture in this period needs to focus on strategic, variously successful attempts at hegemonization, while at the same time never forgetting the contingency and dynamism of this process, down to the micro-level of subjective experience. In the following chapters, by looking at various aspects of musical mass publicity—the *Schlager*, "serious music" in mass culture, and the figure of the gypsy—as they were configured in the 1920s and 1930s, I will propose various ways to develop a more historically precise concept of mass publicity in Germany of the Weimar and Nazi periods that attempts to retain this balance. This will provide not only a new perspective on the period in question, but also offer some new interpretive suggestions for the question of musical mass publicity in general.

and personhood in capitalism. The study of the musical mass culture of this period thus needs to begin the more difficult project of disentangling the various strands of this multidimensional historical process that terms like "the Weimar Republic" and "the Nazi period" tend to obscure.

The objection here is thus not merely "empirical": if the narrative on musical mass culture in fascism is not only merely historically misleading, but is also a tool in quite specific forms of ideological work, the ideological work shows that popular music in particular serves as a key nodal point for the continuing reproduction of oversimplifying figures of repression and resistance that underwrite a metaphysics of authenticity. Indeed, a kind of "repressive hypothesis" continues to haunt the study of popular music in this period, by which authentic popular music and popular culture flows as a constant stream, only occasionally dammed by the repression of external forces. Of course, like all dams, this one is bound to eventually break. This repressive hypothesis naturalizes popular music as a zone of authentic expression, usually linked to "the body" in a more or less direct fashion. The continued predominance of a vocabulary that refers to jazz and other black music, for example, as "more embodied" is astonishing, and the circulation of these stereotypes in discourse about popular music in Germany is particularly steadfast. Like its cousin repressive hypothesis analyzed by Foucault in his history of sexuality (Foucault 1984), I would suggest that the constant reproduction of a certain dominant narrative of the development of popular music in the Third Reich suggests that we continue to hold an intense investment in upholding this repressive hypothesis. The goal of this book is to try to displace this stubborn narrative, and provide new ways of thinking about the role of music in German mass culture in the 1920s, 1930s, and 1940s. In examining the period, we will look and listen behind these audiovisual icons and reflexively examine their own ideological function. At the same time, I hope this book can offer a new approach to the sonic traces of this period that genuinely retains the critical element in the present tense of its writing, which is increasingly lacking in studies of fascism and its emergence. If, as Benjamin writes, history is always the "object of a construction located in a place not in homogenous and empty time, but a place filled with the present (*Jetztzeit*)," this project attempts to return to our conception of the history of this period an explosive encounter with the present.

A further desideratum of studies of music in the Weimar and Nazi period is the question of mediacy and publicity. Not only do the new approaches to music in the Nazi and Weimar period still tend to focus on questions of musical or discursive "content," they also only marginally treat the new forms of musical publicity—radio, recording, and sound film—which truly molded the everyday "sound" of the period. For Kater, for example, these media are simply seen as modes of transmission, either available or not accessible to musicians of the day; in this view, not only is the role of the media in music *production* underestimated, the concomitant transformations in modes of musical *consumption* are also given little notice. In other words, not only should we concentrate on questions of *what* was listened to; equally important to our analysis of musical mass culture is the study of *how* listening took place. In order to accomplish this task, we need to look at music in general as a component of mass culture and place it more precisely in the consumer culture of the period. In order to do this, this book will focus on a number of different aspects of the question of musical mass culture in Germany from 1924–1945. In the rest of this introductory chapter, I would like to sketch out the theoretical starting points for this exploration, beginning with the question of "national sound" itself.

National Acoustics and Publicity

Nations sound. In his seminal work on the nation, Benedict Anderson (1983) coined the word "unisonality" to describe the sound nation.[7] As an example of this simultaneously empirical and imaginary sonic phenomenon, Anderson chooses the national anthem.

> Take national anthems, for example. Sung on national holidays. No matter how banal the words and mediocre the tunes, there is in this singing an experience of simultaneity. At precisely such moments, people wholly unknown to each other utter the same verses to the same melody. Singing the Marseillaise, Waltzing Matilda, and Indonesia Raya provide occasions for unisonality, for the echoed physical realization of the imagined community. (132)

Anderson's brief explication of the nation's sound provides a useful point of departure. In addition, however, to grasping the idealized sonority of unisonance, the level of the imaginary, we understand the sound of the nation more in depth if we complement Anderson's analysis of the experience of the nation's sonic simultaneity with a description of the varied history of this experience. In other words, not only does the national imaginary itself need to be historicized, but the technologies of its production, like "unisonality," also need to be placed within a historical context. While it might well seem a given that the national public, its history and present tense, can be invoked in sound, one of the goals of this study will be to try to grasp the particular history of this imaginary, in order to return it not to some kind of empirical history, but rather to tease out the traces of social antagonism that determine its seemingly perfect resonance. The affect of "community" in sound seems here to be taken for granted, removed from historicity, and by extension, social antagonism.

In an attempt to historicize this kind of simultaneity, Eric Hobsbawm suggests the importance of mass culture in the formation of the modern nation. National presence, publicity, and "sonality," Hobsbawm argues, need to be contextualized within the history of various forms of mass mediation.

> National identification in this era acquired new means of expressing itself in modern, urbanized high-technology societies . . . The first, which requires little comment, was the rise of the modern mass media: press, cinema, and radio. By these means popular ideologies could be both standardized, homogenized, and transformed, as well as obviously exploited for the purposes of deliberate propaganda by private interests and states . . . deliberate propaganda was almost certainly less significant than the ability of the mass media to make what were in effect national symbols part of the life of every individual, and thus to break down the divisions between the private and local spheres in which most citizens normally lived, and the public and national one. (1990, 142)[8]

While Hobsbawm's account of modern nationality does offer insight into one of the nation's primary sites of historical process, the field of mass culture, his attempt to inject history into the conception of the nation by mobilizing mass culture as the site of the nation's historicity fails to remember the historicity of mass culture itself. Indeed, in his account, the methods and mechanisms through which the national was produced in the early-twentieth-century moment of mass culture and participated in the transformations of publicity and its structural complement and *sine qua non*, privacy, "require little comment."

Recent work on the history of mass culture, however, indicates precisely that these developments cannot be taken for granted, and do indeed require a great deal of comment.[9] We are presented with two distinct problems by this trajectory of thought on the sound nation. First: how was the affectual nation historically tied to a certain kind of sonic experience, and how can we theorize its historicity? Second: how can we talk about the role of mass culture in the implantation of this sonic fantasy in ways that respect the complex historicity of mass cultural formations themselves—their institutions, practices, and publics? In other words, while the history of German mass culture has often forgotten the historicity of the nation, the history of "nationality" has in turn neglected to focus on the specific historicity of mass culture. In this book, I will seek to explore both these modes of historicity by engaging the question of publicity. The large body of work dedicated to the study of *Öffentlichkeit*, or publicity, has proven especially fruitful for thinking about the nation on the diachronic plane, giving its development historical contours, and for theorizing its synchronic operation as a space of both affect and social action.[10]

In the German case, publicity has long represented a special problem for historians and social theorists, particularly, or implicitly, in terms of accounting for the history of the twentieth century. Publicity has been a key term in what we might call the diagnostic literature: one of the classic liberal accounts of German history, the *Sonderweg*, saw the specificity of German publicity as indicative of the more general specificity of the German "special path" through the historical process. Already in the 1930s, Helmuth Plessner began to develop a theory of the specificity of German history, which he reformulated in the 1950s as an explicit theorization of what he called the "late nation" (1959). Arguing that while nations like France and Britain "have their roots in the baroque," Germany's self-consciousness of nationhood could only come to fruition in the industrial age, which itself took place "late" in German history. With a bourgeoisie overly dependent on the aristocracy in a fragmented "Germany," the foundations of a liberal state could not be established in Plessner's view. Although not so much explicitly addressing the question of publicity, Plessner's analysis certainly hints in the direction: ultimately, Plessner suggests that the ideal "Western" public sphere, as existed in both France and England in the eighteenth century, was lacking in backward Germany. In that the German Protestant traditions in particular fostered private religious experience over public engagement, a uniquely German "depth" and insistence on "honesty" was unable to embrace the more pragmatic requirements of modern democratic culture. Plessner even offers a spin on the relationship of German musical history to this problem, arguing "German culture in modernity preferred music and philosophy as their areas of expression," two areas of cultural production which "lie in conflict with normal linguistic communication."

> The essence *[das Eigentliche]* of music cannot be put in words. Vocal music is always on the surface. It experienced its heyday in Italy, not in Germany. Only where speech is silent does music begin. And only where speech disintegrates, when it is removed from the over all accompanying communication and is made the object of contemplation, does philosophy begin. (1974:103)

Of course, in many ways Plessner's account of musical history is fatally flawed, not only in accepting the notion that the symphonic tradition is "German," but more importantly in projecting late-nineteenth-century notions of absolute music back into the roots of modern musical development. Nonetheless, this passage is nothing if not provocative, and opens up the interesting question of the relationship between publicity and music and their role in German history.

Plessner's more or less vague descriptions of the development of a historically specific, yet ultimately unified, German "national character" in modernity were given more depth and complexity in the work of Ralf Dahrendorf (1965). Dahrendorf, redeploying Plessner's theoretical interventions, suggests that German society failed historically to produce the kind of national subject required of the publicity specific to liberal democracy, that is, an autonomous, abstract subject engaged in debates about issues of emphatically public concern. While Plessner tends to remain on the level of religious or intellectual history, citing "Protestant depth" as a seemingly transcendental cause rather than something in need of explanation, Dahrendorf in contrast seeks the roots of the "problem" of German publicity in a more institutionally grounded history. Arguing that the "predominance of private virtues" inhibits the establishment of democracy, and that this predominance is only to be had at the expense of "public virtues," Dahrendorf seeks the social roots of this situation in Germany. He looks first at the German educational system, particularly the relationship between family and school, in which the family is privileged at the expense of the school—for example, late schooling, short school days, and the early end of mandatory school attendance. Further, he argues, the lack of the encouragement of "social" activity in the school—from sport to cooperative learning—leads to a profound distrust of the "public" itself (1971, 343). He draws the conclusion that this lack made German society especially vulnerable to fascism and other authoritarian structures. While this diagnosis ultimately rests on a similar notion of "national character," and is thus unavoidably subject to the critiques of this kind of logic that have been rehearsed elsewhere, it is interesting when read as a possible explanation of a particular local, historical development, suggestive of the ways in which the decay of public forms of sociability can have grave impact on political developments, even when these forms of sociability seem to have no direct link to the properly political.

It is indeed this kind of generalization of the problem that makes the question of publicity in "the German case" interesting. While Plessner and Dahrendorf are explicitly engaged in a kind of diagnostic project of the specifically German case, Habermas takes a more international view, focusing perhaps too much on English and French models of the public sphere in order to trace out the specific historical constellation of its modern emergence. Although in contrast to Dahrendorf or Plessner, Habermas himself is strangely silent on the question of fascism, his interpretation of the public sphere implicitly questions the diagnostics of a specifically German problem. In his groundbreaking work on the public sphere, which predates Dahrendorf's investigation of the German social *Sonderweg*, Habermas refuses the all-too-easy reliance on the national framework that characterizes the *Sonderweg* theorists. Instead, he argues that in order to understand the specifics of any one political scenario, we have to understand the development of the public sphere as rooted in the general condition of capitalist development, which, although in every case uneven, tended to follow similar models all across Europe and North America. Suggesting instead that the emphatic moment of Enlightenment publicity was in decline in all Western states, Habermas understood the moment of German fascist publicity as but a special case of a more widely distributed mode of mass cultural publicity common in the larger industrialized nations of the West (1989, 141ff.). He suggests that mass culture operates within an internal contradiction inherent to the construction of the public sphere itself: that the separation of the public and private so essential to the historical development of the public sphere is weakened by the very structures of consumption which from the beginning characterized the operation of the public sphere. The shift from a "culture debating" to a "culture consuming" audience ultimately leads to the decay of the public sphere itself.

While Habermas' broader account is certainly more useful for a critical investigation, his account of publicity has two distinct problems. First, his story of the decline of publicity fetishizes one specific mode of public sphere, the liberal moment of the Enlightenment. In their response to Habermas's theory, Oskar Negt and Alexander Kluge rethink the emergence of the public sphere as part of the establishment of bourgeois hegemony.

> The "dictatorship of the bourgeoisie" is expressed in the compartmentalizations, the forms of this public sphere. Whereas the bourgeois revolution initially does make the attempt to overcome the limits of the capitalist mode of production, the forms—for instance the separation of powers, the division between public and private, between politics and production, between everyday language and authentic social expression . . . prevent the mere mention of social critique, counter publicity, or the emancipation of the majority of the population. There is no chance that the experiences and interest of the proletariat, in the broadest sense, will be able to organize themselves amid this splitting of all the linked qualitative elements of experience and social practice. (Negt and Kluge 1972, 14)

Revising Habermas's account in a form of internal critique, and redeploying his reliance on the specific forms of experience proper to ideal publicity, Negt and Kluge suggest that the ideal public of Habermas's account was specific to bourgeois domination, and refuses constitutively other forms of social experience. More recently, feminists have further interrogated Habermas's account, seeing in his idealized form of abstract publicity an apparatus of power, by which the "marked" body of the female subject was excluded from full participation (Fraser 1985, 1992). In a similar vein, race scholars have described the color of the abstract public citizen: the white subjects of traditional publicity built the logics of their "uninterested" public reasoning on the constitutive exclusion of black specificity (Spillers 1987; Berlant 1993). A critical account of publicity needs to be aware of the conditions of its operation, to locate the structuring moments of power that determine the formation of various kinds of public sphere.[11]

Second, Habermas's account of the decline of publicity fails to engage properly with the specificity of the mass cultural moment. A number of scholars are now attempting to theorize the problem of mass publicity, its specific modes of subjectivity and its forms of collective agency. Miriam Hansen's work on the public sphere and cinema offers a way of thinking through publicity and mass mediation not as technologically determined historical givens, but rather as dynamic, contested, but nonetheless policed forms of social experience, and thus contributes a certain density to the potential of the public sphere as a tool for critical cultural studies. "The political issue is whether and to what extent a public sphere is organized from above—by the exclusive standards of high culture or the stereotypes of commodity culture—or by the experiencing subjects themselves, on the basis of their context of living *(Lebenszusammenhang.)*" (1991b, 12). Citing Kluge, Hansen argues that the possibility that this public sphere can allow alternative formations is based on the requirement of a "third term—the other viewer, the audience as collective, the theater as a social space, part of a social horizon of experience" (14). Hansen thus sketches out a more refined way of thinking about agency in the public sphere, in ways that reformulate the cultural studies tropes of "resistance" and opposition.[12]

While theorists like Michael Warner have begun to explore the visual culture of publicity, the sound of publicity remains largely untheorized. Warner makes the point that publicity in the West, which might be rethought as the dialectical relationship between the subjectivities of spectatorship/citizenship and stardom, requires iconicity for its intelligibility (1992, 385). We might say as well that to be public in the West means to have a resonance, to resonate, to reverberate. The differential access to publicity that Warner (and others) argue is central to its historical trajectory and function is marked (or unmarked) by its audibility as much as its visibility. The kind of voices that are heard in the institutionalized public sphere, the very way voice is constructed as a locus of agency and subjectivity, the registers of the material conditions of certain forms of embodied publicity, and the relationship of voice to body—each contributes to the way we think about publicity as both a differentially distributed resource and a selectively localizable burden.

In order to direct attention toward the sonic aspects crucial not only to the constitution of a vague sense of national affect, but specifically to the formation of national public spheres, I have chosen to focus my study on what I have called the acoustics of publicity. The usefulness of this perhaps not so felicitous phrase lies in the ambiguous meanings of acoustics: acoustics is, on the one hand, the physics of sound, a descriptive science that claims to model the empirical phenomenon of resonance itself. But, at the same time, acoustics are normative. There are "good" acoustics and "bad" acoustics, acoustic distributions and architectures that are more or less appropriate to engendering certain kinds of subjective experience. My discussion of acoustics will encompass both of these meanings: a description of the "empirical" sound of the nation, as well as an investigation of the various kinds of sound nation that competed for hegemony. In other words, a study of the "acoustics of national publicity" suggests an empirical description of the ideological conditions—material and "cognitional"—that determined the sonic experience of the public, as well as a historical look at the competing conceptions of how those conditions should be molded or transformed in various ways.

Habermas argues that musical performance was crucial to the formation of bourgeois publicity. More than simply one realm in which this historical transformation can be traced, Habermas suggests that music was in fact the locus of social practice where this transformation registered most profoundly:

> The shift which produced not merely a change in the composition of the public but amounted to the very generation of "the public" as such, can be categorically grasped with even more rigor in the case of the concert-going public than in the case of the reading and theater going public. ([1962] 1990)

Habermas's more or less general propositions about the role of music in the history of the public sphere have been supported by recent empirical work on the eighteenth century. James Johnson's investigation of listening in Paris clearly positions music in the center of the formation of new kinds of public capable of serving as a challenge to more traditional conceptions of both politics and aesthetics:

> Like public opinion in political discourse, the musical public effectively challenged traditional absolutist patterns of judgment by

offering a third source of musical arbitration apart from both the
king and the opinions of disconnected groups. (1995, 93)

What emerges here is a dialectical relationship between the historicity of musical practice and the history of publicity's social formations.
Transformations in publicity impinged on the social organization of
musical practice, and changes in musical practice contributed to the
historic constitution of those social formations known as publics.[13]
In theorizing the acoustics of publicity we can gain insight into the
historical dynamic of these developments by grasping elements of
the "experiential conjunction" of publicity in ways that go beyond the
traditional fetishization of speech as a possibly pure form of communication, looking at the ensemble of social practices that make the very
idea of communication, and the resonant subjects that communication
requires, possible.

The Case Studies

Recent musicological work on the Weimar Republic and the Third
Reich has been mainly concerned with elite musical practices, sites,
and repertories.[14] This work has certainly broadened our understanding of the role of musical culture in both the development of fascism
and its hold on power, going a long way to complicate the oversimplified opposition of Weill versus Wagner that seems to structure our
commonsensical understanding of music in the Weimar and Nazi periods. But the focus on these issues has tended to obscure the importance and complexity of more thoroughly mass-mediated forms of
musical practice. At issue here is not merely the opposition between
elite and "popular" musical cultures: a more in-depth consideration
of both popular and elite musical practices in this period needs to
come to terms with the simultaneously ideological and technological transformations in musical publicity that characterize this period:
radio, sound film, and recording.

It is important to distinguish between a study of "popular music,"
understood as the music industry defines it—a canonical corpus of songs
and stars—and a study of "music in mass culture." A study of music
in mass culture must include a close study, in other words, of the conditions under which music resonated in mass cultural environments:
musics both of a lasting and a profoundly fleeting nature. This means
that seemingly "major" figures or events play a marginal role in this

study, in the interest of focusing on what might at first seem the more banal aspects of popular music. But, as I hope this study will show, it is precisely at the level of the quotidian where a study of "music as mass culture" can be the most fruitful. This means on the one hand a focus on seemingly "minor" figures, who might seem "musically" uninteresting, as well as a deeper look at the function of music in various modes of social practice. While of course figures like Marlene Dietrich played roles in the mass culture of the Weimar Republic, a historical look at this period reduces their stature remarkably in the context of other problems and issues. While putting these things in perspective might irritate the reader who was expecting to learn more about those stars he or she was already more or less familiar with, I hope it will also open up new vistas for thinking about the history of popular culture in the first half of the twentieth century in ways that avoid the clichés all too readily called to mind.

In order to open up this field of discussion, this historical and theoretical intervention is structured as a set of case studies, each using readings of films. This strategy is useful for two reasons. First, the cinema represented one of the key acoustic environments of national and public experience: any historical encounter with the acoustics of national publicity in this period needs to place the cinematic moment of mass culture at the center of its project.[15] Secondly, film also provides a rich source for an examination of the contradictory ideological field of mass culture. Allowing the popular music of the period to be seen within the primary mode of its consumption, a look at the sound films of the Weimar and Nazi periods enriches our encounter with these musical texts, and can serve as a key for opening up new perspectives of interpretation.

The illustrated journals of the period are a second primary focus of research. In particular, advertising offers a rich source of cultural excavation. Reflecting transformations in the audience of its address, and at the same time serving as a normative tool to form that very audience, print advertising was one of the central guides for the audience in negotiating the emerging system of mass culture in the 1920s and '30s. This is especially true in the case of the illustrated weeklies of the period. Distributed at kiosks, on the street, and in railroad stations, these magazines, which stood out from other publications of the time because of the sheer number of photographs and illustrations, had by the early 1930s come to hold a central place of importance in the German media landscape. By 1931, the *Berliner Illustrirte Zeitung* (*BIZ*), the most successful of the "illustrateds," had reached a readership of two million (Kirchner 1962, 357), a number that—to use a crude comparison in order to give a sense of magnitude—far surpasses the readership of any sort of comparable German weeklies today. Although primarily addressed to the growing audience of white-collar employees (Marckwardt 1982), this newly dominant mass medium grew astronomically in the 1920s and was definitely also accessible to the working-class audience of the period. The *BIZ* and its counterparts like *Die Woche*, linked advertising and reporting closely in their layout, and represented a central support in what Horkheimer and Adorno term the "culture industry"; indeed, in many ways the *Illustrirte* served as a paradigm for addressing and constructing a new mass audience. In addition, the "illustrateds" concentrated to a large extent on other forms of media practice, and thus served as a kind of metamedium, crucial in maintaining the links among what Horkheimer and Adorno called the three pillars of the culture industry in the 1930s: "films, radio, and magazines" (1969, 123).

The first case study focuses on the relationships among "the nation," mass culture, and modes of publicity by dealing with radio and cinematic depictions of radio. The standard account of radio's almost all-powerful role in the German national public relies on an ahistorical conception of the German audience and an oversimplified conception of mass culture's relationship to the state. Especially in the realm of popular music, we find that—throughout the Weimar and Nazi periods—radio was not a simple medium for delivering propaganda to the people, but rather represented a tense, contradictory social field. By beginning with radio, I hope to provide a useful sense of periodization. The start of continuous German radio broadcasting on October 29, 1923, was contemporaneous with what Peukert (1989) has called a period of "deceiving stabilization," i.e., was contemporaneous with the establishment of a new and briefly stable form of hegemony. Not only did the years 1923–24 represent a possible break with the baggage of World War I, these years also symbolize the beginning of what many historians regard as a traceable course toward the development of fascism and the fall of the Weimar Republic. Tracing out radio as a site where this hegemony was composed and contested will be the aim of the first chapter.

In the subsequent chapters, I begin to reconstruct a model of how to understand the acoustics of publicity in this period. Chapters 2 and 3 are both concerned with the dialectical relationship between publicity and privacy in musical practice, and especially with the installment of new forms of both in the 1920s and 1930s. First, in chapter 2, I describe one particular zone of musical publicity: the *Schlager*, or "hit song." If the kind of mass publicity that radio exemplified needs to be historicized before being fully integrated into any national narrative of German history, a look at the *Schlager* provides a key to commenting on the specificity of mass culture in the 1920s and 1930s in Germany. The *Schlager* is often caricatured as the epitome of bad mass culture—key in the establishment of fascism and its continued hold on power. Using films, magazines, and novels of the period, I suggest instead that the *Schlager* represented what Oskar Negt and Alexander Kluge have called an "organ of experience." This model, I will argue, allows us to grasp both the historical specificity and indeterminacy of this form of mass cultural music, refusing the ahistoricity and telos of both "resistance" and "false consciousness."

The next chapter then examines the relationship between "serious" and popular music in German mass culture of the period, and shows how "serious" forms of musical practice were inserted into mass cultural structures of listening. On the one hand, the "classical" music tradition was articulated to the mass national imaginary provided by the acoustics of radio and cinema. In broadcasts of national art music events, for example, the intent was to produce an acoustic fantasy of the German mass not only for the domestic market, but also within an international context. But it would be a mistake to focus on this relatively marginal aspect of the question. As I will show, this was not the dominant role of "serious" music in the mass culture of the period. Instead, in many ways approaching the structures of address familiar from the *Schlager*, art music was inserted into a new, emphatically modern musical privacy. The installation of a new form of interiority in "classical music" and its popular consumption assembled a disciplinary structure of musical privacy that would later come to dominate modern musical consumption in capitalism in general. By looking at the use of art music in the cinema and advertising in particular, I will trace out the emergence of this complex apparatus of subjectivity around art music, and suggest ways in which it shows how music played a central role in the ideological structuring of diverse practices of everyday life and notions of publicity and privacy.

The final chapter focuses on the question of "race" and its role in the German musical public sphere, by looking at the case of so-called gypsy musicians and musicality. A highly saturated locus of ideological production in Central Europe, gypsy music provides a counter-example to oversimplified accounts of the operation of race in the German public sphere of this period that tend to see the German case as a uniquely pathological development. While gypsies were subject to industrialized mass murder by the Nazis, gypsy music and musicality were also deployed in Germany's national acoustics as sonic placeholders for both a "lost" *Heimat* and the lure of the exotic. The striking similarity of this racial regime to other racial regimes in the West should remind us of the very real dangers involved in seemingly more innocuous forms of symbolic appropriation and fetishization in popular music.

2

—— • ——

The *Schlager* and the Singer Film: Organs of Experience and the History of Subjectivity

The previous chapter illustrated that Germany's radio publics were by no means once and for all established with the invention of the technology, nor were they later trapped by a "totalitarian" radio practice able to instrumentalize radio technology in uniquely powerful ways. An adequate history of the medium needs to chart out a series of recurring struggles and a history of constant renegotiation, in which radio's operation as a site of publicity and its role within the overall acoustics of publicity were far from secure. Reconceptualizing the placement of the radio in social practice and the structure of radio as a mass medium is a crucial step in framing a more critical and more properly historical account of acoustic culture in this period. This "technological" approach, however, is merely one side of the issue. Just as the placement of sound technologies and the structure of various media like the radio determine the parameters of "content," these media are in turn structured by specific forms of acoustic practice, which are situated in those media and through which these media are constituted. If one of the most cherished assumptions about the acoustics of publicity in Germany of the 1920s and 1930s is a profoundly *unmediated* conception of the radio as a medium, no less cherished assumptions cling to this mainstay of radio broadcasting's "content" already in its early years: the German *Schlager*.

In ways arguably unparalleled by other forms of musical practice, the *Schlager*, roughly translated "hit song," came to form the bulk of radio programming and dominate other forms of acoustic culture in the late 1920s.[1] But the *Schlager's* key role in mass culture was not only due to its purely acoustic presence. Linking older forms of print culture, i.e., printed music and advertising, with the newer mass media, the *Schlager* in the late 1920s can be understood as a central point of articulation within the system of "films, radio, and magazines," or a main connecting link in the switchboard of what Horkheimer and Adorno termed "the culture industry" (1969, 123). A focus of attention and alarm in both the general and the music press, and a central theme and "technique" of novelists such as Irmgard Keun (*Das kunstseidene Mädchen [The Artificial Silk Girl]* [1932]), Alfred Döblin (*Berlin Alexanderplatz* [1929]), and Gabriele Tergit (*Käsebier erobert den Kurfürstendamm [Käsebier Conquers the Kurfürstendamm]* [1931] [Tergit 1978]), *Schlager* and *Schlager* singers were at the heart of mass culture and came metonymically to represent the particular brand of modernity of late Weimar culture.

Although the German *Schlager* enjoyed its heyday during the late 1920s and 1930s, the term itself dates from the late nineteenth century. Probably adapted from Viennese retail jargon, the term was originally used in the 1860s and '70s simply to indicate those songs, usually from the context of an operetta, that achieved a certain level of commercial success with the audience, which in turn was intelligible as "popularity" (Worbs 1963). Between 1900 and 1918, however, the meaning of the term underwent a transformation: *Schlager* were now understood to constitute a genre (Schär 1991, 33).[2] This transformation was not determined by any clear change in style or the "taste" of the German-speaking audience. If anything, *Schlager* were in musical terms more variant and diverse after 1918, due to the jazz-like elements in the popular music of Germany in the 1920s and 1930s and the speed at which new trends in popular music established themselves in the more developed mass culture of the Weimar period.[3] Most importantly, however, the new *Schlager* represented a different kind of social site of musical production and consumption, no longer primarily associated with operetta. With the beginning of radio broadcasting (1923) and sound film (1929), the technological and ideological transformation of the mass media during the 1920s disrupted the former context of the hit song and its former function, replacing these with forms of public experience at odds with the traditional publics of the operetta stage and the musical print culture that had developed around the operetta.

Scholars have not ignored the centrality of the *Schlager* in the late Weimar Republic and the Nazi period. On the contrary, it has been conceptualized as one of the most powerful techniques of a manipulative distraction in the late Weimar period, which encouraged the German population to ignore economic hardships and to lose themselves in escapist fantasy. This account further suggests that the German *Schlager* represented an almost unique refusal to engage in the properly political sphere: the *Schlager* is granted agency in this account, and is scripted to play a central role in the establishment of a fascist state.[4] Dietrich Kayser's book on *Schlager* is paradigmatic for this approach. Capitalist society "produces a strong, widespread need for distraction *(Ablenkung)* and entertainment," and the *Schlager*, for Kayser, fulfills this need.

> The *Schlager* takes on . . . the function of playing over obvious class contradictions and connecting their supercession to the correct authority, destiny. The petit-bourgeois accepts this illusion because of the incapability of recognizing himself as a member of the proletariat; only too gladly does he meet here a world without class-barriers and the full acceptance of the existing *[des Gegebenen]*. (1975, 25)

Echoing in many ways the standard account of radio policy in Weimar, Kayser focuses on the monopolistic tendencies of the *Schlager* industry (22–23).[5] *Schlager*, in other words, have a quite specific social function: instrumentalized by the agencies of monopoly capitalism that dominated mass cultural production in the late Weimar years, *Schlager* were, in this logic, indeed designed to inhibit properly critical cognition on the part of the petit-bourgeois listener, and readily achieved this goal. If *Schlager* are seen as being forerunners of fascist mass culture, seemingly both "cause" and symptom of the end of a potentially democratic mass culture in the Weimar period, an equally clear ideological role tends to be assigned to them in the historiography of Nazi mass culture (Wicke 1987, 419). *Schlager* in film, radio, and phonography served in this account as the ultimate means of distracting the population from everyday concerns; the term *Durchhaltelied* in particular, literally "hold out song," is used to describe *Heimat*-laden songs from the latter war period.[6] Mass cultural music is here seen as successfully directed by the Nazis to the last detail, keeping the "mood" of the masses optimal for the war. Even after other forms of popular culture have been subject to attempts at critical redemptive recuperation, the German *Schlager* continues to play an almost exclusively negative role.

Critics and historians have tended to come down especially hard on the *Filmschlager* and early sound film. Marc Silberman's (1995) account of the "coming of sound" to Weimar cinema casts the *Schlager* and the early German musicals as the opposite pole to a progressive modernist use of mass culture. In a negative comparison to the explicitly modernist aesthetic of films like *Kuhle Wampe oder wem gehört die Welt?* *[Kuhle Wampe or Who Owns the World?]* (Dudov/Brecht 1931; music Hanns Eisler), Silberman interprets the bulk of early sound film as directly manipulative. Intimately linking musical comedy with "the middlebrow ideologies of social harmony and classless statism proposed by the National Socialists" (40), Silberman forgoes the kind of intense textual work he expends for a filmic text like *Kuhle Wampe* for the entire category of "mainstream" musical film. In so doing, he reduces the play of sound and image in these commercial products to mere elements in both the "escapist" plots of the films themselves and the emplotment of German political history itself. Indeed, for Silberman, the fact that musical films like *Die Drei von der Tankstelle [The Three from the Gas Station]* (Thiele 1930) dominated early sound film production seems to prove the homologous relationship between monopoly capital and the destruction of any potentially critical film culture or practice. Ultimately, this path leads to the trap of an overly schematic and arguably paradoxical dichotomy between critical modernism and manipulated modernity.[7] Surely, there is something to be said for regarding *Kuhle Wampe* as an almost unique moment of critical filmmaking in the early sound period, particularly in its use of sound. But if this status is guaranteed by opposing it to an oversimplified understanding of mainstream film production and its effects on "the audience," we are simply reproducing the low/high dichotomy in a pseudopolitical register. Not only does this approach allow us to learn little about the operation of mass culture as a social field, it blinds us to other kinds of potentially critical formations in this period, particularly those made possible by the contradictions and fissures within acoustic mass culture.[8]

It should not be overlooked that these accounts of the *Schlager* and early musical film do have the advantage of placing ideology at the center of their concerns. However, this literature fails to explicitly *theorize* ideology in the realm of mass culture. "Ideology" in this account reads as the space of epistemological illusion about the nature of the social. The real content of the social form, for these commentators, is veiled by the nonsense of the classless *Schlager* fantasy. But, as Slavoj Žižek has argued, echoing the work of Althusser, "ideology must be disengaged from the 'representationalist' problematic: ideology has nothing to do with illusion, with a mistaken, distorted representation of its social content" (1994, 7).[9] Ideology, in other words, is not a different plane of existence, where the social is "commented" upon. Instead, ideology must be seen as an integral component of the social itself: there is no outside to its operation, and more or less "critical" representations of the social "real" are also implicated in ideological production and dependent on ideology for their meaning.

Not only is the theory of ideology in the standard account inadequate to the problem at hand, in that it hinders our view of the complexities of mass cultural musical practice, this account also fails to address adequately the question of the *Schlager*'s historicity. While mentioning in passing the new technologies of reproduction and their tendency to saturate the music market to an extent unprecedented in the commodification of musical practice, these authors fail to locate the *Schlager* in the context of more thoroughgoing changes in the form of publicity in mass culture. The question of historicity should involve first of all the nature of the "audience": in the standard account, the "German" audience of the *Schlager* seems to be an ahistorical, class constant: the petit-bourgeois appears in this account as a fully intelligible personality, with a function that is obvious and desires that are not only ahistorical, but also quite readily manipulated. Moreover, we need to *theorize* more precisely the nature of the historicity of mass culture, in particular the historicity of the *Schlager*. If it is a mistake to look to the economic instance as determining the social in an unmediated fashion, it is certainly a grave error to map the effects of the political (the "state" in liberal discourse) as completely determining the mass cultural sphere, even in protofascist and fascist Germany of the 1930s and '40s.[10] Rather than making the arena of mass culture ultimately subject to a synchronicity with the "properly" political, we might want to ask what kinds of publicity can be traced in the arena of mass culture that operate according to a different temporality.[11]

While we need a more nuanced theoretical grasp of the role of ideology in mass culture to truly illuminate the *Schlager*, we should consider this a two-way street. By looking at the question of the *Schlager*'s specificity, we can also contribute to a re-theorization of ideology. In order begin to capture the nature of ideology in popular music practice, we need to locate the specific structures of subjectivization *(assujetissement)* on which these musical practices depend. As in the case of radio, this requires looking at the *Schlager* as a specific mode of musical publicity that both depended on and engaged in the production of certain historically specific arrangements of collectivity and of subjectivity. In this chapter, I will engage the specific effectivity of the *Schlager* by theorizing the hit song in terms of the historicity of publicity and its relationship to the subject. In order to do this, we need to look beyond the *Schlager* as a body of musical texts; while much of the literature on *Schlager* has focused on the lyrics, a focus on "the music" would also not solve the problem that these analyses have: the textuality of both *Schlager* lyrics and music itself needs to be framed. The *Schlager* needs to be historicized and theorized as part and parcel of this moment of modernity; to paraphrase Miriam Hansen, if we position the *Schlager* within a history of sense perception in modernity, we can recast the debate on "resistance" and the nature of the mass cultural audience in more specific historical and political terms (1995, 365). In order to focus our attention on "heterogeneity, nonsynchronicity, and contradiction" in the *Schlager*, I will show how the *Schlager* represented a moment of crisis and transformation in the configuration of publicity. Then, returning to Habermas's account of publicity and the subject, I will trace out how the *Schlager*-subject can be seen as the prerequisite and product of this crisis. Finally, returning to theoretical questions of agency and indeterminacy, I will discuss the *Schlager* as an "organ of experience," theorizing how we might move beyond the simple dichotomies of "resistance" and manipulation in our understanding of music in German mass culture.

"The Musicalization of the World"

In 1931, Oskar Bie, a prominent German music critic, attempted to come to terms with the *Schlager*, or "hit song," and its role in late Weimar mass culture. In an article entitled "A *Schlager* Travels around the World," appearing in one of the main illustrated weeklies, *Die Woche (The Week)*, Bie specifically characterizes the new quality of the *Schlager* in the age of sound film. The sound film, he writes, needs but "eighteen to twenty-four months" to circumnavigate the globe; "the operetta was never able to achieve this." The critic continues to describe the *Schlager* and its principal mode of dispersion, the sound film, as part of a larger process, which he called the "musicalization of the world."

> The musicalization of the world through the sound film is without precedent. The tempo is accelerated, the saturation absolute. The *Schlager* today has its fastest and surest dispersion. (863)

It is worth spending some time on Bie's description, written at the height of the *Schlager* craze. Not only did Bie, known at the time for his books dealing with the opera and the concert, provide a particularly rich contemporary "ethnographic" account; more importantly, he left behind a profoundly symptomatic text that allows us to engage a deeper reading of the *Schlager* as a zone of social experience.[12] More than merely offering a number of interesting synchronic insights into the way the *Schlager* was read by contemporary observers as holding a special place in the social, Bie's account also unwittingly gestures in the direction of the diachronic, suggesting a number of different transformative processes around the *Schlager*. The accelerated tempo and absolute saturation of the *Schlager* are for Bie not simply unprecedented phenomena in the social organization of musical practice; the "musicalization of the world" represents a more thoroughgoing transformation of the experience of both time and space in modernity. Central to Bie's account of this more general condition is the role of technology, but also the "social situation" of this musical practice in the urban scene.

> One hears it from loudspeakers, it sounds from a window on the gramophone, it parades in the music stores, it is posted on the advertising columns, the Berlin cobbler's apprentice *[Schusterjunge]* sings it, the worker has it in his mouth when he goes home, the young ladies sing it at tea, it is struck up for dance. (864)

This description of the acoustics of urbanity in the age of the hit song is illuminating for a number of reasons. Bie's *Schlager* is grammatically elusive, both subject and object. While on the one hand it sounds and parades on its trip around the world, seemingly independent of human agency, on the other hand it is heard, sung, posted. From the abstract acoustic space of the modern city, loudspeakers and gramophones heard through windows, the *Schlager* comes down to earth as part of the seemingly more concrete experience of *flânerie*. Bie's description thus evokes a contradictory serial simultaneity. From the cobbler's apprentice to the gramophone, simultaneity is produced in the multiple technologies of dispersion that come together in the *Schlager*. Bie's description also maps a trajectory from properly public modes of presence to a more complicated kind of now-public realm: the body of the listener.

Bie opposes the new *Schlager* not only to operetta, but also to "folk music": the main difference for Bie between *Schlager* and "folk music" is that the *Schlager* is "set in the world artificially" (864). Bie focuses his attention on the journey of the *Schlager*:[13]

> The journey of a *Schlager* is a part of modern technology, like the trip of the folk song was a part of old romanticism. The *Schlager* is thus more than fashion, it is in a certain sense the expression of a modern musical conception *[Musikanschauung]*, that prefers a short and effective melody to a long evening of opera, in which its happiness and its desire are reflected without too much cultural pathos . . . Beginning and end might be sometimes romantic, but the trip itself has the tempo of flight. (864)

Bie's description picks up on the complex, nonsynchronous temporality of the *Schlager*. The *Schlager* might begin and end with the romantic, but this now-nostalgic mode of sociality is thrown into the "tempo of flight," an emphatically modern form of technologized experience. Moving between already familiar kinds of musical sociality and a more distracted, mass-cultural moment of musical pleasure, the *Schlager* in this account marks a moment of transformation that Bie's phrase, "the musicalization of the world," only begins to grasp.

Bie's "musicalization of the world" is a particularly rich but by no means unique example of how the *Schlager* was seen in the late 1920s and early 1930s as a radically new kind of musical publicity.[14] Another valuable source for tracing out the complex social field Bie is here attempting to describe can be found in advertising from the period. As was the case for radio, advertising again played a central role in structuring the *Schlager* as a realm of social experience, and presents us with a rewarding archive of the kind of contradictory formations that Bie seems to want to sketch out. The presence of the *Schlager* in advertising of the period took a number of forms: visualizing the mass audience and its relationship to the *Schlager*; establishing the forms of mass subjectivity appropriate for the emerging audiovisual star system, and inserting the *Schlager* into modern technologies of sound. One genre of advertising techniques specifically figured the relationship of the musical object or star to its audience. In Figure 9, an advertisement for Parlophon Records from 1930, we see one example of the way this new public was represented.

Proclaiming to the reader that "listening to Parlophon and being in the mood are the same thing," and advertising specifically "the new dance *Schlager* played by Barnabas von Géczy and his orchestra," one of the most popular German bands of the 1930s, this image depicts an infinite crowd of dancing couples beneath a larger-than-life gramophone playing a Parlophon record. This depiction shows a mass extending infinitely in three directions, not anchored to any one place. We are told that Géczy plays in the Hotel Esplanade: if we imagine Géczy playing in this hotel, one of the most famous Berlin hotels then located at Potsdamer Platz, this might serve to ground the experience of listening in more traditional modes of publicity anchored in specific locales of modern life. But this scene is not pictured here: there is no "place" visualized in this advertisement other than the space occupied

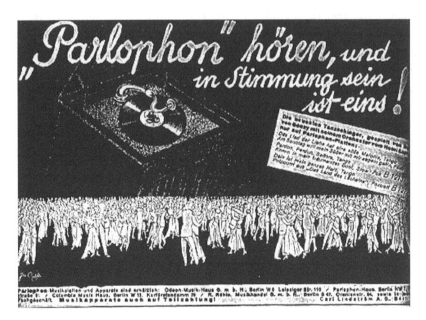

Figure 9. *"Listening to Parlophon and Being in the Mood Are the Same Thing!"* Advertisement for Parlophon record players in Die Woche, *January 18, 1930.*

by the mass, produced by the record and its technology of reproduction. This example shows that the pleasures of the new *Schlager* were no longer tied to the experience of publicity that characterized more traditional forms of musical performance, where the sound of the musical performance resonated in an environment designed to gather the public in one place, limited in its extension. Instead, the *Schlager* "took place" in its own fantasy architecture with a new kind of delocalized acoustic, the physics of its "sound" determined not by the constraints of walls or ceilings but by the distribution of the mass, centered around the new technologies of musical distribution.

The Parlophon ad also makes clear that the purchase of the *Schlager*'s banally material manifestation was to be understood as the purchase of a much more complex commodity, popularity, or access to an experience of popularity. The new concept of *Schlager* indicated a genre of songs, not necessarily from the context of a larger work, that were understood as having been designed to be popular, and the pleasures of the *Schlager* were dependent on the experience of their popularity. Still other advertisements used the *Schlager* as an icon of popularity to sell other commodities. An example of this practice were *Schlager* contests; sponsored by corporations intent on selling anything from swimsuits to cigarettes, these contests invited both professional and amateur *Schlager* composers to submit their version of a new jingle or song singing the praises of the corporation's product. The winning "hit" would be printed, along with the composer's name, as the prizewinning *Schlager*, as can be seen in the examples of these advertisements reproduced in Figures 10, 11, and 12. These ads represent both the continuity and change of this complex formation in the Weimar and Nazi periods. The first one, from 1924, is an advertisement for a company that makes women's swimsuits, Rosenberg and Hertz, and the brand name "Forma."

The song's iconic status is linked directly to the physical experience of fashionable dance by its title: "Forma Shimmy." The text to this "hit," written by a certain M. Velin from Dresden, speaks in many ways for itself:

> Ich könnte dich noch jahrelang in Forma seh'n
> und würde selbst im Winter mit dir baden geh'n
> zu Wasser und zu Lande bist du himmlisch schön
> drum könnte ich dich jahrelang in Forma seh'n

(I could see you for years still in Forma
And I would even go swimming with you in winter
In water and on land you are heavenly beautiful
So I could see you for years in Forma)

The rhythms of this dance song, emphasized by the rhyme of the text, intimately associate the movement of dance with the fit of this new swimsuit; the wearer of this swimsuit is then promised a popular body, in sync with the hyper-present tense of musical mass culture. The "Forma Shimmy" is not only available here in full piano accompaniment; in the corner of the advertisement, band leaders are offered free copies of the arrangements for piano and salon orchestra of "our Forma Shimmy," as well as the right to play the song without paying royalties. The advertisement not only enlists the music to this dance *Schlager* as a visual icon of its product; it also hopes to encourage the band leaders of the *BIZ* readership to participate in the "event" of this hit by adding it to their repertoires.

The second advertisement engages in different strategies to produce the affect of mass publicity that it wants to associate with its product. The *Schlager* is merely a "four-liner" jingle; less concerned with appearing up-to-date than the "Forma Shimmy" example, this presentation of a fairly simple melody engages instead with a form of nostalgia.

This nostalgia is also indicated by the composer of the "hit," Walter Kollo. Depicted at the left playing his new hit on a saxophone for a pig (presumably the icon for Buchholz Brandy), this composer, along with other aging operetta composers like Paul Lincke, belonged to the grandfathers of popular music in the 1930s.[15] But this advertisement is also engaged in a commercial mode of national fantasy.

> Already this weekend, on March 26th, 3000 bands will play in
> German . . . the new Kollo *Schlager*-Song "Come, Bend Your Head
> Towards Me" for the first time, and the guests bring home with
> them a lovely memento of this evening and the loved Original
> Buchholz Brandy.

This device makes the *Schlager's* arrival into an event; the kind of mass public that this "new *Schlager* song"—a mere advertising jingle—was supposed to produce and address has become the tool by which the product is to be sold.

If the marketing of the mass public as a kind of event in this case

Figure 10. Advertisement for Forma in Berliner Illustrite Zeitung, 1924.

Figure 11. Advertisement, Ur-Buchholz Weinbrand, 1929.

Figure 12. "There's a New Magic Word: Alva, Only Alva!" Advertisement for cigarette brand in Berliner Illustrirte Zeitung, 1934.

remained at least in part structured by more familiar, older forms of musical experience, the transformation of the *Schlager* from a public event to the event of a public was quickly adapted to the new technologies of musical reproduction. The third example, "There is a new magic word: Alva, only Alva!" is an advertisement for cigarettes that appeared shortly before New Year's Eve, 1934.

Like the 1927 example, this "first hit of 1935" is also by a prominent composer, Willi Meisel.[16] But unlike the kind of simultaneity organized by the Albert Buchholz AG in 1927, or the possibility of buying the music to this "classic" hit, here the reader is offered a "10 cm record of this hit, played by the famous dance orchestra Oskar Joost, sung by Erwin Hartung and the Humoresque Melodios." Joost was a very popular jazz and swing musician in the 1930s in Germany; playing both in a hotter style and a more popular *Schlager*-dominated repertoire, Joost was one of the central innovators in popular music from the period.[17] This example includes both verse and refrain:

> When one today as a man anytime and anywhere needs a pick-me-up
> one knows how to do it so that our hearts smile: one smokes Alva.
> Even the woman likes to smoke Alva like the men, because they [are]
>   mild and beautiful
> Aroma and the Format are a true achievement
> Smoke and you'll see!
>
> There is a new magic word that makes all worries disappear
> Alva! Only Alva!
> You were maybe already often in love. Who shows you that there is
>   fidelity?
> Alva! Only Alva!
> At the fireplace you dream of sweet harmony, the cigarette Alva,
>   it will never disappoint you
> There is a new magic word that makes all worries disappear
> Alva! Only Alva!
> Alva! Only Alva!
> You will never change from Alva.[18]

The configuration of publicity and popularity that enabled—and was enabled by—the *Schlager* in the late Weimar Republic was produced by and contingent on the new experience of mass cultural modernity, a structural complement to the visual spectacle of the "mass ornament" (Kracauer 1995). The advertising techniques that used the *Schlager* not only revolved around the popularity of the various composers who wrote these *Schlager*, but also depended on the experience of popularity that the *Schlager* represented to market other products. The new centrality of the *Schlager* was predicated on transformations in the ideology of popularity; rather than being attributed to "opinion," in which a given public sphere chooses to "enjoy" a certain song, popularity came to be understood as a mode of address dependent on the mass publics that characterized the Weimar period. The kind of listening practice on which the *Schlager* now relied corresponded to a newly configured public that understood itself as constituted precisely by its embrace of the latest popular musical product.

Commodity and Publicity: Public Events or the Event of a Public?

Of course, since its emergence in the eighteenth century, modern musical publicity has always been centered around the commodity form. Describing the change in function of the concert from a form of "representative publicity" characteristic of the *ancien régime*, Habermas notes that the commodity form of music in the new concert form was key to the development of critical publicity. While Habermas points out that "admission for a payment turned the musical performance into a commodity," he also argues that this was the prerequisite for the emergence of autonomous music itself. This contradictory autonomy of the musical object in turn allowed for the emergence of musical taste.

> Simultaneously, however, there arose something like music not tied to a purpose. For the first time an audience gathered to listen to music as such—a public of music lovers to which anyone who was propertied and educated was admitted. Released from its functions in the service of social representation, art became an object of free choice and of changing preference. The "taste" to which art was oriented from then on became manifest in the assessments of lay people who claimed no prerogative, since within a public everyone was entitled to judge. (1989 [1962], 39–40)

In other words, the commodification of the musical performance was the condition for an ideal collection of equal listening subjects, subjects who understood themselves as participating in, *being* a public. The very concept of musical taste was dependent on this arrangement; the abstract character of the musical work, necessarily obscuring its nature as social practice, was required for the corresponding abstractness of the listening public and the pleasures or displeasures this body might find in the work "itself."

If the commodity form of musical performance as found in the concert was crucial in the historical formation of Western publicity and the abstractness that it requires,[19] the reconfigurations of publicity in the age of mass culture, and the transformed conception of musical practice as commodity that these reconfigurations entailed, can be seen equally to involve musical practice. In the 1920s and 1930s, neither the concert form nor the operetta performance continued to represent the central mode of musical publicity or served as the primary site at which the commodification of music was staged. This shift in modes of commodification in turn produced a new kind of musical audience, inhabited by new forms of listening subjectivity. In the concert form, opera, and operetta, the musical event "happens" in a retroactively produced, dehistoricized public, which then forms an opinion about the musical work; the concert requires and produces a certain claim to continuity, and as such, masks the commodity character of publicity by turning musical consumption into something more. But the *Schlager* is a different case entirely. Here, the music is not a public event, but rather, the music serves to inaugurate the event of a public. Thus, this is not a mere reversal of terms: the public that "happens" in the *Schlager* has a discontinuous relationship to earlier modes of musical collectivity, indeed insists on its extreme contemporaneity as a break with all previous musical commodities. The idealized public of the concert is here fractured by the multiple forms of commodification that determine its operation. From the imagined infinite public not dancing in the Hotel Esplanade, to the more intimate interaction of the swimsuit wearer and her admirer, to the smoking gentlemen and the fans of Buchholz Brandy, each new advertisement presents the moment a new public "happens," and offers the consumer a new and radically fragmented way of *experiencing* publicity.

This is then not only a transformation of the logic of space, but also of the logic of time. On the one hand, the multiple musical publics of mass culture cannot be gathered in any one place, as is the case in the ideal form of bourgeois publicity, but are defined by their fragmentary relationship to the commodity form. There is no ideal concert hall which might theoretically house all the "members" of these musical publics. Instead, each emerging fragmentary musical public requires its own fantasy architecture. On the other hand, the temporal continuity of the Enlightenment public sphere—at least its claim to temporal continuity—is resolutely refused by these forms of musical public, where the sense of time indeed seems to be serial—the hit song of 1924—but in fact recurs in a constant now, a hyper-present tense. While the concert public is at least imagined to have an existence that extends beyond the concert hall in both time and space, the *Schlager* audience is continually reinvented; both audience formations and the *Schlager* themselves seem subject to disposal and reconfiguration at an astonishingly rapid tempo.

It was precisely the self-referential newness of this formation which made the new *Schlager* of each year so attractive for advertising: the constant "modernity" of the *Schlager* served as a musical allegory for the new commodities awaiting consumption and linked the transformation of the public sphere directly to the acceleration of modern forms of consumer life. The kind of fascination with the *Schlager* that these advertising practices express is well represented by the sound films of the late Weimar and Nazi periods. Not only was the sound film crucial to the new *Schlager*, but the *Schlager* was also central to the new pleasures this medium offered. Indeed, as Bie's account suggests, the *Filmschlager* became the main location where the full experience of a mediated publicness in radio, recording, and sound film could be enjoyed. One good indicator of this is the prominent iconic use of *Schlager* music in the illustrated film programs of the early sound period.

While printed *Schlager* music retained its iconic status in film programs up through the 1940s (Figure 13) early sound films like *Die Drei von der Tankstelle [The Three from the Gas Station]* (Thiele 1930) not only arranged their plot description around the *Schlager* from the film; they also featured complete piano arrangements in montage with production stills and other star images. If the program focuses our attention on the centrality of *Schlager* in the film, the film itself does not fail to deliver on its promise. It elaborately integrates the technological rhythms of modern life and the *Schlager* it features. As Kracauer described it:

> An unmotivated waltz invited workers clearing out the friends'
> unpaid-for furniture to transform themselves into dancers, and
> whenever the amorous roadster approached, its horn would emit

a few bars which threaded the film with the stubbornness of a genuine leitmotiv. (1947, 207)

This is echoed in the advertising practices Electrola used to sell "the *Schlager* that everyone sings from *The Three from the Gas Station*" (Figure 14). The reader is shown two production stills from the film, the first of Oskar Karlweis at the gas station, and the second of the Comedian Harmonists, the famed male sextet who were prominently featured not only in this film, but in many shorter and full-length films of the early sound period.[20]

Here again, music and image themselves do not make up the focus of publicity; the film is not merely a public event. Rather, the *Schlager* of this film become the nodal point where a hyper-mediated public happens. The stills from the film might be said to "sell" the songs, but the songs equally "sell" the film—any simple conception of directionality falls short of elucidating the problem. What this advertising practice really attempts to produce is the experience of "everyone" singing, listening, watching, reading: the *Schlager* makes up the center of this new experience.

As a by-product of this phenomenon, a particularly popular subject matter in various media contexts was the "life of a *Schlager*." Even as late as 1938 in *Es leuchten die Sterne [The Stars are Shining]* (Zerlett 1937–1938), we still witness an obsession with the social technologies

Figure 13. Film program The Three from the Gas Station *(Thiele 1930).*

of popular music in film. The number *"Haben Sie den neuen Hut von Fräulein Molly schon gesehen?"* ["Have You Seen Miss Molly's New Hat?"] (M: Leo Leux, L: Zerlett, a.k.a. Hanns Hannes) represents an elaborate explanation of the "life of a *Schlager*."[21] In this backstage musical, this sequence is supposed to represent the scene of filming. But like almost every other scene in the film, we are privileged ultimately to hear and see the fully edited version of the intended film product.[22] In the series of shots depicted in Figure 15, we see this *Schlager*, supposedly "inspired" by the accident of an omelet falling on "Miss Molly's" head, move through each of the stages of its "life."

Featuring not only the composer of the song, but also the film and singing stars Max Hansen, Hilde Hildebrand, and Rosita Serrano, this sequence is syntactically organized by dissolves: the series of scenarios is intended to give us an idea of the *Schlager*'s trip "'round the world." From its "birth," through multiple modes and languages of distribution, this sequence climaxes in an extended rhumba version of the song featuring a barely clothed, dancing La Jana surrounded by a girl revue with maracas. This highpoint of the "life of a *Schlager*" is followed by its rapid demise, as in the next shot we see an organ grinder wistfully playing the song on a lonely street; the crumpled sheet music to the song blowing in the wind at his feet.

Figure 14. *"Tank Up on Good Feelings." From* Berliner Illustrirte Zeitung, *1930.*

Shifting between its own status as a new form of musical mediacy and older conventions of the acoustic commodification, such as sheet music, this vision of the "life" of a *Schlager* removes it from any kind of proper agency. Its ultimate cause is an accident of fashion, and its travels from scene to scene are staged as protonatural. The final resting place of the *Schlager* as city trash disassociates this form of dispersion from the "folk"; the *Schlager* is a passing event, ultimately productive only of waste. At this point in the film, the *Schlager* also disrupts plot: not only does this number seem totally disassociated from the film in terms of thematic interest and character development, but the extraordinary length of this sequence also breaks the narrative rhythm of the rest of the film in ways that far surpass the revue film structure. The public that this scene fantasizes into existence thus breaks with the temporality of the film musical as a whole. In a certain sense both inaugurated and dissolved by the syntax of this scene, the *Schlager* public emerges here as far from easily assimilable to what Rick Altman (1987, 200–249) might describe as the idealized public audience of a backstage musical. A fleeting, disposable formation, like the *Schlager* itself, this audience cannot be conceived of as "community," but rather disrupts the temporal requirements of any experience of "community," and finds itself in the end a waste product, discarded onto an ever growing trash heap of *Schlager* publics.

While the fascination with the transformative role of *Schlager* and sound film in the experience of modern life are certainly illuminating for understanding how they were perceived, the overwhelmingly enthusiastic spin on this phenomenon that I have explored thus far found its complement in more critical accounts of this transformation. Even in a by-and-large technophile account like that of Oskar Bie, a kind of nostalgia for older forms of musical public makes itself felt, as in his comparison of *Schlager* and folk music.[23]

[Folk songs] survive in the vernacular *[Volksmund]* through the most different ages, they accompany the great events of world history on a private basis, they come from the soul and touch the soul and fill the heart *[das Gemüt]*, without always singing the praises of love, with the expression of joy and suffering, that touch us daily, in all situations remain the same and in music find an eternal consolation. Sometimes this little piece *[Stückchen]* comes from a local *Posse* . . . sometimes the little song *[Liedchen]* doesn't simply land on the piano at home, but also through the beloved organ grinder *[Leierkasten]* and there achieves its popularity. The whole situation is much more idyllic than today. (1931, 863–64)[24]

Not only are both folk song, or even the "alley song" *[Gassenhauer]* "if it were of a more lowly sort"(863), dependent on the slower, communal process of oral transmission, which can take "years and decades," they are, according to Bie, prone to last for a longer period of time; this implies a quite different relationship to history and the experience of private subjectivity on the stage of history. The contingency of the popular that a film sequence like "Have You Seen Miss Molly's New Hat?" finds so attractive is here cause to mourn the loss of permanence that Bie sees as having been embodied by the folk song tradition.

The centrality of the *Schlager* in mass culture was also the focus of debate and attack in the musical and nonmusical press. One example of this appeared in the journal *Die Musik* in July 1932, entitled, "Do *Schlager* have artistic value?" (Connor 1932). The author of this article, music critic Herbert Connor, had published articles on the same topic in other forums, most importantly in *Die Weltbühne*, an influential

Figure 15. "Have You Seen Miss Molly's New Hat?" Number from Es leuchten die Sterne (Zerlett 1937–1938).

left-liberal journal of Weimar urban culture. As in his earlier articles in *Die Weltbühne* (Connor 1931a, 1931b, 1931c), Connor takes the reader on a tour of the *Schlager* industry. Starting from the position that there is "no inherent reason at all to equate *Schlager* with musical trash" (1932, 749) Connor goes on to explain the fundamental difference between *Schlager* of post–World War I Germany and popular music of earlier periods. He focuses on the blatantly commercial nature of the product, and the monopolistic character of the music industry:

> 99% of all *Schlager* that are played today are artificial productions of an industry that feeds off the exploitation of the copyrights of its products . . . According to the governing trends, the *Schlager* publisher switches from touching Rhine songs *[Rheinlieder]* to fresh, happy military marches. Because of the royalties, lately text and music are written by the publisher and the authors together . . . The heart of the *Schlager* company is the propaganda office. From here, the threads are spun to the radio, to sound film, to the record industry, to the big culinary establishments, to the performers. (750)

In Connor's polemic, the new *Schlager's* lack of artistic value illuminates the decay of modern capitalism. Connor ends his bitter criticism with his diagnosis of the root of the problem: the "speculation" on the lower instincts of the masses that Connor sees the *Schlager* "industry" engaged in, and the products it produces, combine to produce a horror vision of the modern, big city, rootless and tasteless. The hit song for Connor is indeed both a symptom and an agent of this perceived transformation: "the *Schlager* of the twentieth century is not only without artistic value, but also is one of the main reasons for the ever growing hollowing of taste of a broad spectrum of social groups" (751).

On the one hand, Connor's critique might seem to participate in a familiar, and undoubtedly necessary and worthwhile critical topos, reading popular music as both symptom and guarantor of the dominance of capital and its distorting influence on the public sphere. But the vocabulary in this article indicates that Connor's critique also needs to be placed in another discursive context. Particularly in Germany of the 1920s, the corpus of writings complaining about the decay of "*Gemeinschaft*" due to the forces of industrialization and modernity seen metonymized in the organs of mass culture came to approach something of a genre in its own right. But Connor's diagnosis of the problem appeared later that year in a quite different context. In November

1932, the Catholic *Volkswart*, a journal—unlike *Die Musik* and opposite *Die Weltbühne*—with a resolutely antimodern stance and traditionalist audience, dedicated to the "struggle against public immorality," published an article under the name Eva Maria Blume titled "The *Schlager* Industry—a Look behind the Scenes of *Schlager*-Production." Reading this article after Connor's polemics in the liberal press, one begins to notice that the text has a familiar ring. On closer inspection, the reader would realize that either Blume is Connor's drag incarnation or a plagiarist; Blume's article is essentially identical, word for word, to Connor's polemic (Blume 1932b).

The fact that the same text could appear in what seem to be such different contexts illustrates the degree to which this discourse about popular music was institutionalized in the late Weimar Republic. The tendency to demonize the figure of the *"Schlagerfabrikant"* [*Schlager* manufacturer], *"Schlagerclique,"* or *"Schlagerspekulant"* [*Schlager* speculator], was also present in the pages of the Nazi-dominated radio journal *Der Deutsche Sender [The German Radio Broadcaster]*. The ostensibly liberal democratic arguments of an author like Connor or the seemingly more traditional "moral" concerns of the mysterious "Eva Maria Blume" find here their repetition in a fascist dialect. Commenting on *Mein bester Schlager [My Best Schlager]*, a radio show in the *Berliner Funkstunde* [Berlin Radio Hour], the author writes:

> The self-flattery of these *Schlagerfabrikanten* on the Berlin Radio Hour, so good at advertising themselves, is slowly becoming a scandal. Why does the radio administration allow, of all people, these more or less Jewish *Schlager* producers time before the microphone, as if it weren't an issue of values that cannot be lost to the *Volk?*—One only needs to listen to the purely business form . . . of this nonsense once to remember the character of this *Völkchen*, that without shame in order to stuff its own pockets fills our ear with this obnoxious doodling *[Gebudel]* and Jew-dling *[Gejudel]*. (Anonymous 1932a)

While the latter text uses its polemic against the *Schlager* as part of a clearly fascist and anti-Semitic agenda, the "analyses" of the two earlier examples are similar in form, if not in content, to the linkages made by *Der Deutsche Sender*. The earlier articles also saw the composers of *Schlager* as alien to *Gemeinschaft*, and as a threat to the values of the "German" community only interested in lining their pockets at the expense of a general decline in good taste. If *Der Deutsche Sender* makes the anti-Semitic character of its antimodern polemic explicit, the figure of the "foreign," "exploiting," "money hungry" musical industrialist in Connor is driven by the same motive and enabled by a strikingly similar social fantasy. These accounts of mass cultural music share, in other words, the projection to a social "other" of a contradiction they refuse to find in the social.[25]

At stake in each of these commentaries is not simply the nature of this particular set of mass cultural products. The need for each of them to displace the "cause" of decay onto a foreign agency only emphasizes that what these authors were reacting to was an issue that was far less isolable than their fantasies of *Gemeinschaft* imply. These commentaries illustrate a fear of the kind of mass audience that was forming and being formed around the figure of the *Schlager*. The wide dispersal of this critical discourse on the nature of *Schlager* and their harmful effect on community and subjectivity suggests that the concerns being articulated here are more substantial in nature than any simple fears of a decline in taste. What was it about the *Schlager* that allowed it to be perceived as such a fundamental threat, across the political spectrum? What was the kind of mass audience that these commentaries were afraid of?

The *Schlager* Subject

If the *Schlager* represented a redefinition of what musical publicity means, this also indicates that the *Schlager* can be located in a longer history of subjectivity as manifested in and sculpted by specific forms of musical publicity. For example, James Johnson's work illustrates that the formation of a musical public in France was not a question of the musical gathering of already constituted listening subjects—divorced from the historical process—in new social formations. Instead, Johnson argues, the formation of a musical public had everything to do with the constitution of "private" affect and subjects able to operate as the locus of that affect.

> The discovery of an additional stratum of expression, one which had gone largely unacknowledged by earlier generations, encouraged spectators to turn inward to feel the emotions the music evoked. In so doing, it articulated a shift from an objective recognition of the sounds of nature to a more subjective experience of empathetic response. (1992, 221)

It became, in other words, important to "feel" with the music of the opera, rather than merely to enjoy the spectacle; character took on a new importance both musically and theatrically in the staging and reception of French opera. This shift, Johnson argues, produced the kinds of subject that could participate in the public moment. The ground for a new kind of collective experience, this new mode of private subjectivity put the experience of emotion at the center of public musical life. Moreover, Johnson emphasizes how this experience registered in the ideological space of the spectatorial and listening body: the weeping opera-goer that Johnson finds in late-eighteenth-century France not only represented an affectual break with the past, but in a profoundly material and physical way a new kind of embodied subjectivity.

In this context, we should also recall that Habermas's description of the rise of the public sphere in the eighteenth century mobilizes the patriarchal family as its affectual ground, required for the production of appropriate modes of subjectivity (1990, 43). Further, Habermas describes the transformation of the intimate subject's relationship to the commodity form as key to the collapse of publicity's classical mode.

> The bourgeois ideal type assumed that out of the audience oriented subjectivity's well-founded interior domain a public sphere would evolve in the world of letters. Today, instead of this, the latter has turned into a conduit for social forces channeled into the conjugal family's inner space by way of a public sphere that the mass media have transmogrified into a sphere of culture consumption. The deprivatized province of interiority was hollowed out by the mass media; a pseudo-public sphere of a no longer literary public was patched together to create a sort of superfamilial zone of familiarity. (162)

What Habermas and Johnson here are addressing is the problem of ideology in publicity in general, and by extension, the problem of ideology in musical publicity. By this I mean not the more or less idealistic version of the ideological that Habermas himself mobilizes (and Negt and Kluge critique) in his story of decay and decline, where it is understood in opposition to the grand "idea" of the public that he sees as truly containing the potential for critique and enlightenment.[26] Habermas's conception of the ideological in publicity is based on his notion of an increasingly apparent process of deprivatization in the age of mass culture, which in turn removes the potential for any kind of truly critical subjectivity.[27] Constantly forced into the spectacle of public opinion, the mass cultural subject, according to Habermas, no longer can construct a position from which he can truly perceive the state of the social condition. The postulated move from a "culture reasoning" to a "culture consuming" subject, which Habermas admits was always lurking in the structure of even the most "ideal" Enlightenment public sphere, not only dehistoricizes the *conditions* of subjectivity by identifying an exclusively Enlightenment conception of "humanity" with the possibility of critique, but also reifies one particular construction of publicness and privacy. As an alternative, I would like to mobilize a conception of the ideological as operating primarily in the social space of subjectivity. This approach was most famously developed by Louis Althusser, who argued that *"the category of the subject is only constitutive of all ideology insofar as all ideology has the function (which defines it) of 'constituting' concrete individuals as subjects* [italics original]" (1971, 171). By tracing the subject's role in the formation of publicity as the history of different ideological arrangements, we can disable both the Habermasian pathos and the Althusserian penchant for ahistoricity by grasping more concretely the indeterminacy of historical process.[28] In order to accomplish this task, we need to attempt to conceptualize the *Schlager* as an ideological transformation in the private realm, understood as a historically specific zone of both domination and subjectivity.

Returning for a moment to the "musicalization of the world," Bie sees this process not only as a shift in the staging of public acoustic culture, but also remarks on the insertion of situated subjects in new forms of *Schlager* public. In order to concretely ground his description of *Schlager*'s serial modes of dispersion, at first reliant on depersonalized technological forms of public presentation, Bie begins to introduce a set of characters: "the Berlin cobbler's apprentice *[Schusterjunge]* sings it, the worker has it in his mouth" and "the young ladies sing it at tea." By tracing out this motion of the *Schlager* from the singing boy into the mouth of the worker, and finally to the young ladies at tea, Bie ties the scene he is describing not only to an abstract social scene of urban acoustic culture, but also to a staging of specific forms of subjectivity. This subjectivity is however always compromised by its intersection with the materiality of everyday life in the urban landscape: the shared substance on lips and in mouths is also the stuff of advertising, plastered to the advertising columns *[Litfaßsäulen]* around the city, metonymically linking the space of the body to the mass cultural architecture of modern life (Figure 16).

Figure 16. Advertising column, with posters for Comedian Harmonists, Kassel, 1931.

We see how these different characters are differently situated in this public moment. The "young ladies" do not have "it" merely in their mouths, nor are they simply partaking of a standardizing hyper-present tense of the *Schlager*. Instead, they "sing it at tea," indicating a different relationship to the publicity of the *Schlager*, and suggesting the nonsynchronicity of modes of consumption even in the hyper-present tense that Bie is otherwise describing.

But the anti-*Schlager* polemics are even more illuminating for grasping the kind of shift that this moment seemed to represent in the history of subjectivity. While on the one hand these polemics alert us to the transformations in the larger scope of public experience in the late Weimar and Nazi periods, they also provide a kind of negative image of the *Schlager* subject. In a different *Volkswart* article, "The *Schlager*— a Harmful Product of the Times That We Struggle Against," Eva Maria Blume again railed against the *Schlager*'s role in Weimar modernity (1932a). Describing the musical life of the nation as a "chaotic mess," made worse by the "unbounded possibilities for distribution" that the radio and gramophone represent, the mysterious author here denounces this "typical product of the times" that attracts listeners away from a "higher world of . . . sounds" (89). *Schlager* include all the worst things of modernity, writes Blume, "from the rhythmic bubbling, sonically sensuous intoxication, to nerve-wracking, decadent, vulgar thrills, to the most barren meaningless kitsch" (89).[29] But this time, Blume does not limit her images of a tasteless dissolving *Gemeinschaft* to the generalities of her plagiarized exposé of the *Schlager* industry, but focuses on the transformation of perception.

> Thus the *Schlager*, grasping the senses, flies effortlessly into the ear and just as easily issues forth from the lips—it's no wonder that it spreads so quickly and in no time flat may rule a whole city. (89)[30]

Like Bie, Blume tries to comprehend the presence of the *Schlager* by situating it in relationship to some kind of experience of embodiment. While Bie's ultimately nostalgic take on the *Schlager* eventually grounds it in the "young ladies singing"—a kind of modern *Hausmusik*—Blume's account provides a sketch of a radically different kind of subject. This is not a subject that can more or less choose to sing or hear the hit song; rather, the hit song occupies that space that Blume sees as once having been inhabited by the "autonomous" subject. The senses are not tools of the *Schlager*'s listener, but rather appropriated, "grasped" by the *Schlager* itself. The body of the listener serves ultimately as a conduit for this commodified experience of a public personhood, as the song slips from the mouth of the unsuspecting *Schlager* subject. Blume is describing a kind of subjectivity that transforms the relationship between individuality, collectivity, and by extension, the moment of domination: ruling a city "in no time flat." Blume recognizes the *Schlager* as a new kind of social experience, both predicated upon and productive of a new kind of subjectivity. These "products of the time" travel through the bodies of their listeners, making a new kind of link between the publics "ruled" by these hits and the embodied experience (and physical possibility) of subjecthood.

But unlike Bie's more general rhapsodies, or Connor's cultural pathos, Blume is concerned about one audience formation in particular: women, or more exactly, girls. Blume is outraged by an article that appeared in a provincial newspaper (*Kassler Neueste Nachrichten*) that told of a recent exhibition of the exams of a girl's school: the article reported how the girls put on a fashion show to the music of the song "*Das gibt's nur einmal*" [That only happens once]," the main *Schlager* from *The Congress Dances (Der Kongreß tanzt)* (Eric Charell 1931) and one of the most popular songs of this period of German mass cultural music. Blume writes the following about this "scandal":

> How pleased Lilian Harvey [the female star of the film] would be, if she were to see that not only were they many "doubles" [English original] here, but also were to hear her Viennese *Freudenliedlein* "*Das gibt's nur einmal das kommt nicht wieder*" as the highpoint of this splendid fashion show. Should we really consider such derailments as only harmless child's play? Or did a not so insignificant institution of education believe it was necessary to highlight itself in this kind of a timely fashion??! If Germany's future youth leaders and mothers receive their A in *Schlager* singing and film star imitation, then we can't expect too much of them. (90)[31]

Blume's concern here is specifically for a gendered audience, and the danger is the loss of a properly "motherly" generation of girls for the future of the nation. Expert in mimicking the latest film stars and singing the latest film hits, these girls, Blume fears, fail to imitate the proper roles that both the nation and the family expect. While Blume of course overestimates in her negative polemic the utopian potential of popular pleasures, the ensemble of experience that Blume fears seems to have had a potentially disruptive relation to the proper reproduction of the national family and the attendant economic order that its reproduction secured.[32]

Both the moment that Blume polemicizes against and Blume's own polemic are structured around imitation. "*Schlager* singing and film star imitation" are perhaps not subjects that girls can get an A in, but they certainly are engaged with the ideological in ways not entirely dissimilar from the pedagogical model of social reproduction that Blume thinks is so vital in the history of the nation. Blume associates "*Schlager* singing" with the disruption of motherhood; she locates, without intending to, a fissure between two quite distinct ideological apparatuses of recognition. Blume's nervousness about this state of affairs begs to be over-read, and thereby understood as something more interesting than a mere polemic: while on the one hand the *Schlager* points to the disruption of one particular ideological apparatus of subjectivity and collectivity, on the other hand it inaugurates a new level of the saturation of personhood with the stuff of commodity capitalism. Unlike the imagined abstractness of the concert public, Blume grasps that the *Schlager* public is recurrently supplied with new forms of "modern" embodiment: prosthetic personhoods that can be discarded with the next new hit song, new dance, or new dress. "*Schlager* singing and film star imitation" are practices, in Blume's account, that fail to adhere properly to the ideological production and recognition of things like femininity and privacy, instead showing the disruption of these apparatuses by the circulation of commodities in the reterritorialized terrain of the new *Schlager* subject.

Blume's critical take on this subject is by no means our only witness of this transformation: novelists in the style of the New Objectivity *(Neue Sachlichkeit)* used the *Schlager* to develop both character and setting in ways that reflected the emergence of this scene of subjectivation. Alfred Döblin mobilizes specifically the female *Schlager* subject in *Berlin Alexanderplatz*. This time, the *Schlager* which appears repeatedly in Döblin's depiction of Weimar modernity,[33] participates in the commodification and spectacularization of the female body, while at the same time disabling a moment of heterosexual intimacy. Franz Biberkopf, the "hero," finds himself in the room of a prostitute "who even has a gramophone." She sings for him in "Bamberg's nylon stockings," but "without a blouse." This seminudity materializes the conjuncture between commerce and intimacy on the space of her body; the couple continues switching between mass cultural and "intimate" dialects of personhood. But before her performance, she describes when and how her singing takes place:

"You know where? Where I feel like it. I have no engagement at the moment, you know? I go in nice bars and ask. And then, my *Schlager* I have a *Schlager.*" (1961, 27)[34]

Döblin's scene goes on to assert a new kind of feminine identification with the mass cultural product:

"Don't tickle." "Hey, come on." "No, don't touch. That destroys my business. My *Schlager*, be nice, my sweetie, I hold an auction in the bar instead of passing around a hat: anyone who has the cash can kiss me. Crazy, right?" (27)[35]

Prostitution and the *Schlager* are intricately linked in this passage;[36] the woman has her own *Schlager*, through which she is able to sell her own thoroughly commodified mode of intimacy. But in the context of this specific business transaction, her *Schlager* takes precedence over the claims of Biberkopf on the female body. While the *Schlager* does not represent a form of feminine autonomy, it certainly interrupts the "normal" relationship of the commercial transaction of the sexual act that prostitution is supposed to operate within. Her *Schlager* itself comments on the form of this intimacy:

She puts on a top hat, crows in his face, shakes her thighs, the arms close at her side: "Theodor, was hast du bloß dabei gedacht, als du gestern nacht mich hast angemacht? Theodor, was hast du bloß damit bezweckt, als du mich einludst zu Eisbein mit Sekt?" ["Theodor, what were you thinking, when last night you made your move? Theodor, what did you intend, when you invited me to Eisbein (knuckle of pork) with sparkling wine?"] (27–28)[37]

As she moves to sit on Biberkopf's lap, taking cigarette after cigarette, she continues the commercial "seduction" with another *Schlager*: "Weißt du, was das heißt, Heimweh? Wie das Herz zerreißt, Heimweh? ..." (28). The entire act seems accompanied by a musical score, approaching the structure of a revue: "She hums *[trällert]*, stretches herself out on the sofa. She puffs on her cigarette, strokes his hair, hums, laughs" (28).[38] But while the Theodor in her *Schlager* represents a kind of abstract model of heteronormative masculinity, Biberkopf himself fails to perform.[39] Biberkopf first feels himself "imprisoned" again by this scene of intensely commodified intimacy, imagining in a Berlin accent "they ain't gonna release me. I still ain't out" *("Sie entlassen mir nich. Ick bin noch immer nich raus")* later explaining to the prostitute, who has been continuing her commodity revue, "I'm not human anymore."[40] Döblin soon moves into a quite different register: by inserting a passage describing the scientific causes of impotence and the possibilities for treatment, the male body comes on display as a scientific curiosity.

> Testifortan, protected trademark Nr. 365695, sexual medication from *Sanitätsrat* Dr. Magnus Hirschfeld and Dr. Bernhard Shapiro, Institute for Sexology, Berlin. The main causes of impotence are: A. insufficient charge due to a disturbance in the function of the inner secretion gland; B. too great resistance through overly strong psychic inhibitions, exhaustion of the erection center. The time when the impotent patient should resume attempts can only be determined individually on a case-to-case basis. A break is often valuable.[41]

Here again, a commodity, the impotence drug Testifortan, takes center stage, its commodity character reinforced by the citation of the trademark number. If the missing Theodor from the song text is a placeholder for an abstracted masculinity in the *Schlager* fantasy, the very singing of the *Schlager* disrupts Biberkopf's relation to his own masculinity, and would require the investment in another commodity to restore its functioning. The female *Schlager* subject's disruption of the proper habitus of gender thereby disables the emplotment of a properly masculine relationship to the female body, the ideological emplotment, in other words, of heteronormatively determined, patriarchal intimacy.

If in Döblin's version of modernity, *Schlager* and their female fans are part and parcel of the decaying structure of a seemingly autonomous subjectivity, the prerequisite and product of a historically masculine bourgeois publicity and its claim to bodily abstraction, Irmgard Keun's *Das kunstseidene Mädchen* (1932) consistently portrays its protagonist as experiencing private emotion, indeed the very possibility of a physically embodied privacy, primarily through the citation of the latest hit song. Something of a *Bildungsroman* about a young employee, Doris, and her exploits upon moving from a "middle-sized" to a big city, *Das kunstseidene Mädchen* also uses the technique of *Schlager* citation but this time in the first person narrational voice.

At any event, Jonny Klotz can teach me the new tango this evening, so that I stay on the top of things in every way. I feel all nervous and irritated *[kribbelig]*—the whole day with nothing to do and I am eager for the coming of darkness—and I have the melody constantly ringing in my ears: I love you, tan Madonna, in your eyes the sunshine glows . . . And the violinist in the Palace Club sings like soft flour— God, it feels so—and need to devour a night with music and lights and dancing and the like, 'til I can't take it anymore—as if I had to die the next morning and would never get anything again. I want a dress made out of lavender lace with silver trim and a dark red rose on the shoulder—I'll try to get a job as a model, I'm a yellow star— and silver shoes . . . ah, what a tango fairy tale—there's such wonderful music—if you're drunk, it's like a slide on which you're speeding down. (1979 [1932], 19)[42]

The dizziness of this passage in orthography, description, setting, and narrative movement evokes in multiple registers the experience of the *Schlager* listener, "speeding down" a slide of "such wonderful music." One might be tempted to dismiss Keun's device as simply an artifact of a perhaps overly self-conscious modernism, which in turn inadvertently places the distractions of modernity in the female character and thereby echoes the problematic character of much antimodern discourse of the period. But her text is illuminating for the way it conveys "subjectivity" through the distracted circulation of the *Schlager* and the imitated voice of the singer. Both of these are attached to private affect only insofar as they are equally linked to consumer desires reified in the material of the fantasy dress or the voice of the singer, soft like flour. Keun's figure might then be read on the one hand as an object lesson in the confused emotionality of the young female employee, both the protagonist of the novel as well as the symptom that this morality tale seeks to isolate. In this passage, however, an economy of distraction and its linkage to commodity consumption become clear. Right at the beginning of the passage, Keun's narrator wants to participate in the "event of a public" that the *Schlager* inaugurates: "so that I can stay on top of things." But this desire to be modern, to participate physically in the event of a public, interrupts her own embodied experience of proper femininity, replacing it with a nervous waiting, constantly accompanied by the melody of a *Schlager*. Again here, this bodily participation in the *Schlager* public emerges as a zone of intense commodity fetishism: she not only wants a "dress made out of lavender lace with silver trim and a dark red rose," she also needs to "devour" *[auffressen]* a night of glamour. The ultimate goal of all this is a reconfigured personhood, a new, "popular" body: "I am a yellow star." Jonny Klotz has become just another instrument in Doris' insertion into the realm of commodity capitalism: and ultimately, her body, first imagined as the "tan Madonna" that a voice echoes in her head, and later imagined to "speed down" a slide in a drunken state, refuses to conform to the more banal structuring of gender that the passage's beginning attempts to make clear. This moment is what I believe the polemics against the *Schlager* reacted to: where the affect of subjective interiority that mimics the bourgeois subject is disrupted by the complete serialization and standardization of bodies and feelings, where privacy is exposed as part of the commodification it pretends to avoid.

Considering the way Keun's character orchestrates multiple planes of social experience in the citation of the *Schlager*, it seems that the standardization of privacy, the condition Adorno diagnosed as "pseudo-individuality" was perhaps available to make material the experience of standardization and serialization in the very moment of private affect.[43] The point is not that Keun's character is a model of proper political agency; rather, the fact that Keun's modernist style mobilized this mode of subjectivity seems to indicate the presence of this kind of experience (in mediated form) in the social sphere. Most centrally, the kind of nervousness that is engendered by the style of this text is also what was seen by the anti-*Schlager* crusaders as the central problem of the new form of mass cultural music: Connor, for example, calls *Schlager* the products of a music industry "that speculates on certain culture-antagonistic characteristics of our nerve-destroying times" (1931, 67). The scenes that Blume, Döblin, and Keun each describe place the *Schlager* at the center of a drama of recognition for reader and character. To return for a moment to Blume's polemic, the girls identify with the singing film star in their own imitation of her voice and they also recognize themselves in her commodified image. The reader of Blume's text, and Blume herself, are also implicated in this game: by naming the *Schlager* itself, Blume brings her readers into this scene of recognition: we "hear" the event of a public that these girls are so infamously a part of. But in Döblin and Keun, the recognition of *Schlager* texts displayed by or around character also brings the reader firmly into the experience of this new kind of public, recognizing *themselves* as the mirror reflection of both the circulating commodities and the fractured moments of musical publicity that the *Schlager* citation calls up. By looking at the cinematic working through of this problematic, we can learn more about the central role of the *Schlager* in the "nervous" system that was mass culture in the 1920s and 1930s.

Singer Films and Recognition

In an article published in *Melos,* a prominent left-leaning music journal of the 1920s and early 1930s, the musicologist Hans Mersmann attempted to describe the role of "*Schlager* records" in the molding of personhood and forms of subjectivity.[44] While jazz had "aided the development of music for use," Mersmann wrote in 1931, early sound film and revues were pushing developments in the other direction, focusing instead on "personality": "In the series of *Schlager* records produced in the last period, the concept of personality is more prominent. Sound film offers particularly useful material" (1931). At stake here for Mersmann is the same dynamic of recognition that interested Adorno and Kracauer. But Mersmann's diagnosis is more precise: he looks primarily into the role of "personality" in the linkage between film and the *Schlager*. Not the *Schlager* alone, but its insertion into an elaborate apparatus of audiovisual publicity made it so powerfully operative in shifting forms of subjectivity. As Mersmann suggests, the audiovisual star figures manufactured in the film industry were particularly involved in these transformative processes, placing a new structure of "personality" at the center of attention.[45] As we have already seen, however, the new "personality" of the star cult was matched on the other end by new forms of modern personhood in capitalist consumer culture, particularly as they adhered to modes of mass musical publicity.

One example of the increasing linkage between "personality" and musical publicity in the cinema is the 1933 Joseph Schmidt film *Ein Lied geht um die Welt (A Song Goes 'Round the World)*, one of the many so-called singer films of the early sound period. *Singer films* centered around the problem of recognition in popular song. Rapidly consolidating to form a genre readily intelligible to the cinematic public of the early 1930s, each of these films features and centers on one of the radio tenors from the period, most prominently Jan Kiepura, Richard Tauber, and Benjamino Gigli. These radio tenors were not dissimilar to earlier popular stars of the opera stage like Caruso, whose fame was also primarily secured through recording. Although clear comparisons can be drawn between these singers and more recent mass cultural mani-festations like the "Three Tenors," any possible similarities are out-weighed by a major distinction: through their participation in sound film, this group of singers came to be emphatically identified not with the vague fetishistic notion of "having a beautiful voice," which can be used to sing any number of arias or songs, but instead, as suggested by Mersmann, these tenors came to be identified with the particular popular songs they sang and the cinematic characters they portrayed. Although both the genre and the nature of this kind of stardom required that these films focus on both opera arias and popular music, one or two *Schlager* ultimately dominate the film: for example, "Ich liebe alle Frauen [I Love All Women]" in the film of the same name (Carl Lamac 1935), and "Heute Nacht oder nie [Tonight or Never]" in *Das Lied einer Nacht [The Song of One Night]* (Anatole Litvak, 1932). *Schlager* were so dominant in the singer film, that already in 1932 this characteristic of the genre found itself parodied.[46] *Ein Lied geht um die Welt*, in turn, fea-tures a number of operatic arias, serving the needs of plot and atmo-sphere, as well as participating in the "*Schlager*ization" of opera music in this period; but ultimately, the *Schlager* has the last word: the love song "Frag' nicht [Don't Ask]" (M: Hans May, L: Ernst Neubach) and the "theme" song, "Ein Lied geht um die Welt" (May/Neubach) are the central moments of musical performance in the film. The moments of opera or *Lied* that this film uses indeed force "classical" forms of musi-cal expression into the *Schlager* form. Used as nondiegetic background music or narrative devices to develop the character of the singer, *Lieder* or arias are disassociated from any larger work or context.[47]

The film is set in Venice, allowing Oswald to supply the spectator with a number of outdoor scenes of the stars roaming around that city's canals. Ricardo (Joseph Schmidt) and his friends Simoni (Fritz Kam-pers) and Rigo (Viktor de Kowa), live together in their mansard. The three have hit hard financial straits, and Ricardo needs to find an en-gagement. After a scenic walk, where the spectator is given a number of montages of outdoor shots of Venice accompanied by music, Ricardo/ Schmidt winds up at the radio station. He asks the doorman for per-mission to see the director, and the short, unspectacular looking Ricardo is of course denied a hearing. On hearing the provocative words of a nearby conversation, "if someone wants something, they have to try something extreme," Ricardo stands on his platform shoes in the lobby of the radio station and begins to sing an aria.

This is the first moment of misrecognition in the film: the guard and the other characters populating this scene have thus far failed to take the short, unattractive Ricardo for what he "is": a singing sensation. The moment of song clears up this problem: after his triumphant performance in the lobby, Ricardo is ushered upstairs to the director; after hearing his glorious voice, the director asks: "Why didn't you come to me sooner?"

This first moment of (mis)recognition brings on the second (Figure 17): the next sequence begins with a shot of a spinning Ricardo Parlophon record and a superimposed title informing the spectator of the character's intervening period of success. This title not only tells us of Ricardo's success, but also informs us that the star "was never seen by the public."[48] With the title still on the screen, the cinema public sees the now-successful Ricardo/Ricardo walking into a Parlophon record store: walking up to the record player, the source (we shall learn) of both the last shot and the soon-to-be dieceticized sound, Ricardo removes his hat. On a cut, another shot of the record on the turntable is shown, identical in composition to the earlier shot, and, as the spinning

Figure 17. Beginning of record shop scene, Ein Lied geht um die Welt (Oswald 1933).

comes to a halt, the music stops. The record stops just when the text on the record is perfectly horizontal, allowing the spectator to see both Ricardo's name and the name of the song we just heard: "Ricardo sings 'Am Brunnen vor dem Tore.'" This stages recognition in its proper mode. The character from the prior scene, now given a specific kind of subject trajectory by the intertitle's biographic explanation of his success, is clearly identified for the spectator with the sound emanating from the record. While the relationship between Ricardo's heard voice and his body, "never seen by the public," is also established as a problem, the encounter of Ricardo with his own appropriated, reified labor seeks to ameliorate this problem, reestablishing Ricardo as indeed an autonomous subject.

In the next shot this technology is placed between Ricardo and Nina (Charlotte Anders), the woman who is to become the object of his desire. Nina is a record saleswoman, a figure also common to other films of the period.[49] This figure in a certain sense encapsulates the instability of older forms of subjectivity in modern mass culture. While the stopping of the record in both visual and sonic space allows their dialogue, the work of proper identification and recognition that the sequence has accomplished by linking record and Ricardo is undone: Ricardo asks Nina if he might listen to his own objectified voice. "Dear miss, I would like to hear Ricardo's new records." As this dialogue begins, the background noise in the shop instantly becomes audible. Bodies and records now make more than music, they also make noise; the sound of the records slipped out of their sleeves and the sound of Nina and Ricardo walking seem almost excessively marked as they make their way to the listening room. The camera tracks the two as they move through the store, and she offers one of the many Ricardo records she has in stock, "a German folk song, 'Am Brunnen vor dem Tore.'"

As the music of the orchestrated version of this Schubert *Lied* begins for the second time, we cut away from the record player to a shot of Ricardo and Nina looking down at the record player. This cut inaugurates a pattern that structures the rest of the sequence: multiple shots are used to produce the scene of listening, while single shots are used to depict the more banal moments of plot and dialogue. Music, it seems, has entered the scene as another character, "embodied" by the "thingness" of the record player, indeed the record itself. Music "expresses" itself through the excess of shots used during the musical moments that this sequence depicts. As Ricardo's voice begins to sing the words,

Nina picks up the remaining Ricardo records, clutching them to her breast, and smiles (Figure 18).

Here we are given the opportunity to see Nina and her fetish object(s): Ricardo is, in this moment, like the spectator, voyeuristically engaged in her pleasure. By the end of the first line, we cut to a differently angled shot of the pair. Nina continues to look at the record, and Ricardo at Nina. This time, on the words "sweet dream," the camera points our attention to two star photos hanging in the background. One is male, one female: their placement aligns with that of the two "real people" in the scene, mapping out the room according to the coordinates of the heterosexual matrix. But the scene in this room nonetheless seems to exceed that logic.

Almost at the end of the song's first strophe, we cut to the scene outside the listening room. No change in acoustic space marks this cut: as will be the case for the entire film, all moments of technologically mediated musical performance fill the imaginary sound space of the diegesis, to the exclusion of all other distracting sounds. The eyes of each of the other customers are directed towards the listening room. A woman enters the store, and after a few (unheard) words with another

Figure 18. Record shop scene, Ein Lied geht um die Welt.

saleswoman, she also looks towards the point of the sound's emana-tion. She gestures toward the man behind the counter, who wordlessly answers (on a cut) by pointing towards a Ricardo/Parlophon label on a record jacket.

Back in the listening room, the record stops. On a cut, we see the stopping record; this image reminds us once again of the one and only way "Ricardo" is visible to "the public," as a name on a record label. After returning to a shot of the couple, the film then shows us Nina directing her attention lovingly toward the record player, as Ricardo looks at her with almost threatening desire. "Is that not a wonderful voice?" Nina is quick to offer a second record to fill the sonic void: Strauß's "Launisches Glück." Quickly after the opening chord, Nina turns away from the record player, and we cut back to the outside scene at the counter. On the last beat of the introduction, Nina walks to the right, away from the record player—and Ricardo—record in hand. Ricardo also walks to a chair, on the opposite side of the room (left and back). Now, the record player, as well as the two photos on the wall depicting (presumably) singing stars, break up the space between the two figures. These media interrupt both the voyeuristic encounter between the two characters and our own potential identifi-cation with Ricardo, as we find ourselves attached less to character than to the scene of mediation and its commodity traces.

The shots are now more rapid in succession, Ricardo in a middle range shot looking over at Nina, followed by a middle close-up shot of the people outside by the counter, moving towards the camera and the site of emanation. The one remaining woman at the counter ges-tures toward the salespeople for what we can only presume to be all the Ricardo records Parlophon has to offer. In a flurry of activity, the woman and man behind the counter both grab at least twenty records from the shelves. As the scene continues, the shots orchestrate the inten-sifying focus of the scene towards the "private" interaction between Nina and her record, bringing the "public" to gaze in at the spinning turntable, only to break the spell as the record comes to an end. Then we not only see the fetishistic relationship of Nina to her recorded Ricardo, but we are also, as spectators, brought into the voyeuristic pleasure of the "public" inside the record store.

But the voyeuristic pleasures that this scene cinematically produces are never those that it diegetically depicts as integral to character, those of Ricardo. Ricardo is "surprised" by the intrusion of the public. The intrusion of the record store "public" into the scene of his own voyeur-istic pleasure, staged by the commodified trace of his own voice, allows the spectator to see his voyeurism disrupted by the intrusion of the spectator's own visual investments. More importantly, the one "real" point-of-view shot in this "love" sequence is not staged as part of a shot–reverse-shot relation depicting any "human" intimacy: this shot is from the *record's* point of view. This is then the scene of "recogni-tion" that Kracauer describes: it is not Nina recognizing the voice of Ricardo, but the record framing the subjectivity of the listener, Nina, iconized in the rhetoric of this shot. The cinematic spectator, sutured to this site of "vision," thus finds herself "recognized" by the commod-ity. As the film continues, one moment of (mis)recognition leads to another. One of the central topoi of the singer films is mistaken iden-tity. In films like *Ein Lied für Dich* (Joe May 1933), *Ich liebe alle Frauen Das Lied einer Nacht*, and *Das Lied vom Glück* (Carl Boese 1933),[50] the singer is misrecognized by the female lead as a mere man, confused with the other central male character of the film. Often featuring other tech-nologies of musical stardom, the radio and recording, the plots of these films revolve around the various comic situations that the confusion of identity implies. True to the form, in this film, the confusion of iden-tity is linked directly to the technologies of the *Schlager*, radio, and gramophone, and thus illustrates many of the issues that the new form engendered. But if other films tend to use this confusion to propel their diegesis, this film cuts short the primary drama of misrecognition soon after it begins.

While the misrecognition of Ricardo in the record store serves to set the film's love story in action, this next scene of misrecognition dis-rupts the normal plot line of this kind of narrative of mistaken identity. In other singer films, the question of "true" identity serves as a denoue-ment; in *Ein Lied geht um die Welt*, the issue is settled immediately. Nina takes up Ricardo's invitation to meet the great singer. When the woman arrives for tea at Ricardo's home, she mistakes Ricardo's friend, the more attractive musical clown Rigo (Victor de Kowa) for Ricardo himself. The characters sit down to tea, and, on hearing a mando-lin player outside playing "Santa Lucia," Nina insists that Rigo (her Ricardo) sing. Rigo attempts to keep up the masquerade, insisting first that he is out of voice because of the crumbs of cake, and second that the piano is out of tune. Ricardo, sitting at the piano ("it's not out of tune at all!") insists that Rigo sing. Rigo painfully attempts to sing "Santa

Lucia": but soon Ricardo himself breaks into song. Nina recognizes the voice as "Ricardo" the recording star. But while on the one hand this scene seems to reassemble Ricardo as a full subject of publicity, Nina's "recognition" of a complete Ricardo in fact makes clear that *this* Ricardo is not "Ricardo" at all. The Ricardo on the records that Nina caressed in the shop has now disappeared; the man before Nina is somehow someone else.

But while the confusion of Ricardo and Rigo is solved at the beginning of the film, the basic confusion of recognition, the assemblage of the singer belied by the record, remains to haunt the plot. The rest of the film documents Nina's growing frustration with this mismatched voice and body, Ricardo and "Ricardo," while simultaneously tracing out Ricardo's growing infatuation with Nina. In a second climactic scene of exposure in the film's penultimate sequence, after a long day of sightseeing in Venice with Nina, Ricardo is supposed to make a radio appearance: Nina, who has no radio of her own, appears offscreen at the door to Ricardo's and Rigo's apartment to listen to the concert. Nina and Rigo move through the apartment to the Reico radio in the center of the room: Rigo touches the radio, closing on Nina, and in response, Nina rushes in to turn on the radio (Figure 19). Her reaching for the radio dial is a moment of panic; it is as if the love scene that Rigo seeks to initiate is wrong without the mediation of the radio, and Ricardo's voice.

As in the earlier scene in the record shop, mediated music is accompanied by multiple shots. As Ricardo starts to sing, the series of shots appropriates his voice as the sound track for a love scene: as earlier in the film, the sound of technologically mediated music is accompanied by a series of shots in an accelerated rhythm. The earlier shots of the scene stage the developing love scene around the radio by alternating shots of Nina, Rigo, and for comic relief, Simoni in the kitchen. Rigo has his hand on the radio as Ricardo is singing; in a way, the film suggests that Rigo needs to ground his own lovemaking on the basis of Ricardo's stardom. By the second refrain of this song, "Frag nicht," a song which earlier in the film accompanied the "lovers" Nina and Ricardo through Venice, the syntax of the shots changes: Nina and Rigo now appear as a couple. After a series of three shots, the couple kisses. But on the climactic high note near the end of the song, the camera pans around the room to the door, the starting point of the scene. With shots now positioning Simoni, the radio, and the couple in relation to

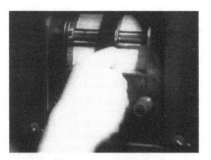

Figure 19. Disrupted love scene, Ein Lied geht um die Welt.

the door, we see Simoni's reaction shot, and then Ricardo, looming in the doorway. Accompanied by a shot of the couple around the radio, the female voice of the radio announcer explains his presence: "Attention, Attention. We now end the Ricardo record concert *[Schallplattenkonzert]*. The indisposed artist canceled at the last minute." Nina repeats the words, "Records?," as she turns toward the doorway and is shocked to find Ricardo standing before her.

But the film only unwillingly departs from Nina's fetish: the reified voice that she (mis)recognizes as Ricardo. If the love narrative of Ricardo and Nina is doomed to failure from the beginning of the film, the fetish object of "Ricardo's" voice remains. As one commentator of the period said of the audience's reaction to this film,

> This film was made for and around Joseph Schmidt. It is carried by the singing. When he sings, he fills the screen. Because of the voice of the radio tenor one hopes that great masses of curious radio listeners will want to see this film. There were many perfume-scented women present, who made it clear through their frenetic clapping that they would certainly not have acted as Miss Nina—Charlotte Anders—did. (Anonymous 1933a)[51]

We need to ask, however, whether this commentator's reading of the climactic moment of the film might not be a misreading on two levels. On the one hand, does Nina simply "choose" the prettier, vocally less able Rigo, or is something more perverse going on? While she was romancing Ricardo the voice and Rigo the body, separate in space and yet mediated by the furniture of the radio, she was clearly not choosing Rigo the person, but Rigo the stand-in, an attempt to disguise her fetishistic relation to the commodified voice of the singer. When she is seen by Ricardo, this inaugurates the disintegration of her fantasy love-object: the word she speaks, "Records?!," bring Nina's perverse love back into the circulation of commodities.

At the same time, the commentator's reading of the film's reception also opens up more questions than it answers. It seems more likely that the "frenetic" response rather indicates that the audience in fact gleefully shares in Nina's fetishistic obsession with the possession of Ricardo's records; the singer film's obsession with the problem of voice and body make the love story behind it pale in comparison. The female spectators in this account are in rapture not for the person of Schmidt, but are engaged in their own fetishistic relation to the reified object of his voice.[52] The shock that Nina expresses on seeing, and being seen by, Ricardo, is not the shock of being found out merely in the embrace of another (mere) man, the empathetic concern of the good girl Nina for the hurt feelings of the great singer. This commentator's certainty that the women in the audience would have acted differently attempts to contain the specter that the film has let loose: a voice with an unimaginable, invisible body, and the misfit between the fantasy world of the commodity and the bland, interpellative structures of heteronormative everyday life, where the men are more likely than not both unable to sing and are certainly at least as "unattractive" as Ricardo/Schmidt. "Real" men can only satisfy if they themselves are equipped with a shiny new prosthetic personhood that can capture the glamour of the world of commodities. The frenetic applause of the audience that the commentator here registers might be better understood as a frenetic moment of self-recognition in the perverse pleasures of Nina. What this film seems to illustrate, in other words, is the structure of the *Schlager* as a mode of interpellation that disrupts the very consolidation of a structured intimacy. Both the cinematic techniques and techniques of emplotment that characterize this film might at first merely seem to be genre conventions in the context of the comedy of mistaken identity.

But, it is precisely the developing system of genre conventions around the singer film's comedy of misrecognition that is revealed to be an unwitting allegory of the modern division of labor and its complement, the phantasmagoria of commodities.

The love story, whose heterosexual coupling is supposed to conclude this allegory, is given a radically reflexive perspective through its own technologies of representation and narration. The voice in this film is then definitively *not*, as Mary Anne Doane has argued, "freed from the potential trauma of dispersal, dismemberment and difference" that is engaged by the technology of sound film" (1985, 171). Žižek offers a more persuasive model for thinking about this problem; less focused on the technological determination of the cinema than the tradition of apparatus theory, Žižek suggests that the split between voice and body might lie at a deeper level: the audiovisual contract blocks out an "orginary chasm that divides the body and 'its' voice." This chasm takes on a historically specific form in this film, in which the body and its "singing" voice are continually naturalized only with the help of various forms of mediation. On the one hand, illustrative of the culture industry's attempt to "provide . . . the semblance of the human" (Negt 1993 [1972], 17), this film also points to the dissolution of the ideal subject of bourgeois publicity and the moment of possibility that this dissolution entails.

Organs of Experience

We have now seen how the *Schlager* can be interpreted as part of a contradictory, shifting site of subjectivation. In particular, it should be clear that this is a highly dynamic process: providing different modes of (mis)recognition, the subjects produced around the *Schlager* are only fleeting at best; like the publics constantly reassembled around the latest hit songs, the *Schlager* subject is profoundly disposable, thrown out with the new season, or even, the newest record. How can we more precisely conceptualize the functionality of the *Schlager* as an inter-pellative drama of recognition? In a seeming reflection of the audio-visual logic of the singer film and its use of *Schlager*, Adorno and Kracauer privilege the process of recognition in their analyses of the *Schlager* and its relationship to mass culture more generally.

> The listener who retains a *Schlager* and recognizes it again, becomes, through this, in an imaginary but psychologically very loaded region,

the subject, for whom the *Schlager* ideally speaks. As one of many who identify with this subject, the musical ego, he feels at once his isolation ameliorated, joined to a community of *fans* [English original]. (Adorno 1973, 42)[53]

Adorno's understanding of the processes of subject formation through identification in the *Schlager* provides us with a good point of departure for an investigation of the specificity of this new kind of public. His account points out how we might further explore this specificity: what is required is an understanding not only of the "community of fans" as a historically specific moment of mass publicity, but also the kind of *Schlager* subject that Adorno sees as both constituting and constituted by this public. But Kracauer has a much more interesting take on the problem. To begin with, in his ethnographic exploration of employee life in the late 1920s, Kracauer names his *Schlager* "listener," and describes her character in more detail:

> I remember a girl who is called "Heimchen" by her friends. Heimchen is a proletarian child who lives in Gesundbrunnen and works in the registry of a factory. The magic of bourgeois life only reaches her in its most tawdry form, and without thinking she takes all the blessings that fall down to her from above. Characteristic of her is that, whether in the dance hall or the suburban cafe, she cannot listen to any piece of music without twittering the *Schlager* text written for it. (1971 [1930], 68)

In this scenario, recognition operates with a different vector.[54] Kracauer turns the usual conception of the pleasures of popular music on its head: instead of describing, as Adorno does, the mere moment of "I know that song," Kracauer describes the way the *Schlager* recognize the listener:

> But it is not she who knows every *Schlager*, but rather the *Schlager* know her, bring her in and beat her softly to death *[erschlagen sie sanft]*. She is left in a state of total numbness. (68)[55]

Punning on the suppressed undertones of the German root of *Schlager*—*schlagen*, to hit—Kracauer depicts this scene of recognition and the pleasures that it entails as a site of violence. His theorization of this experience might be read as a simple dismissal of the female employee, but the transformed *Schlager* subject in this scene is also potentially aware of the intrusion that the *Schlager* represents. This awareness, or cognition, is structurally dissimilar to that of the autonomous public subject of Habermas; by bringing the suppressed meanings of the *Schlager* to the surface, Kracauer reveals an embodied experience of the violence of mass culture. His reading of this moment refuses the "illusions" that many commentators see as the central pleasure of the *Schlager*, placing the listener in a less romantic, more brutal kind of scene.[56]

Both Adorno and Kracauer are here describing what Althusser would call interpellation in the scene of mass cultural pleasure. Like Althusser, they are linking the moment of recognition to the production of specific kinds of subjectivity—and, through this, the reproduction of ideology. Kracauer's description of the listening pleasures that constitute the *Schlager* as a set of social practices echoes in interesting ways Althusser's discussion of the nature of ideology as such. For Kracauer, the operativity of the *Schlager* in the production of mass cultural pleasures is secured by a structure of recognition and the subjection/subjectification which that moment of recognition entails. But complementary to its function as an apparatus of recognition, the *Schlager* also became the place to work out the problems entailed by misrecognition: Althusser locates recognition and misrecognition as the two "functions of ideology as such" (172). The case of the *Schlager* shows the unstable, indeterminate relationship between these two ideological moments.

If we consider the *Schlager* less as an isolated song text, and more as part of a transforming apparatus of publicity and subjectivity, we soon realize that an interpretation of the *Schlager* as a simple form of "manipulation" or "illusion" ultimately misses the mark. But we need to hold on to this historical moment of subjectivity as one of contradiction: The *Schlager* themselves were by no means—regardless of their seemingly antifascist aesthetic—inherently oppositional moments in mass culture, nor were they always successful attempts at steering popular pleasure in time to the needs of the Nazi regime, or more generally, capitalism. It is crucial to understand the *Schlager* as registering the *possibility* of resistant formations that could make material and experiential the conditions of modernity that the critics of the *Schlager* sought to erase, or, in the Nazi form, to harness. The tendency to read *Schlager* as one-way tools of manipulation rests on a "functionalist notion" of consciousness (Postone 1996, 38). Likewise, the attempts to read other forms of popular music ("jazz") as critical in fully positive manifestations places opposition somewhere outside of history "conceive(s) of capitalist society only as reified and deforming, and treat(s) critical thought and practices as historically indeterminate" (38).

By no means do I want to simply "positively" evaluate the singer film as "critical": I do want to allow for the possibility that the female audience of this kind of film was capable of a historically specific form of critical engagement with this form of cinematic representation, an alternative form of spectatorial publicity.[57] These films were part of a new possibility for experience within the history of sense perception in modernity, as Miriam Hansen has described it, a new mode, to place oneself in a totalizing, modernized image of society, providing a form of embodied consciousness that makes the social contradictions typical of capitalism ("class") and its gendered articulations available for a certain form of collective experience (1995). This collective experience might well not map onto bourgeois notions of cognition, but at the same time it is an oversimplification simply to dismiss its formation as a simple "distraction" from the "real." If in our present readings of these films their historical role remains limited to an idealistic form of "ideology critique," this kind of bourgeois criticism of the traces of these potentially alternative forms of consciousness should be itself understood as a form of reactionary nostalgia.

Negt and Kluge have offered a tool to describe this kind of phenomenon: "organs of experience." Moving from Engels's description of historical embodied experience, where the social transforms the organs of cognition, Negt and Kluge seek to expand their understanding of the sense-producing capacities of the subject in capitalism to include "the head, the body, the nerves, the senses, the feelings . . . ; these [experiences] must be able to work on the historical relationship as a material object" (777).[58] They see the transformed body of the subject in history as the battleground for social antagonism (782). The social moment of the *Schlager* should be linked to the contradictory form of the organ of experience, a thoroughly ideological site, both for veiling existing social relations (and their conditions of reproduction) as well as for grasping the relationship of the subject to these conditions.

> On the one hand, the wage laborer, who stands opposite the capitalist, in relation to the Fronde worker [*Fronarbeiter*] in the middle ages, suffers a loss of experience regarding the clarity of that which happens to him. On the other hand, he gains however new organs of experience. The form in which the work process societalizes [*vergesellschaftet*] shows him a large number of other individuals in the

same situation. The domination that affects him is not experienced as willful or accidental pressure, but rather as something produced and artificial. (1981, 780)[59]

Not only does their pithy description of the ways mass culture functions simultaneously to take away and provide forms of experience *[Erfahrung]* (to be understood as experiential cognition) parallel (and make more precise) Kracauer's frustratingly vague theoretics of 'distraction' (Petro 1987, 137), it also reminds us of the true complexity and critical edge of Benjamin's discussion of the social organization of cultural production and perception, often lost in the still circulating anti-Adorno caricatures of Benjamin's work.

The relinkage of ideology theory with a concept of the historicity of experience, I would suggest, is a promising way to further develop the critical theory of mass culture, and in particular to theorize acoustic culture. Registering the loss of experience that is the condition of modern forms of wage labor *and* providing a new form of social experience in the emphatic sense: i.e., a new form of making contradiction material, *Schlager* represent the place of the production of domination, its cognition, and the possibility of its refusal. This new organ of social experience was not necessarily assimilable to the reproduction of the existing relations of production. In other words, if, in the classic Althusserian formulation, ideology, "represents the imaginary relationship of individuals to their real conditions of existence," the panic produced by the *Schlager* both in the critics and in the "recognizing" spectator, is indicative of the form's disruption of this imaginary relation, making contradiction material in the new kind of experiential relation of the "individual" to the conditions of (re)production. But the *Schlager* also introduces new "imaginary relations"; thus the political meaning of the *Schlager* ultimately emerges as radically undecidable. Like the labor process, *Schlager* consumption also provides a mode of "experiencing" the role of the situated consumer in the production of the social. The historical eruption of this new organ of experience made possible a new subject of mass publicity, refusing the kind of romanticism that their texts seem to provide by disrupting the sentiment of *Gemeinschaft*. The intrusion of commodity fetishism into the supposedly private production of subjectivity can thus expose interiority and "individuality" as zones of profound contradiction.

Schlager thus represented a new kind of publicity that disrupted the operation of ideological apparatuses like the family and femininity by staging a new form of subjectivity which linked *Schlager* production to commodity capitalism, and providing a new organ of experience to make this social reality a "lived" part of the everyday. This being said, we now need to return to the question with which I began this investigation: if the *Schlager* does not represent any simple kind of mass manipulation, we equally need to think about its relationship to the concept of "resistance." The model of resistance as an explanation of the ensemble of social practices that we know as popular culture is especially attractive in discussing the Third Reich. We have an investment in locating popular culture as ultimately independent of the state: mobilizing a kind of "repressive hypothesis" of the pleasures of popular music, we would like to script the role of certain kinds of popular musical practice as the expression of those social forces that the state, a kind of autonomous, alien organism, chose to repress.[60] But, as I have shown, if the *Schlager* cannot be read as any simple form of mass manipulation, it is equally problematic to read the *Schlager* moment—particularly in its more or less "jazzy" forms—as one of fully self-present alternative publicity, that is, decontextualized "resistance."

While Detlev Peukert's work is usually sensitive to this problematic, his discussion of the *Schlager* and its relationship to formations of resistant collectivity precisely inverts the model of mass culture operative in the standard account of the *Schlager*. Using a "popular" approach, Peukert has argued that the *Schlager* provided a social space of resistance for German youth in the 1930s, specifically for those gangs known as the Edelweiss Pirates. The Edelweiss Pirates made their first appearance in Germany in the late 1930s; a more or less loosely organized group of youth gangs organized in a number of different western German cities, they were seen by the Gestapo as a significant threat to the regime's efforts, represented by things like the Hitler Youth, to monopolize youth culture in the Reich. Having arisen spontaneously at youth gatherings, these groups tried to re-function leisure—and indeed the developing concept of youth itself—against the desires of the regime. In his work on the Edelweiss Pirates, Peukert has pointed out that one of the ways they produced collective affect and the possibility of an antifascist working-class politics was by singing the melodies of Nazi movement songs with altered lyrics as well as *Schlager* of the period.

> In these evenings people killed time, gossiped, told stories, played
> the guitar and sang songs—especially hiking songs or popular hits
> *[Schlager]*, with words that spoke of foreign lands, adventure, 'rough
> fellows', beautiful girls. No cliché of commercial entertainment was
> left unused; but the Edelweiss Pirates also appropriated these banal
> stereotypes for their own ends. For one thing, they were not singing
> the Hitler Youth songs prescribed as 'suitable for young people' or
> the fighting songs of the chauvinistic German military tradition;
> they were singing the songs that were permitted to the citizenry as
> non-political compensation for the burdens imposed by the regime—
> adult hit songs *[Schlager]*, which dealt furthermore with adventures not
> allowed to the young, the pleasures of boozing and love. In addition,
> the Edelweiss Pirates developed a remarkable knack for rewriting the
> words of the hit songs, inserting new phrases or lines or whole verses
> which catapulted their own lives into this dream world. The hits thus
> became a means of articulating longings and demands for an existence
> other than the grey reality of war. (1987, 157)

Further, certain forms of popular music which had a complicated relationship to the ordering of fascist hegemony, particularly swing, found
popularity in other kinds of oppositional or semioppositional groups.

If the Edelweiss Pirates were inclined to re-function *Schlager* as tools
of some kind of resistant practice, we need to put this in context. It
would be both a political and a theoretical error to locate the stuff of
resistant practice in the hits themselves, in their status as musical texts.
It would also, however, be a mistake to view groups like the Edelweiss
Pirates as a fully formed resistant collective independent of the interpellative operations of mass culture. To put the Edelweiss Pirates in a
kind of context, let us consider by way of a conclusion another film that
dramatizes the issue of song and collectivity. *Tanz auf dem Vulkan [Dance
on the Volcano]* (Steinhoff, 1936) is set in Paris on the eve of the 1830
revolution. The plot revolves around the activities of a certain actor,
Debureau, played by one of biggest stars of German stage and screen,
Gustaf Gründgens.[61] This star of the Paris stage leads a double life,
and serves as the point linking two different "publics": a more or less
proper theatrical public, where the hierarchy of monarchy continues
to determine the placement of subjects in relation to both stage and
state, and a resistant underworld of political intrigue.

Crucially, this linkage is made through popular song. One song,
"Die Nacht ist nicht allein zum Schlafen da [The Night Isn't Just for

Sleeping]" (M: Theo Mackeben, L: Otto Ernst Hesse), in particular finds favor with the Paris audience: the central song in Debureau's stage act is used not only within the theater, but also outside. Debureau distributes alternative lyrics to the verse of this song, all insulting to the king. One example of these "mock verses" is the following:

> König Karl auf Frankreichs Thron
> Wirst den Kopf verlieren
> Doch wer keinen Kopf mehr hat
> Braucht sich nicht rasieren

> (King Charles on France's throne
> You will lose your head
> Indeed, he who has his head no longer
> Doesn't need to shave)

The linkage between popular song and political publics is made not only by the workings of this film's plot; cinematic devices are also employed to this goal. The film begins with historical background: after "explaining" the politics of France in 1830 through the use of titles superimposed on images of the film's central characters, another title tells us that "one went to the Funambules Theater." The next title introduces Debureau: "The magnet was the genius Debureau, the darling of the Parisians." The image of the theater that was introduced with the prior title then dissolves into a huge poster of the actor, and this image lingers on the screen, superimposed on the theater public itself. The public site of the theater becomes, the film suggests, the person Debureau. Accompanying the image track is the music playing in the theater, the central *Schlager* of the film, and we see the audience singing this song along with the as-yet-unseen stage presence, Debureau. As the song comes to a close, the "mock verses" are distributed from the balconies of the theater. Soldiers are waiting outside the theater, expecting these verses to be distributed to the departing audience. When it becomes clear that the audience has already received the mocking verses and is already reciting them, the soldiers attempt to quell the insubordination of the crowd, and a riot ensues. At the end of the film, when Debureau is about to be executed, Charles has already fled Paris. A montage of the "people" of Paris is set to the rhythms of Debureau's song. Debureau is to be led to his execution, and the climax of the film occurs when Debereau's execution is called off. "Sing, Debureau, sing," the crowd screams. And sing he does: the mass, now gathered as a triumphant public, sing with Debureau the "real" words to his hit song.

Ultimately, this film argues that this counterculture of *Schlager* is able to form an authentic collectivity, strong enough to topple a king. This film's use of the *Schlager* to argue ahistorically for a new kind of radicalized "counter-public" seems to model the kind of public that Peukert sees as resistant in the Edelweiss Pirates. The use of the popular song to script a "resistance" to the existing social order is in other words not by any means unique to "alternative" social formations, but rather makes up a central part of the way *Schlager* were conceived more generally. The similarity between these two conceptions points out that in fact the kind of collectivity represented by the Edelweiss Pirates was by no means one necessarily critical of mass culture. To the contrary, the kind of "critique" we want to see in this sort of practice is better understood as operating within the contradictory terms of mass culture itself. This is not to suggest that there was no possibility for modes of counterpublicity around the *Schlager*, nor that the *Schlager* was ultimately "repressive" in its function. It does suggest, however, that we need to complicate how we view the role of *Schlager*: the idea that a resistant collective can "express" itself publicly through the use of the *Schlager* in a profoundly dehistoricized, commodity-free "folk"-like use of the medium, is one that is engaged by the logics of mass culture itself, and in particular, the populist logics of mass culture's depiction of the political during German fascism. The contradictory moments of the *Schlager* lie elsewhere: not in the production of an authentically resistant collective, but in the transformed relationship of subject, commodity, and public that the *Schlager*, as an organ of experience, represents. The destabilizing moment of the *Schlager* is to be found on what Postone has termed "the theoretical level of . . . possibility"; in our readings of "the musicalization of the world," it is our place to critically reconfigure that moment of possibility, in the hope that we might better recognize similar moments in the present.

3

"Musik" and "Musick": "Opus Music" and Mass Culture

> The unity of the two spheres of music is that of the unresolved contradiction.
>
> —*Theodor W. Adorno, "On the Fetish Character in Music and the Regression of Listening"*

Schlager and *Schlager* singers clearly dominated musical mass culture during the Weimar Republic and the Nazi period. Their apparent radical newness as a media formation made and makes them seem particularly able to capture something of the "spirit" of the time, encapsulating essential components of social experience and shifts in the historical construction of subjectivity. All the same, despite the pivotal position of *Schlager* in the acoustics of publicity, it would be a mistake to ignore the crucial role played by other forms of musical practice in the expanding realm of musical mass culture between 1920 and 1945, in particular that of so-called "serious" or "art" music. First and foremost, art music itself was subject in this period to dramatic forms of intense commercialization and new modes of distribution by means of the new acoustic technologies. Not only had recording already produced a vastly expanded star culture centered on instrumental virtuosity and vocal expertise—Caruso being here the most obvious early example—radio now played a central role in further widening the circles of serious music's fans. Serious music in both recorded and live forms made up a central part of broadcasting throughout the period, shifting between daytime broadcasts of "light" music and early evening concert presentations and opera broadcasts. Secondly, the sphere of serious music was also highly present in the illustrated press. This was particularly true of advertising, which increasingly mobilized both the star cult of opera stars and conductors as well as the glamour of musical events themselves to sell various products, not only of a musical nature. Finally, the cinema used the world of "art music" in a number of different ways, both as a narrative tool and as a thematic source of material. In considering the acoustic culture of the period, we need to realize that not only was the spread of *Schlager* a new phenomenon in the organization of publicity; the formation of new, mass cultural audiences around serious music also needs to be considered in a properly historical fashion.

On first look, these shifts seem primarily related to the question of *access* to musical publicity or a broader familiarization of the wider public with the rituals of art music consumption. If access to earlier forms of bourgeois musical publicity in the nineteenth century was extremely limited by financial factors, the newer technologies obviously made certain kinds of musical sound available to a broader audience.[1] But we should be wary of this kind of "obviousness": while from a certain perspective the new acoustic technologies seemed to radically democratize older forms of musical culture, the transformed acoustics of musical publicity that these shifts entailed also meant that the music itself could no longer be considered the same object. In other words, this was not a democratization or opening of access in any concrete sense, but part of a more thoroughgoing transformation of music's role in everyday life. The very role of music as and in social practice—as the hub of various media networks and systems of economic exchange—began a dramatic process of transformation, wherein older structures of sociomusical experience which had been enabled by older technologies of reproduction and distribution, in particular sheet music and the domestic piano, would increasingly become obsolete.

Some of these shifts had direct consequences for the pseudonatural opposition of art and popular musics. It could be argued that the general field of musical practice had already long been divided into two primary categories. This was certainly true of elite discursive production: prior to the gradual emergence of "absolute music" and more modern conceptions of the musical work of art, the opposition between religious and secular music had been central. But since the early nineteenth century, musical practice was increasingly understood as being made up of *Unterhaltungsmusik*, or entertainment music, and *ernste Musik*, or serious music.[2] These terms, used in various forms of expert or semiexpert cultural discourse, formed an opposition that would become increasingly central in organizing the field of sociomusical practice. This was especially true of the new constituencies beginning to participate in one way or another in the mass cultural acoustics of publicity.

Although this kind of dichotomy is familiar to us as well, apparently corresponding to the more Anglo-American distinction between "classical" and "popular," the opposition in Germany of this period can only be said to map roughly onto current notions of "popular" and "classical" musics. *"Unterhaltungsmusik"* was understood to include not only the new *Schlager* and dance music but also forms of musical practice that in the modern sense could easily be considered "serious music," if not at least "art music." March music, older operetta music, more traditional forms of dance music like the waltz, as well as various kinds of folkloric musical practice, from Viennese *Schrammelmusik* to gypsy music,[3] each were equally considered to belong to the category of "light" music. "Serious" music, in contrast, was a far narrower category, if not in musical style, certainly in the social conditions of its production and consumption, stretching from opera to chamber music. This binary opposition not only played a role in structuring musical performance, determining performance sites and performer habitus, it also crucially organized the acoustic economy in terms of distribution and reception. From radio programming to record production, each of the emerging zones of the acoustic economy was grouped into these two primary categories of musical practice. The hardwiring of this opposition, from corporate structures to musicians' organizations, helped to make the distinction between the two realms ever more firm (Stapper 2001, 68–70).[4]

It is a well-established consensus within music historiography, if not music aesthetics, that any conception of these categories as denoting ahistorical characteristics of musical "quality" or style is at best misleading, and at worst facetious. Adorno is one of the clearest writers on this question, arguing "the tidy separation of the social field of music is illusionary" (1973a, 20).[5] This, however, is not the same thing as deeming the opposition irrelevant or nonexistent: it would equally be an error to simply ignore this opposition or to pretend that this binary had no reference to social reality at all. Contrary to some romantic views of popular culture, these distinctions are no mere arbitrary invention of the elite, but are in a real way articulated to and reflect real distinctions in the social structures of musical practice on every level of production and consumption. As Adorno also remarks, "it would be just as easy *[bequem]* to conceal the break between the two spheres and to assume a continuum that would allow progressive education *[Erziehung]* to slide without danger from commercial jazz and *Schlager* to the cultural goods *[Kulturgüter]*" (1973a, 20). In order to truly grasp this problematic, we need not only to consider how serious music was inserted into the developing apparatuses of musical mass culture, we also need to look at how the relationship between art music and the popular was explored, charted, and experienced in the period under question. This entails investigating how the very category of serious music itself was sculpted by the consumption of music in modern mass culture.

Like the popular music of the period, the publics addressed by art music were marked by the attendant changes in forms of listening practice that these publics underwent during the 1920s and '30s. This was due in part to the spread of participation in musical mass culture, but also to fundamental changes in social structure that realigned the system of "distinctions," class habitus and taste, and itself allowed modern musical mass culture to emerge. The emergence of various forms of class-specific habitus in modernity, most importantly that of the newly prominent class of white-collar workers—Kracauer's "employees"—played a key role in this process. While some fractions certainly reveled in the showy taste for all things modern, certain other fractions of this new class were particularly characterized by the more or less conspicuous consumption of what they perceived to be "cultural" goods. This confusion of the consumption of musical commodities with participation in an elite musical public, schooled in what Bourdieu calls the "aesthetic disposition," in many ways approximated the proud display of cheap reproductions of the "great masters" in lower-middle-class households. The cultural techniques involved in the consumption of serious music certainly did serve to elaborate strategically a set of distinctions marking the difference between the *petit bourgeois* and those lower in the social hierarchy. At the same time, this strategy was doomed to reproduce the logic of the hierarchy itself, and in so doing to reinscribe what Bourdieu would later call the "objectively and subjectively 'unhappy' relation" to culture that characterizes the position of the "employee" in the broader social scheme (1984, 327).

What makes middlebrow culture is the middle-class relation
to culture—mistaken identity, misplaced belief, allodoxia.
Equally, one must avoid treating this . . . relation in substantialist
fashion, although it always betrays itself, in the eyes of the
dominant, by the most incontestable and objective indices of a
manner and mode of acquisition . . . What makes the petit-
bourgeois relation to culture and its capacity to make "middle
brow" whatever it touches, just as the legitimate gaze "saves"
whatever it lights upon, is not its "nature" but the very position of
the petit bourgeois in social space . . . determining his relation to
legitimate culture and his avid but anxious, naïve but serious way of
clutching at it. (327)

As we shall see, many aspects of musical mass culture were tailored to
foster this kind of "unhappy" reception. The complex of acoustic culture, ranging from the illustrateds use of musical stardom to the phonograph record, offered numerous ways of reinforcing a musical canon
of seemingly legitimate culture. The presentation of proper scenes of
performance and the inculcation of appropriate forms of "serious,"
semireligious listening that formed this complex allowed the lower-
middle-class audience to "clutch" at the pieties of high art in an "avid
but anxious" way. This was at least in part accompanied by an explicitly nationalist tone that would find it easy to settle in the new hegemonic arrangements of post-1933 Germany. But not all responses to the
cultural hierarchy of musical practice simply affirmed the hierarchy of
taste by aspiring toward upward mobility. The emergence of the obviously slippery category "opus music," as so-called serious music was
negatively termed in a populist dialect during this period, itself indicates the rise of new audiovisual media networks and new forms of
musical consumption which could support the establishment of what at
first seems like an either/or approach to musical taste. Serious music—
and its distinction from "light" music—should then be considered a
crucial part of what Bourdieu termed the "classification struggles" in
the cultural field (1984, 483), classification struggles that again complicate any black-and-white picture of the role of music in the historical shifts before and after 1933.[6] In particular, this makes the study of
the relationship between these two slippery categories telling indeed.
As we shall see, this opposition was overdetermined by other contradictory structures, most prominently the production of national identity and the concomitant fashioning of modern consumer subjects. By

examining the differing ways in which "art music" was staged within musical mass culture, we can thus gain insight into a number of different zones of the social.

The Nationalization of Music and New Modes of Commodification

Art music held and holds a central position in the structuring of the German national imaginary. In particular, between the wars, German music criticism and musicology were characterized by a heightened attempt to forge a notion of "German music."[7] As Pamela Potter emphasizes, this development must be seen in continuity with earlier musical discourse in "Germany": a notion of musical Germanness was key to the production of the German national imaginary before, during, and after the founding of the Reich in 1871 (1998, 202).[8] This project was continually plagued with difficulties, both in national and musical terms. Like all projects of national invention, the attempt to fill German national identity with any kind of positive content was highly problematic. Indeed, the problems in the German case were particularly extreme. Continually shifting between linguistic, ethnological, racial, and political claims to peoplehood—i.e., multiple contradictory apparatuses of local and national identity—German nationalism found itself on particularly rocky ground.[9] These problems were compounded when the object of nationalist interest was "German" music history. Not only was the compositional practice of "German" composers like Bach, Händel, Haydn, and Mozart profoundly cosmopolitan in terms of musical style, the musical cosmopolitanism of these composers was compounded by contrary claims on the central canonic composers of other national imaginaries. Händel in particular was already claimed by the English national tradition, and Mozart and Haydn could just as easily be mobilized to underwrite either nostalgia for the multinational pomp of imperial Austria or a local Austrian sense of national identity in opposition to that of more northern "German" climes (202). This meant that any attempt to map national identity onto musical characteristics inevitably had to resort to vague claims about particularly German musical qualities like "masculinity" and depth, particularly where the more familiar repertoire of the eighteenth and nineteenth centuries was concerned (203).

It would seem that all solutions to the "problem" of German music must have opened up many more questions than answers. Nineteenth-century solutions relied more on defining what was not German: from anti-Semitic tirades about "Jewishness" in music to the stereotyped denigration of "effeminate" French or Italian musical traditions. All the same, musical commentators "nevertheless had faith that [German music] existed, and they feared its impending extinction at the hands of over-rated foreign imports" (Potter 1998, 202). Beginning in the period following the First World War, the notion of German music began to take on many characteristics found in post-1933 official national discourse. One example is Hans Joachim Moser's three-volume survey *Geschichte der deutschen Musik*. In this monumental work, Moser attempted to label particular musical characteristics as specifically German, a notion which here took on emphatically modern "racial" characteristics (Potter 1998, 207). As Potter writes, particularly in describing later musical developments, Moser "lapses into vague descriptions that are more poetic than technical" and focuses on binaries of weakness and strength that articulated well with the increasingly popular notion of a German "race" (207). Moser's work also was part of a general trend in musicological discourse to mobilize clear notions of racial threat and a vocabulary of degeneracy: this was especially embodied by the notion of *Musikbolschewismus*, which, as Eckhard John suggests, rapidly surpassed the limits of political discourse and took on racializing qualities. This discursive field, while related to and dependent on the history of other forms of nationalist discourse, also marked a subtle shift toward a more clinical sense of pseudobiological threats against the musical "body" of the German people. In the 1920s, the field of German music was thus characterized by the constant threat of "foreign" elements of jazz and atonality, each of which was understood to have some kind of relationship to "alien" Jewish forces (John 1994).[10]

In its most benign form, the racialist logic of music discourse implied that the cultivation of this "German" racial quality was the "peaceful" destiny of the German people, a kind of gift to the world:

> Music was seen by many as a uniquely German capacity; and seemed to be the best way for the German nation to claim its place of pride in a new world order. (Potter 1998, 4)

These idealized goals at the beginning of the Weimar period were in part fulfilled, with the vast expansion of amateur and youth music-making activities, an increasing interest in musical pedagogy, and impressive state funding for musical institutions. Through these and other measures, the Weimar Republic was in some ways able to establish a musical culture that was indeed singular in Europe of the 1920s. But this benign form of "positive" racialism was always accompanied by the lurking exclusion of musical and racial others from participation in this uniquely "German" gift. It would be a huge leap to automatically link the racial thinking in the concept of "German music" to the mass murders of the Nazis. All the same, the kind of nationalizing articulation of musical practice here at work did help to make biological notions of nation and race intellectually and emotionally concrete and thus central to the German national imaginary. In this quite specific sense, musicological discourse, as a force in crafting the social field of acoustic culture, did play a direct part in the establishment of the racializing epistemologies that would in part contribute to the developments that culminated in the mass murders and mass incarcerations of the Nazi period.

But the powerful, if unstable, ideological construction of "Germanness" in music could never have been produced merely by expert forms of discourse around musical practice. Musicology was by no means alone in contributing to the "nationalization" of German music, nor was the organization of concert life in Germany the central zone of music's national imaginary in 1920s and 1930s. The new audiences of "serious music" were in part implicated in the process of the nationalization of society, in that the use of art music in the German mass media was attached to a national pedagogy of musical "pastness." Radio programming in the 1920s clearly attempted to link national affect to art music. This was exemplified by live radio broadcasts of public ceremonies and concert performances that used "German music" to stage an acoustic fantasy of national presence on the airwaves. A Berlin program on November 8, 1927, for example, honoring Constitution Day, began with Wagner's overture to *Die Meistersinger*, continuing with performances of choral works by Beethoven and Schubert (Schumacher 1997, 485). Not only does the use of the *Meistersinger* signal the nationalist tone of this event, the selection of works further mines the nineteenth-century tradition of the male chorus and its central role in the event culture of German nationalism.[11] At the same time, a more pedagogical impulse could be heard in the various educational broadcasts that dealt implicitly or explicitly with the question of art music and national identity. Radio shows like "German Classicism, German Romanticism," broadcast in Breslau in 1925, or the series "The German Symphony," broadcast by the Cologne station West German Radio (WERAG) in the late 1920s (Großmann-Vendrey 1997, 747, 749), were perhaps not intended to serve as nationalist statements. Nonetheless, they participated in and were dependent upon the production of German national fantasy, fabricating a link between particular musical practices and styles and an affect of national musical "pastness."[12] Musical programming of Weimar radio was often instrumentalized to mobilize a nationalist affect. This was not unlike many of the "historical lectures" presented in Weimar radio by right-leaning scholars, politicians, or journalists, who tended to cultivate a nationalist reading of the aftereffects of the First World War, and thus transport a barely disguised political agenda behind a veneer of neutrality. More dramatic and effective national linkages still were made around musical festivals, in particular, the annual opera festival in Bayreuth, which was broadcast to an international audience, played a central role in the musical staging of national fantasy (Anonymous 1931, 1932). As Großmann-Vendrey has pointed out, not only the national and international prestige of Bayreuth was a factor here, but the status of Bayreuth as a site of national representation also played a key role in the staging of the radio broadcast in the German public sphere (1997, 782).

The recurrent re-"nationalization" of certain forms of musical practice was a linchpin in the placement of art music in German mass culture in the 1920s and 1930s, far beyond the world of radio broadcasting alone. Advertising again was central in structuring this process. While, as discussed in the previous chapter, the music to hit songs—or rather, jingles parading as hit songs—was often printed in advertisements and used to visually iconicize various products, from brandy to swimsuits, "serious music" was also used to sell various products. Already in an advertising series from 1930—here for the Austrian state tobacco monopoly—various composers were mobilized as part of a German national symbolic. In one of these ads (Figure 20), the reader was presented with Haydn as the composer of the music to the German national anthem.

Presumably, Haydn is gripped in the process of composing that very anthem as the reader catches him in his lonely candlelit chamber. The text in the advertisement reads as follows:

Figure 20. Advertisement, Österreichische Tabakregie, 1930.

The German perfect anthem. Joseph Haydn, Mozart's ingenious predecessor, opened the series of great Austrian composers. His *(formvollendet)* classical compositions still seem so alive today, although with none of these was he able reach such a level of folk-ishness *(Volkstümlichkeit)* as he did in the Austrian people's hymn, the simple and grippingly noble melody *(Deutschlandlied)* has become the shared property of the entire German people.

Just as old as the Austrian people's hymn is also the Austrian tobacco monopoly.[13]

This advertisement seeks to assure the consumer that the cigarettes from the Austrian tobacco monopoly are a prestige-product by simultaneously marketing a national canon of music history. By referring to the common musical material of the Austrian Imperial Anthem, from Haydn's Emperor Quartet, and the later re-texting of the same music in 1848 by Hoffman von Fallersleben for a German national anthem, this ad at once illuminates the fragility of German musical nationalism—indeed the German national imaginary in general—and seeks to pedagogically mobilize an imagined commonality of noble musical Germanness to sell Austrian cigarettes. Like the use of *Schlager*, which linked products to multiple forms of sociomusical practice, this advertising technique also played a central role in structuring the social experience of the illustrated weekly's mass readership. Inserting a nationalizing function into the calculus of cultural capital, the reference to art music in advertising would have a double pedagogical effect. On the one hand, this kind of reference participated in the (re)nationalization of a certain German musical canon, at the same time providing a self-serving guide for the mixed readership of an illustrated weekly through the complex terrain of cultural capital.[14]

But this marketing is itself also part of a new star system around the figure of the composer. Haydn, as he is here depicted, presumably in the process of composition, is a figure from the world of popular music biographies, a genre of popular textual production around the composer subject later increasingly supplemented and arguably replaced by the composer film. Similar to the biopics of popular song writers in America, the German composer film repeatedly resurfaced in a number of different forms in the 1930s. These films ranged from the fairly straightforward early films like *Aufforderung Zum Tanz* and the Austrian film *Leise flehen meine Lieder*, which had as their main character a single canonic composer—here, respectively, Weber and Schubert—to a later film like the tragic *Friedemann Bach* (Müller, 1941).[15] The question of art music and its relationship to the cinema will be dealt with in detail later in the chapter, but for now let it suffice to remark that the cinema partook both directly—by means of explicit narrative strategies—and indirectly—by means of a tacit reliance on cultural fluency—in the discursive (re)production of "German music."

At the beginning of the Nazi regime, the national tenor of musical discourse and musical practice in Germany took on a newly strident tone. In January 1934, a "cultural offensive" began with the broadcast of a Beethoven cycle (Drechsler 1988, 58), marking the 165th anniversary of Beethoven's birth. The nationalist pathos surrounding these broadcasts linked Beethoven the hero to the new, "pure" Germany, and claimed that the sprit of Beethoven's music had finally found its home in the new German people. The *Völkischer Beobachter*, for example, included the following text in the month before the first broadcast:

> Now we can again look up to Beethoven . . . We can today, on his 165th birthday, place at his feet the adoration of a purified Germany . . . We are looking for Beethoven the man. We feel tied to him in his struggle, his belief, his patience, his strictness with *[Härte gegen]* himself. (Drechsler 1988, 64)

Followed by later focuses on Wagner, Bach, and Händel, the broadcast of "German" music, particularly in the so-called "Hour of the Nation," and later radio shows like "Music of the Great Masters," was repeatedly linked to maintaining and propagating the myth of "German" musical superiority.[16] But beyond that, these radio shows, simultaneously broadcast by all German radio stations, attempted to make a link between musical authorship and national community, wherein the struggles of composers to achieve self-fulfillment mirrored the struggle of the German people to do the same. Seeking a reflection of the ideal soul of the German people in the acoustic manifestation of the nation that a radio broadcast pretended to provide, this use of art music on a mass scale pushed nationalist discourse regarding music to new limits.

This nationalizing aspect of art music in mass culture was certainly quite prominent, and might lead us to believe that the use of art music in the 1920s and 1930s was quite unequivocal and effective in its nationalizing operation. This is further supported when we look at "official" discourse of the Nazi period: the opposition between "serious" and/or folk music and *Schlager*, or hit songs, for example, was often linked to nationalist content in certain kinds of discursive production. This can be seen primarily in the *Reichsmusikkammer*—the mandatory organization for all musicians and composers during the Third Reich—especially in the writings and speeches of Paul Graener, Richard Strauss's successor as head of the Composer's Section and one of the chief musical ideologues of the Nazi period. In the "building up of the *Volksgemeinschaft*," Graener wrote:

> We have a dangerous enemy: that is the crudeness *[Plattheit]* of so-called "people's music" *[Volksmusik]*, the hit songs *[Schlager]*, sung everywhere, especially by the youth. I call on all fathers and mothers not to tolerate it when their children bring hit songs home. (1938, 112)

Often, this kind of discourse was explicitly linked to fantasies of race and national identity. Fully in the spirit of *Gleichschaltung*, *Die Musik* published an article in 1933 entitled "The Nationalization of German Music," where we read of the crisis in the "German musical feeling."

> Negro rhythms foreign to our essence *[wesensfremde Negerrhythmen]* jazzed up and frazzled the German feeling for music, raised with Bach, Mozart, and Beethoven, to excess. No nation wandered so far as we, the natural, grounded race *[Art]* into the atonal waters. (Hille 1933, 666)

But despite the seeming self-evidence of their character, we need to be cautious in interpreting these kinds of statements. In contrast to the many sources, relatively easy to locate in the canonical archives, which illustrate this kind of polemic, many more, perhaps less obvious and subtler sources indicate different positions on the nature of popular music and its relationship to the German musical tradition. Discourse on popular music itself was quite varied. Often the attempt was made to "Germanify," at least in name, cosmopolitan musical forms—as in the case of "German swing"—or the question was averted entirely and replaced with a pragmatic focus on musical production as a quasi-industrial problem. In other words, successful competition with foreign products was more the issue than any question of cultural integrity.[17] A typical example of this kind of remark can be found in the journal *Reichsrundfunk* in 1942:

> Music is, however, also a question of generation . . . (e)ven the
> waltz was once new and had to establish itself against older forms
> of dance, the young generation demands a tight, modern rhythm.
> (Anonymous 1942)[18]

This is not merely a case of shifts in discourse over time during the
Nazi regime. Although it is the case that "official" discourse in the 1940s
was far less concerned with the question of cultural purity in the realm
of the popular, we can trace out an alternative approach to serious and
popular music throughout the period. This had its roots in earlier models: the use of art music in 1920s broadcasting, for example, was not
always attached to pedagogical intent. Instead, art music was often
mixed with "lighter" genres: the very first radio broadcast is the earliest example of this phenomenon.[19]

The usage of more or less "absolute" musics in this kind of context
inevitably served the invention of a new genre of musical practice. Based
on traditions familiar from salon music, it now made sense to group
marches and waltzes with Brahms *Lieder* and Beethoven Romances in
the broadcasts of the "afternoon concerts."[20] These afternoon concerts
often not only mixed genres, but also used arrangements of "classical
hits" for smaller ensembles. The use of these arrangements was practical for a number of reasons. For example, the afternoons did not enjoy
the same listener attention as broadcasting in the morning or evening,
meaning that the use of a full ensemble would have entailed an exor-
bitant financial investment for relatively minimal audience returns. At
the same time, the afternoon concert was often called a "tea hour,"
and the intimate associations of this social context would have made
the use of an orchestra ridiculous, to say the least. Nonetheless, these
afternoon concerts soon met with some opposition. The critic Felix
Stiemer, for example, made his distaste for such afternoon concerts
quite clear in a 1928 article in *Der Deutsche Rundfunk:*

> Of course, there is nothing in the least to be said against light
> entertainment music, but these afternoon programs are often so
> unbearably uniform *[eintönig]* and played so carelessly *[lieblos
> heruntergespielt]*, and when then the four or five men attempt
> Wagner or Verdi—[it is] horrible, truly terrible. (Stoffels 1997, 657)

In contrast, the morning musical broadcasts, particularly on Sundays,
tended to use brass orchestras or *Kurkapellen*, but the mix of musical
styles was similar. Classical "hits" of the period, including things like

Händel's "Chorus and March from Judas Maccabeus," for example, would be mixed with operetta melodies and military marches (Stoffels 1997, 673ff.).

While the beginning of the Nazi period at first was characterized by an attempt to "purify" music's place in radio broadcasting, the extremity of early national musical fervor quickly subsided in the interest of more pragmatic interests. In particular, radio broadcasting recurrently sought to bridge the gap between the "serious" and the popular. By the 1940s, the pedagogical push of German broadcasting looked and sounded quite different than it had in the early years of the Nazi period: As already shown in chapter 1, "classical" music played a prominent role in the *Request Concert for the Armed Forces*. In the *Reports from the Empire* we can get a sense of what role "serious" music played in the reception of this popular radio show in this remark from 1941:

> The 58th Request Concert for the Armed Forces was generally well received. Special mention went to "Träumerei" by Schumann, the songs, which the Mozart Chorus of the Berlin Hitler Youth sung, [*sic*] and the humorous offerings like the Film ABC. (Boberach 1984, 1955)[21]

Here the mixture of a standard from the "salon" repertoire (*"Träumerei"*) with comic sketches seems to have been welcomed by the mysterious "general public." By treating the classical repertoire as a reservoir of musical material essentially not unlike *Schlager* or operetta music, the radio show's producers believed that they could satisfy all listening groups.

If one way of filling the gap between art music and the popular was the radio variety show, other attempts were made to popularize orchestra concerts. In 1941, numerous German orchestras, lead by the Berlin Philharmonic, undertook a massive attempt to bridge the gap between art music and the popular. In this early version of "crossover," a new term was introduced, a term which in itself shows the tendency of the project as a whole. Entitled *"Beschwingte Musik,"* roughly translated "Music with Verve," but also not-so-subtly playing on the English word "swing," the concert organizers clearly intended to play with the increasing popularity of *"beschwingte Musik"* of a different variety, which was becoming more and more popular all the time.[22] The series began in Berlin on October 28, 1941. In the first concert program accompanying the series, we read the intentions of the organizers:

> But no one should think that the music of our great masters is always
> [difficult] . . . No, they could also joke, entertain, and dissolve the
> tension, which they often excited in man's breast, again ready for
> easy amusement. And it is such music which we long for in this
> great time. The worker *[der Schaffende]* wants it, when the sound of
> the machines stops sounding in his ears, and the wounded wants it,
> when he returns to life from the silence of the sick bed. All have
> the same wish: the wish for music with verve *[beschwingter Musik]*.
> (Brückner 1941)[23]

The first concert was held in Berlin for the wounded and workers in
the armaments industry. Evidently conceived at least in part by Goebbels himself, the attempt to sell serious music was not based on mixing
recent popular genres with art music; instead, the concerts featured
music of various levels of "difficulty," but tended to focus on music
which clearly leaned toward the popular: almost inevitably, works by
Johann Strauss, or lesser salon composers like Karl Komzak ended
these concerts.[24] The relatively mild national conservative pathos of the
descriptions accompanying these concerts is distinct from the stridently
heroic nationalism of earlier descriptions of "German" music: indeed,
the "German" character of the music played in these concerts was at
best of secondary interest.

At the same time, even the *Reports from the Empire* register a continuing dissatisfaction with the broadcasting of "serious music." This
was especially true when broadcasts intended to mark the calendar via
reference to the most canonical works of "German music history" con-
flicted with the emerging expectations of leisure in the listening audience. In 1940, for example, the *Reports* reported on the reception of
the Easter program:

> Musically literate circles say that they were grateful that they got
> what they wanted with the St. Matthew Passion . . . but the critical
> voices on the Easter Program come from worker circles and in part
> vacationers with the argument that on Sundays to relax from work
> they would like most to hear operettas and dance music. (Boberach
> 1984 [1940], 987)[25]

Thus, if we consider the complexities of these arrangements, the at
first seemingly obvious ideological function given to art music in the
Weimar and Nazi periods, whereby "German" music served as one of
the pillars of the German National Symbolic, is not sufficient to explain

the larger social function of art music in this period. While nationalization clearly was important in the use of serious music in the 1920s,
'30s, and '40s, this process was always accompanied and more often
than not challenged by shifts in the structures of commodification
around art music practice. We now need to define more precisely the
contours of this process, in order to grasp the multiple levels of the
social implicated in its trajectory.

Musical Mediacy and Privacy

As early as 1925, a little less than a year after the introduction of radio
broadcasting in Germany, the commentator F. Brutz railed against
radio's central role in threatening shifts in musical reception. In an
article published in the *Allgemeine Musikzeitung*, beginning with the
cry, "Radio, you monster!," Brutz charges the radio with potentially
leading to the banalization of music:

> Radio delivers music to the house like pipes under the streets deliver
> water and light . . . Music "on the side," as background noise, as in
> the epidemic of tasteless coffee house music in truly barbaric form
> has spread throughout the entire cultured world. (1925, 635)

Radio's special sin is its tendency to mix: in particular, culture is brought
into dangerous contact with commerce in the perverse new world of
radio broadcasting:

> You [the radio] devour everything you are offered. Stock reports and
> Brahmsian romanticism, party politics . . . This horrible mixture of
> things, which by their very nature call for strict separation! (635)

This audience itself also objected to radio's mixing of musical styles
and genres, albeit quite often with a different valence. The term "opus
music" began to spread as a term of disapproval for art music, most
often in the context of listener response to radio programming. The
very term "opus music" seems to have derived from the style of radio
announcing that accompanies "serious" musical broadcasting: the audience was thus responding not only to the music itself, but also to the
pedagogical apparatus to which this kind of radio listening was supposed
to be attached. Later critics, especially after 1933, tried to reconcile their
demand for cultural pedagogy with the audience's resistance to "opus
music" by adopting a sometimes surprisingly pragmatic attitude. Even

the likes of Herbert Gerigk, musicologist, passionate National Socialist, and the head of the music department in Alfred Rosenberg's *Kampfbund für deutsche Kultur*—in other words, someone not wont to mince words in attacks on musical degeneracy—saw the risks inherent in establishing a too rigid opposition between "serious" and "popular." Writing in the year of the Nazi takeover, Gerigk remarked that while "popular music is the weak point in the structuring of musical broadcasting," he also realized that any new ordering of the radio could not simply ignore the emerging forms of mass public and their new "tastes."[26]

> It would certainly be a mistake not to take those listeners' letters seriously that complain about the "Major and Minor Music," "Opus Music" or "Etude Music" . . . In addition, it should be pointed out that the concept of "the people" for music was only first made possible through the radio. Prior forms of musical performance only reached—even in the best case—a certain social level *[Schicht]*—that is, a fragment of the people . . . His majesty the listener simply wants to be taken seriously. On express order of the highest authority in German radio: the listener is to be given a central place in program decisions. Here the question arises, how far can we give in to the listener, and where does the task of our time begin? (1933, 13)[27]

Gerigk's remarks make clear that he was at least partially aware that the explosion of a musical audience through new forms of listening might make "collectivity" possible—in this case the collectivity of the *Volk*—but only at the risk of introducing new disruptions that threaten to break up any emerging collective imaginary. The job of the radio was then to create modes of broadcasting and listening that repaired these emerging contradictions, to enable the fulfillment of the "utopian" *Volk*. This ultimately entailed a compromise with the existing and expanding world of musical mass culture.

If we consider again the use of Haydn in the tobacco advertising discussed earlier, it seems to insist on retaining an idealized composer-subject familiar from a now-disintegrating musical media network. The fetishistic depiction of the magical link between composer, quill, and paper depict a sense of subjective interiority transmitted from the space of inscription to the paper. Publicity and privacy also play a role in this depiction: the intense privacy of the compositional process as it is here represented, in the lonely light of a single candle, should be understood as a reflection of the privacy of the consumer—a consumer not only of cigarettes, but also of the music itself and the star figure of the composer. Through this, a direct link is established between the inspiration of the composer and the pleasures of listening. While in this kind of iconic representation of composition, the composer-subject literally adheres to the media system of musical notation, the grip of the quill implying the flow of emotion from the composing body to the musical page, the private consumer of both cigarettes and classical music can subsequently reabsorb the sounds of Haydn in his own private sphere. Representing the other end of this process, the consumer is installed as receiver, fully integrated into a totalizing media network of musical traces. Despite the depiction of musical media, the very mediacy of the musical process—implied by the inscriptive system of notation here depicted—is refused, and the direct pleasure of musical inspiration is metonymically linked not only with the lonely pleasure of cigarette smoking, but by extension also with the "true" feeling of belonging to the *Volk*.

These shifts already index the new mass cultural form of musical publicity in a special way. By no means is a "mass" represented here, but the pleasures of mass consumption are staged as intensely private and domestic. The musical publicity of the national anthem should here be enjoyed as a private consumer good, in the comfort of the bourgeois or petit-bourgeois living room. In a similar way, the modern technologies of sound, like radio and phonograph, which produce the voice of a singer, establish and norm a "personal" relationship to the star. The historically specific forms of the collective, traces of which in various ways can still be "heard" in chorale, symphony, and opera, are in this period—particularly after 1933—mobilized to produce national affect, but this affect is not experienced in an uncomfortable "total state," but in the comforts of the bourgeois living room—if necessary by lonely candlelight.

To return however for a moment to Brutz: this earlier critic diagnosed a shift in the constitution of "public" and "private," the mutually constitutive zones of sociality that had previously determined the form of musical modes of reception. Using architecture as a metaphor, Brutz recognized the loss of what others would later term "aura" in radio music; to paraphrase Brutz, a specific "distance"—which ironically for Brutz guarantees "immediacy"—is required for the proper reception of the musical work. But Brutz's criticism in fact went further: his primary complaint with the radio was that it eliminated vital distinctions between different forms of listening practice:

> The loss of all immediacy! Radio shares this, the abolition of psychological immediacy, with the cinema . . . radio music has no kind of spatial frame, and music must be heard in a space that corresponds to its content, if it is to resonate fully. All genres of music require their own spatial distances. A Mozart string quartet is unthinkable in a sports arena or a large theater, a Bruckner symphony unthinkable in a reading room. Radio music no longer has any support in space. (1925, 636)

While Brutz was quite correct in seeing radio as establishing new regimes of listening, he was also quite wrong when he conceived of the radio as a scene of musical address devoid of "spatial frame." For the sounds of the radio did not exist independently of ideological space, but rather were implanted in the multiply determined site of the home, and thus participated in ensemble of linked interpellatory devices that circumscribed this space and organized both the agency and habitus of its inhabitants. This was linked to other social transformations of the period—most importantly what Adelheid von Saldern has documented, an increasing focus on home-life on a mass scale in the 1920s and 1930s (Saldern 1995). As Saldern shows, the establishment of "home life" was combined with intense and elaborate forms of regulation and social production. This was particularly true in Germany, where now firmly established practices of governmentality such as social insurance and public housing entailed a steady increase in the production of welfare discourse and the establishment of new sites of state activity. The domestic sphere was thus by no means a residue, an off-space to the recurring drama of reinventing publicity; the home was also a new invention, governed by new regimes of familial privacy and shifts in state policy that had material effects on the shaping of everyday life. Seen in this light, the domestic scene was a very resonant frame indeed, and would serve to "support" the new practices of acoustic culture in a number of ways.

In the 1920s and 1930s, serious music was especially used in advertising the emerging new sound technologies of the period. But here as well, the synchronic entanglement of multiple media in these advertisements was further complicated by the diachronic references in the advertisements themselves to yet other modes of publicity: One method of selling new sound technologies was through reference to older, presumably more familiar forms of public sphere, as, for example, in the Telefunken advertisement from the year 1936 (Figure 21), "A world full of music."

Also part of a longer series of advertisements, in this advertisement the text redundantly explains the image:

> As in the box at the opera house, so true to the music do you
> hear song and play from the radio receivers from the new year of
> Telefunken.[28]

Seen from the position of the box, only one person is visible besides the consumer unit of the couple: the conductor. No one else is visible in this space. While on the stage itself nothing yet happens, the other spectators are lost in the darkness of the hall, or hidden by the extravagant curtains of their own boxes. Although the radio receivers being advertised were far beyond the means of the ordinary reader, this does not diminish the role this kind of advertising played in structuring ideal forms of listening. In fact, it could perhaps be argued that the fact that these radios were beyond the reach of the "average" reader made these advertisements an even more powerful source of attraction.[29] Faced

Figure 21. "A World Full of Music!" Berliner Illustrirte Zeitung, *1936.*

with this kind of image, we are posed with the following problems: How can we interpret this image in ways that productively preserve the historical specificity of its emergence, and furthermore account for the play between media that this image—and its role as an advertisement—represent? What lies beyond the margins of this advertisement, what kinds of openings do this image—and many others like it—offer for us to piece together a "historical ethnography" of the media culture of this period?

Here, the work of Walter Benjamin is instructive: in his archaeology of the nineteenth century, Benjamin described the domestic as a central locus of historicity. In particular, the separation of the space of living from the space of labor which the salon represented was for Benjamin key in the establishment of bourgeois society, and it was this opposition that established the "private man" as a historical agent, enabled him to "step onto the stage *[Schauplatz]* of history" (1977a, 178). Linking the ideological configuration of domestic space not only to the formation of modern subjectivity, but directly to the development of modern modes of labor and exchange, Benjamin is able to provide a rich historical ethnography that sustains and surpasses the Marxian critique of commodity fetishism and its link to the idealist conceptions of the human. For Benjamin, the "phantasmagorias of the interior represent *[darstellen]* the universe for the private man. In it he collects the distant and the past. His salon is a box in the world *theater*" (177). It would be tempting to simply see in this advertisement continuity with the arrangement Benjamin describes. In the ad, it first seems as if the bourgeois couple's living room has replaced the nineteenth century salon, and the radio has simply replaced the objects collected in the nineteenth century domestic space with a seemingly more direct mediation of the outside world. But this reading can only be considered accurate in a banal way, and explains little about the specificity of this kind of image.

Alternatively, we could understand the image as a symptom of what critics like Jürgen Habermas or Richard Sennett might diagnose as the privatization of public space: in this kind of argument, modern mass culture has turned the theater of the world into a petit bourgeois living room. Sennett argues his case quite persuasively, making an almost Foucauldian point that what he terms the "loss of publicity" has led to a "tyranny of intimacy." Under the cloak of "warmth" and, worse still, with the pretence of an expressive veracity, the intimate subject is a mechanism that serves to regulate "individual" practice and thought in ways much more effective than any standard public sphere. Pretending to offer the possibility of truth, which it claims the public sphere mendaciously undermines, the continuing expansion of privacy ultimately eliminates any emphatic sense of the publicity. In a profoundly Habermasian vein, the condition of the tyranny of intimacy, Sennett argues, results from the misbalance of inherent contradictions within the very notion of publicity. The result of the "erosion of a delicate balance" is a "society . . . burdened with the consequences of . . . the effacement of the *res publica* by the belief that social meanings are generated by the feelings of individual human beings" (1976, 339).

But this kind of reading dehistoricizes our sense of publicity and privacy and returns us precisely to the ahistorical conception of subjectivity that Benjamin (and Marx) sought to critique. Resting on an implicit norm of the "delicate balance" between publicity and privacy, "a balance between an impersonal realm in which men could invest one kind of passion and a personal realm in which they could invest another," Sennett cannot help but construct a nostalgic view of the problem, despite his protestations to the contrary. The universalist anthropology that lies behind Sennett's (and Habermas's) diagnosis itself needs to be the subject of historical critique. In other words, for our purposes, the modern mass cultural readership of the *Berliner Illustrirte Zeitung* could not "lose" a balance between publicity and privacy they never had in any kind of emphatic sense. Instead, as Miriam Hansen (1991) has explored in her study of early cinema, it was precisely the modern mass media that offered contradictory modes of publicity appropriate to the "conditions of living" of the mass audience. Conversely, the "privacy" of this arrangement was not so much intruded on by outside forces as it was at least in part *established* by the modern mass media, sculpted by their caressing address.

I would suggest instead that this advertisement indicates the installment of a new arrangement, which, while seemingly based on older forms of the public/private distinction, instead participates in the production of a new listening subject for modern musical mass culture. If we consider Benjamin's analysis of the nineteenth-century private man more closely, the salon's character as "box in the world theater" is more than mere metaphor; instead, Benjamin's archaeology of the salon places it within a historically specific media apparatus. Benjamin understands the emergence of the private man as occurring within the coordinates of a spatial arrangement that required the theater for its intelligibility. Going beyond a mere metaphorical understanding of Benjamin's diagnosis, the nineteenth century "salon" was thus plugged into a very specific form of subjective experience, linked not only to the architecture of the theater, but also its forms of address and narrative structures. Taking Benjamin's cue in understanding this more modern arrangement, the box represented in the advertisement does not index a specific media apparatus, yet one different from the theater of the nineteenth century. Instead of merely representing back to the reader a reminder of his or her place in the theatrical apparatus, what we are here presented with is far more the *cinematic* representation of such forms of publicity. The mixed readership of the *Berliner Illustrirte Zeitung*, the majority of which was never likely to experience the pleasures of a box— or even an opera performance, for that matter—are not first of all reminded of a "true" opera performance by this kind of advertising technique. Instead, this image referred the reader to then (and now) more familiar, *cinematic* depictions of musical theatrical performance, and, as will be discussed later in the chapter, cinematic depictions of opera spectatorship. This serves to link the cinema to musical reception practices in the other more modern media: radio and recording. In this sense, the claim made by the advertising text is true: the box familiar to the audience addressed by the ad, a box "experienced" from the seat in a darkened cinema, *was* reproduced—or closely approximated—by the experience of radio listening.

Here, the words of Brutz again sound like a useful observation of cultural change: radio did share something quite profound with the cinema, particularly after the emergence of sound film. But Brutz was again, here, also somewhat mistaken: at issue was not a loss of musical immediacy, but rather a shift in musical *mediacy* which ironically established new standards of supposed "immediacy" in the social experience of musical consumption. The role of "art music" in the German National Symbolic was alternately supported and challenged by its positioning in a new realm of "social constitution"[30]—the formation of a modern sense of interiority and privacy depended on the very forms of public mediation. The terms of this shift must be explored. Now that we have begun to describe the linkages among various media through "serious music" in the 1930s, in particular, a closer look at the cinematic use of music can deepen our understanding of how this linkage served as a structure of interpellation, and begin to think about the question of possible political effects. What were the contours of this new musical interiority, and how did the cinema reflect and participate in its installation?

"Classical Music" and Melodrama

The aforementioned "composer film" was only one of the ways in which the cinema used "serious music" in the Weimar and Nazi years. Not only did symphonic and operatic repertoires play a key role in exhibition practice during the so-called silent period, the cinema also attempted to incorporate opera and operetta as sources of thematic material.[31] The links between the cinema and art music traditions were well rooted: indeed, in the presound era, classical references were standard in silent movie accompaniment, a practice that both relied on and instilled the audience's fluency in a developing language of quickly recognizable musical signs. In addition, classical or semiclassical performances often took place "around" the film, making up one aspect of the longer cinema programs in these "palaces of distraction," and further contributing to the incorporation of art music into the audiovisual spectacle of the cinema. The start of sound film further deepened the intricate linkage between these various zones of mass cultural practice. As we saw in the previous chapter, the singer films of the early- to mid-1930s, which starred the famous radio tenors of the day, were basically concerned with staging these stars as both *Schlager* and opera singers. Still other films used art music to structure their plots: Melodramatic films like *Romanze in Moll* (Käutner 1942), *Schlußakkord* (Sierck 1936), and *Heimat* (Froelich 1938) used art music to structure their narratives.[32] In many ways, these films can be said to parallel the Hollywood "woman's film" of the same period.[33] Not only do these films revolve around female protagonists, they also deal with "women's" issues and seem in their address and potential spaces of identification intended for a "female audience." To be more precise: these films continuously reproduced the "female audience" in their interpellative procedures— from the level of the cinematic itself to fan literature and other forms of extracinematic visual and textual production.[34]

One "woman's film" of the late 1930s that makes prominent use of narrative and cinematic levels of "serious music" is the 1936 Detlef Sierck film (*Schlußakkord*). The title of this film, primarily concerned with a narrative of "homecoming," is already suggestive of the investments in sonic metaphors of social consonance and a fantasy of subjective completion that will recur throughout the film's multiple levels of cinematic signification. The film begins on New Year's Eve in New York with the discovery of a body in Central Park. We learn that the dead man was the husband of a certain Hanna Müller; she and her husband had fled Germany after her husband's involvement in an embezzling scandal and since then had been living in New York under the assumed name "Burns." The police arrive to bring the grim news, and in her discussion with the officers, Hanna mentions her child, and the spectator is presented with a shot of Peter's photo.

This photo and the dialogue about her child motivate a scene change: in a sub-sequence syntactically organized by dissolves, we move from an aerial view of New York, across the ocean, and arrive with an aerial view of Berlin. The opposition between the two locales is narratively rooted on both the acoustic and visual planes: "New York" is acoustically represented both diegetically and nondiegetically by a threatening "jazz," and visually iconicized by the figure of the black saxophone player. While the singer films seemed by and large to make no distinction between *Schlager* and aria or *Lieder*—at least they intended to produce a realm of musical consumption in which the distinctions evaporated—a film like *Schlußakkord* insists on the opposition as part of its signifying apparatus. For example, at the beginning of the film, both acoustic and visual elements signal New York as a site of danger and chaos. Sierck uses techniques of montage, dissolve, and extreme camera angles familiar from other films like *Razzia in St. Pauli* (Hochbaum 1932) and the later *Rund um die Freiheitsstatue* (1941) to illustrate the temporal, spatial, and metaphoric moral confusion of American urban life (Vogt 2001, 294–95). The visual codes are matched by an aural code: the soundtrack slips between diegesis and narration, as "jazz," played by a black actor on the saxophone, is first displayed as part of the decadence of the urban, only then to take on the central role of nondiegetic narration. The brassy, jazzy sound of the music serves now as the central mimetic index of New York's urban dystopia. In contrast, the change of space to Germany is marked by both visual and acoustic dissolves. While the expressionist acoustic and visual vocabulary of the New York scenes is replaced by an orderly, restful camera and montage, the sound track offers a sort of musical dissolve into a properly "classical" tonal order as the brass play a chorale-like theme to indicate the return of the narrative to Berlin.

While the beginning of the film is designed to emphasize the distinction of these two spaces, in part by using musical means, very soon the imperative of the film becomes to unify them through the healing properties of radio. Here again, music plays a central role, not only simply in the development of the plot, but also in the means by which the film organizes its affectual economy. As we later return to New York, we see Hanna on her deathbed. Her roommate (?!), an "oratorio singer" whose name directs the spectator's attention excessively to his national identity: Washington Smith, is preparing to hear Beethoven's Ninth played from Berlin, conducted by the previously introduced Garvenberg. Garvenberg is mentioned with a reverence that is only surpassed by the mention of Beethoven himself, and Smith remarks to the doctor on the importance of this broadcast: "The whole world will be listening!" The doctor is more skeptical of the attraction of this media event, and responds, "Don't exaggerate." When later, however, the music begins, the doctor too is taken in by Garvenberg/Beethoven, and we witness him bringing the radio to Hanna's bedside. In a series of shots, Hanna is "cured" of her mysterious illness by hearing the sounds of Beethoven from Berlin, and is thus able to return to Germany. In this film, Beethoven's music serves not only as a sort of individual cure, it also effects a reconstellation of a newly purified domestic scene. In contrast to other forms of mass-mediated music in the film, radio is not a medium of pleasure but of medical magic and spiritual uplift, of familial-national work.

If "[a] medium is a medium is a medium"(Kittler 1990, 229), *Schlußakkord* is obsessed with media and their relationality. Other media make their presence known throughout the plot of the film: the evil Carl-Otto, some sort of nebulous astrologer/soothsayer/magician, who later blackmails the wife of Garvenberg; the child, who mediates Hanna's return to Germany; the mysteriously "other" companion of Frau Garvenberg, who announces the day of the Beethoven concert as one of bad luck. But the radio is the dominant medium of this film: while the other media of the film are either weak or decadent, radio is the medium that establishes broadcaster and receiver in proper, authentically "human" relationship. Earlier depictions of broadcasting, as in the film *Das Lied einer Nacht*, focus on technologies of transmission, showing the communication of sound from the space of its "origin," through radio antennas, through windows into multiple scenes of audition. In *Schlußakkord*, transmission is only "represented" by the naturalizing allegory of the intervening shot of the ocean waves, subsequently only to be represented as reception in one singular domestic scene. The naturalizing allegory of the ocean is furthermore a syntactic block used repeatedly to mark the dual plot of the film's beginning, and represents a resonant gap in the film's texture that is ultimately overcome in the concert hall. This "overcoming" is foreshadowed by the acoustic identity of the two spaces at the beginning of the film.

The child alone is insufficient to reproduce the domestic scene; rather, the domestic scene needs to be called into a national existence by the address of the radio and the "German music" that is broadcast across it. The final scene of the film, musically accompanied by a chorus from Händel's *Judas Maccabeus*,[35] imagines the sort of domestic bliss within the national space that the rest of the film has shown to be an impossibility. As Hanna and her son, placed behind the orchestral apparatus, are elevated to the status of architecture, they become part of the resonant body of the concert hall itself. By approximating the statues that line its walls in their attendant listening, Hanna and Peter literally embody the idealized publicity of the concert hall, itself tied through the radio to a national and international scene. Like the statues in the radio broadcast, which seem to work as natural "antennas" linking the ultimately inseparable mother from the musical, the maternal now seems to support an idealizing national acoustic, able to in the first case cross oceans, in the second, simply all consuming. This national acoustic is however intensely personal: an interior space.

Furthermore, while a film like *Das Lied einer Nacht* had to confront the problem of representing radio's dispersed audience, *Schlußakkord* favors a complete individualization of the relationship between listener and broadcast. Not only does the concert hall where the broadcast is supposed to take place have no visible microphone, the acoustic space of the scene in New York around the radio and that in Berlin are also identical to the film's representation of the acoustic space of the concert hall. While the conductor's wife will never resonate with the sound of her husband's orchestra, the mother—and metonymically through the photograph, the child—return at the end of the film to where they were at the beginning. Radio alone seems to be able to propel the logic of this film's narrative, in many ways because the film insists that Beethoven *immediates* radio: in other words, radio's mediacy is absorbed by a fantasy of acoustic presence. In one scene, we witness a party at the Garvenberg's house, without Herr Garvenberg. The noise of the party wakes Peter, who has by now been adopted by the Garvenbergs. The music playing, first a sort of rhumba, followed by a *Schlager*, is produced by a record player in the corner of the room. We are focused on the spinning of the phonograph as not only an aural but also a sort of visual irritation, enforced by the matching relationship that ties the phonograph to the prior [Sierckean extravagant] crane shot of the child upstairs spinning around on his minicarousel.[36]

This Sierckian fable of musical immediacy and media transparency seems to lend itself easily to an explicitly nationalist ideology. But if we consider the operation of the film more closely, the role of art music is by no means as black-and-white in its relationship to the national as it might at first seem. If *Schlußakkord* seems to insist in its plot on the absolute superiority of art music over the profoundly mediated character of other forms of musical practice, this cinematic argument is considerably challenged by the role of Lil Dagover in the film. Dagover, who at the beginning of the film leaves a resonant gap in the concert hall by her failed appearance, is, in the poster for *Schlußakkord*, the woman figured with Garvenberg in the space of the concert hall. Not the somewhat dowdy mother of his soon-to-be child, but his decadent wife, serves as both identificatory and spectacular focus of the film's narrative. In this way, *Schlußakkord* becomes a nearly direct model of what Doane has described as the musical "love story" in the Hollywood tradition. Like these later Hollywood films, most prominently *Humoresque* (Negulesco 1946), *Schlußakkord* is subject to leakage around the figure of female identification. The wholesomeness of the proper "German" family brought together by Beethoven is constantly threatened by the spectacle of a sloppy, excessively attractive femininity, which refuses, not only to take a seat in the concert hall, but also her proper place as a doting wife and mother. On the one hand, *Schlußakkord* displays the possibility of female spectatorship: as Doane suggests for the American counterpart, the dominance of music in the film, specifically the control of the musical by the male character, serves to displace the implicit feminization to which he is subject. Like *Humoresque*, *Schlußakkord* attempts to display the threat of female spectatorship to the spectacular order of gender by blocking female vision: Charly's/Lil Dagover's absence from the concert, and more importantly her acoustic disturbance outside the doors of the concert hall, briefly disrupt the visual order of a sequence which had previously revolved around the visual anchor of the conductor. Moreover, the excessive display of Dagover in the next scene seems to replace a specific type of femininity firmly in the spectacular position. The threat remains, however, present: the dizzying grammar of shots used to display Dagover/Charly's body strangely echoes the all-around views of the concert hall, with Garvenberg at its center. Even the brief focus on the women in the chorus, which seems at first to displace the spectacularization of the male body with an angelic vision of femininity, is simultaneously a vision of intense feminine "scopofilia." This split between the film's ideological drive to anchor a national family in German music and its necessity to displace the spectacularization of the conductor through the staging of Dagover's body remains an insoluble contradiction that displaces the seemingly straightforward ideological drive of the film.

Furthermore, a film like *Schlußakkord* did not stand alone: the neat operation of a musical ideology of sublime Germanness in this film is disrupted by the fact that other films of the period use art music in a very different way. Particularly interesting in this light is *Heimat* (Froelich 1938), the biggest box-office attraction among German productions of the 1938–1939 season. Primarily a vehicle for the film's main star, Zarah Leander, who since the success of *La Habanera* and *Zu neuen Ufern* had become the central diva of the Nazi film industry, *Heimat*, with a screenplay only vaguely based on the 1893 Hermann Sudermann drama of the same name, was awarded the annual State Film Prize on May 1, 1939 (Rentschler 1996, 248). The film is primarily concerned with a narrative of return: the purportedly American singer Maddalena dall'Orto (Leander) travels to the German small town Ilmingen for a guest appearance in the local music festival; shortly after her arrival, the town discovers that "Maddalena dall'Orto" is in fact a long-lost daughter of the town: Magda. This solves the problem that some of the townspeople see at the beginning of the film; various pillars of the establishment had doubted whether a foreigner should be chosen to sing Bach's St. Matthew Passion during the music festival. But the return of the daughter inevitably, true to the melodramatic tone of the film, engenders problems of greater magnitude. Not only is Magda not prepared to adjust her ways to the provincial morals of the small town, she is also haunted by her past, in particular her relationship to her illegitimate daughter, the father of that daughter, and her own father, who is not yet ready to welcome the long-lost daughter home. Of course, in various ways each of these problems is solved during the course of the film, and at its conclusion the family is again restored:

mother, illegitimate daughter, and grandfather return to their true place in the town, and order is reestablished. The final solution of the film is dramatically staged in the aforementioned performance of Bach's St. Matthew Passion in narrative, visual, and acoustic terms.

This scene is paradigmatic for one use of serious music in the cinema: at first, we see and hear a scene that purports to document an "actual" performance of the Passion, with "real" musicians and a true singer (see Figure 22).

The acoustic of this scene is at first established as that of the resonant, yet architecturally confused church in which the scene is set. At issue here is not whether or not these opening shots are somehow "true" documents of a performance. These shots were also postsynchronized, but by conforming to certain already established standards for the "documentary" recording of musical performance, especially the visual framing of the performers, the scene successfully traffics in the semiotics of a realistic presentation of a musical event.

For our ears, this arrangement then seems initially to be disrupted by the voice of Leander: singing the alto aria, "Buß und Reu", Leander's trademark baritone echoes throughout the church in a most

Figure 22. Heimat *(Froelich 1938).*

unsacrosanct way. Taken out of context, in other words, the voice only sounds like a somewhat ridiculous crossing of inviolable genre distinctions. While in some trivial sense this is all very much the case, we need to ask if actual audience formations of the 1930s and '40s would have experienced this scene in this way. The issues here are more complex: Leander's voice is not only particular for its style, timbre, and extremely unfeminine pitch, but also introduces a different acoustic perspective into the scene of classical musical performance. The shift from the concert acoustic of the previous sub-sequence could not be more dramatic. But considering the immense popularity of this film, what might seem to our ears a radical disjunction might have seemed to many spectators of the period perfectly normal. This in turn suggests that this kind of split is by no means unique to this kind of scene, but instead characterizes sound film production in general, especially in its early years. James Lastra has described two competing models of sound representation in filmmaking in the 1930s. The first, the "fidelity model," insisted on the presence and immediacy of the recorded sound object. The descendent of a long line of metaphors of simulation, in this model "emphasized the literal duplication of a real and embodied (but invisible) auditor's experience of an acoustic event" (2000, 181). The second, which we might misleadingly abbreviate as the "telephonic model," sees the representation of sound as merely part of an overall project of communications, and in its metaphorics traces "its roots to the metaphor of writing, and emphasizes the mediacy, constructedness and derived character of representation" (181).

While the first of these models might also be called the "concert model," cinematic depictions of the concert from the later 1930s continued to be haunted by this split approach to sound representation. This scene is a typical example of this: shifting between two different acoustic regimes, the film struggles to create a new listening space appropriate for both "Bach" and the voice of the popular star. The ambivalence of this scene becomes especially clear when Leander's voice rises in the midst of the chorale. Obviously the soloist's extreme domination of the choral soundscape breaks with more standard performances. This acoustic "zoom in" serves to mark the interiorization of the scene, as the chorus—the collective—seems almost to fade into the background. The paradoxical "genuineness" of the amplified voice had already established itself in the music of the 1930s. The acoustic space of the chorus and that of Leander are not identical: Leander's heavily amplified voice is staged to easily compete with both chorus and orchestra, and fills this strange performance space all the way down to the public scene of familial intimacy between father and granddaughter displayed on the floor of the church (Figure 23).

During the aria, a tear falls from Magda's/Leander's eyes (Figure 24). This tear is one final break with the habitus of "serious music," that code of behavior that precisely refuses the direct staging of the subjectivity of the singer and "the music itself."

A "serious" musical performance, and the linked forms of audience reception, is transformed through this tear to a *Schlager* performance: yet another indulgently soppy Leander hit. At the same time, the very alienating surface that is constitutive for the functioning of bourgeois musical publicity—the abstraction of the performer's subjectivity from the performance—seems to be swept aside, and the barrier between the private spectator in the cinema and the figure here represented is to dissolve. This technique, through which the shine of the tear is supposed to suddenly focus our attention on her face, and reflect the tears that the spectator herself is supposed to be producing. The tear, in combination with the more intimate effect of the amplified voice and

Figure 23. Heimat.

the series of shots that focuses on intimacy, interpellates the spectator visually and aurally into a seemingly private world of depth and authenticity, and thus help to bind him or her to the emotional economy of the scene.

The tear of course also works as a kind of "instruction" through identification, a reminder through recognition that yes, it is now appropriate to shed a tear. At the same time, the shine of the tear is reminiscent of the shine of the star's jewels, and thus unwittingly returns the spectator to the alienating abstraction of publicity that the scene seeks on all levels to obliterate. Thus, even in a film with a musical ideology that at first seems to automatically confirm national socialist notions of "Germanness" and music, we are primarily confronted with modes of listening that do not correspond to an idealized mode of national concert. Instead, we are presented with an arrangement that underscores the production of intimate personal relationship to popular musical stardom, an emphatically modern form of commercial mass culture. This returns us to the question of publicity and privacy: here again, this "private" is by no means one familiar from older social formations. A page from the film program to *Heimat* is instructive on this

Figure 24. Heimat.

point. In a still taken from a scene in the film, in which a meeting between the singer and the Kapellmeister (Paul Hörbiger) takes place at
the church organ, the two central popular songs from the films are
"pasted in" above and beneath the two actors. These iconic references
to the film's other songs—typical of German film programs from the
period—again bring the two areas into intimate contact; they even
seem to allow the "tones" of the *Schlager* to visually resonate in the
acoustic space of the church—a space which in the logic of the film
echoes with the tones of Bach. Combined with the intimate visual
contact of the two figures pictured, staged around the church organ,
this montage again offers the viewer a mode of musical consumption
which refuses any clear-cut opposition between the public and the private, instead depicting the public as an intensely private space. At the
same time, the film insists on a stable listener position for experiencing both the sounds of Bach and the tones of the latest hit song.

The linkage should lead us to rethink our understanding of the operation of ideology in these maternal melodramas. Linda Schulte-Sasse,
for example, in her recent study of Nazi cinema, sees these films as
primarily concerned with the issue of returning home, and thereby links
them in the first instance to a nationalist project:

> The popular topos in Nazi cinema of returning "home" . . . for
> example, illustrates the parallel between the need for spatial
> geographical containment and personal containment. A spatially
> contained, homogenous, "German" environment provides a context
> in which the individual can avoid contamination and in which
> community can come to fruition. (253)

While this is certainly a valid observation of the ideological configuration of a great many films of the period—not only in Nazi Germany—
it might be more productive to see these films as located in a history
of subjectivity as it is installed through the technologies and practices
of mass culture. These films then not only illustrate, but also engage in
the renegotiation of ideologies of musical mediacy through the newly
established *audiovisual* star system and the production of a modern
audiovisual imaginary. The new audiovisual star system, intimately
linked to the acoustic technologies of the day, required what contemporary commentators experienced as a flattening of acoustic experience, so that serious music and popular song could be consumed in an
identical fashion, and so that the counterpart to the audiovisual star,

the sovereign subject of musical consumption, could be granted a coherence only with the help of this audiovisual imaginary. A mutual recognition of "presence" in consuming musical mass culture guaranteed the fidelity of this system, as could already be seen in a radio advertisement from 1930:

> You will buy thousands of happy hours for your family, your friends, yourself . . . The ownership of one of these majestic instruments means calming relaxation from the hard work and toil of the day. The rhythm with which every model transmits in pure tones and true to nature the amusing hit song, the harmonic beauty of serious music, gives the impression of the immediate presence of the artist. (Advertisement, *Berliner Illustrirte Zeitung*, 1930, p. 2132)[37]

A film like *Heimat* also illustrates the lingering contradictions in the attempt to create a homogenous German home for the newly reassembled subjects of audiovisual mass culture. Although the audiovisual imaginary of modern consumer culture makes it possible to link new forms of mass publicity to invented traditions of national musical mastery, this attempt is risky, as shown by some of the responses of contemporary critics to *Heimat*. Consider the following comments made by Ernst Schliepe in an article that appeared in *Die Musik* entitled "Bach as a Film Composer":

> Now to the film *Heimat* . . . In those same deep chest tones, she later sings the famous mezzo aria "*Buß und Reu*"—namely, due to lacking vocal capacity, around a fifth deeper! On top of this it was cut to but a fraction. And at the end, with teary eyes the chorale *Wenn ich einmal soll scheiden*. This film also shows on closer artistic inspection that Bach's music is not used out of inner necessity, but to achieve a horrible effect.

For this critic, the misuse of Bach in the cinematic context is made even worse by the social situation of film reception:

> A half-minute later, the lights come on, the visitors dry their tears— "Please go to the right, keep the middle clear! Chocolate, sour drops perhaps?" To put it briefly: one is crushed. Not from the weight of the film or the falsification of Bach's music, but from the idea that our best cultural good is still subject to every misuse, and in order to achieve superficial effects is dragged into a setting in which it can only be destroyed. (Schiepe, 1939, 376)

This rabid criticism was however in the end a marginal phenomenon: similar forms of what these critics would deride as vulgar popularization in the musical cinema were welcomed in official circles. But the continuing reemergence of this kind of criticism illustrates that the contradictions that continued to mark the role of music in German mass culture required that structures of musical mediacy repeatedly be recast and renegotiated. This kind of criticism also shows that a reading of *Heimat* merely based on its protonationalist plot and nationalized Bach misses the way in which the staging of the nation was alternately supported *and* disrupted by the operation of the film's audiovisual imaginary. In the same article discussed above, Schiepe also took aim at *Final Chord*.

> Of course the conductor film *Schlußakkord* can't do without the Ninth Symphony—as if Beethoven had not also created other truly good works. But in film, only the best will do . . . Ninth Symphony, B-minor Mass, St. Matthew Passion. There is only one positive thing about this profanization and wear and tear: films are so short-lived. Thus, it is guaranteed that these kinds of attacks on taste and sense of art *[Kunstsinn]* at least do not have long-term effects. (376–77)[38]

As we have seen, while national melodrama seems to sound "authentic community" by anchoring it in the family unit via the auditive woman, this acoustic arrangement is far from secure. Haunted by excess in multiple registers, the national claim of these films is constantly in tension with the modern staging of listening subjectivity and the intimate, seemingly "private" relationship to stardom that it requires.

Revue Films: Negotiating the Opposition

A perhaps more stable arrangement can be found in the revue film of the period. Less freighted with the ideological weight of nationalizing films like those discussed above, the revue film could focus more exclusively on musical publicity as a shared zone of imaginary personal interiority. If, on the one hand, *Schlußakkord* and *Heimat* depend upon the installation of modern listening arrangements for their national address, on the other hand they participate in this process of installation by staging modes of audition and casting molds for listener subjectivity. While these films primarily focus on the personal attachment and investment enabled by musical performance and proper modes of listening, the audiovisual network here implied had to be anchored at the other end—the "source" of composition as well. Here the cinema would also play a key role. In various revue films of the period, attention was focused less on performance and reception than on composition. Using the opposition between "serious" and "popular" musical practice—and the resolution of this opposition—as a structure to support the production of meaning on other planes of social life, these revue films center around the figure of the composer and his (or her) capabilities of expression.

The film *Traummusik [Dream Music]* (Bolvary 1940)[39] is typical of this kind of film. Rigidly constructed in three short acts, this film begins in Rome, introducing three of the four central characters, three students at the conservatory: Michele, an opera composer, Ronnie, a *Schlager* composer, and Carla, an aspiring opera soprano. At the beginning of the film, Carla and Michele are established as a couple in a way that secures the typically conservative division of gender roles: Carla sings Michele's music. In the following scene, we are shown the course of their exams at the conservatory, allowing both the key musical and narrative material of the film to be cemented even more completely: Michele's test consists of a performance of a scene from his opera, "Odysseus' Return,"[40] with Carla singing the lead role. Their friend, Ronnie, follows Michele's performance with his own piece, which he calls a "jazz symphony."

After passing their exams at the conservatory, each of these musicians begins to attempt to fulfill his or her career goals in the real, hard-knock world of professional musicianship. Things do not go as imagined, and Carla and Michele have to work as musicians in the nightclub along with fellow ex-student Ronnie and the fourth central character of the film, Odette (Lizzi Waldmüller). Carla, however, is soon rescued from the nightclub, and brought to Milan where her career takes off, while Michele is left behind in Rome to work on his opera. When Michele finishes his opera, he comes to Rome to see Carla's debut performance and, at the same time, play his opera for the director, who had arranged for Carla's breakthrough with somewhat more than music in mind. After being dismissed by the director with the condescending advice to "work on the basics," Michele is indignant. Carla's mother meets with Michele during the intermission of Carla's performance, and asks Michele to leave Carla in peace, as he is a block to her career. After agreeing to do as the mother requested, one final humiliation awaits; in the opera's intermission, Michele over-hears a publisher who had shown interest in his work saying that he only did so at the behest of the opera director. Horrified at being the loser husband to a glamorous opera star, Michele leaves the opera, and returns to Rome, where he teams up with Ronnie and Odette to ded-icate himself entirely to the composition of hit songs. Under the pseu-donym "Mac Dynar," Michele finally achieves international success with his very first musical revue.

In the film's final act, now caught in preparation for the second revue, Mac Dynar/Michele is faced with writer's block, and cannot find the theme song. After a visit from a young composer reminds him of his lost ideals, he decides to sacrifice his opera score for its musical motifs, composing the song "Traummusik" and finishing the revue at the last minute. In the meantime, Carla hears that the Budapest Opera has decided to give Michele's opera a premiere performance. (The detail of how they got the unpublished score is left unanswered.) As happenstance will have it, just when Carla arrives in Budapest to sing the lead role, the three pop musicians also arrive in the city for the premiere performance of their revue. Of course, Carla meets Odette in a hotel lobby, and Carla comes to a dress rehearsal of the revue. She now realizes what has happened, and begs Michele to withdraw the number from the revue. At first refusing, Michele in the end chooses art over commerce, and triumphantly conducts the premiere perfor-mance of his opera instead. As the film concludes, its "to each his own" moral not only has the couples sorted out, but also returns the film's two composers in their proper genres.

The film is a strange product, if only for its extravagant use of inter-media references—one revue scene begins as a television broadcast, marking the early period of limited television broadcasting in Nazi Germany in the late 1930s.[41] *Traummusik* seems to be resolutely mod-eled on the American backstage musical, but is burdened with a some-what unsatisfyingly proportioned revue structure, with its constant shifting between revue numbers and opera performances. Like many German revue films of the period, the numbers themselves take on Berkeley-esque proportions, not only in terms of mobilizing an ex-pansive range of filming styles, but also in terms of mere length. The film also features an almost unique collaboration in its score: while the *Schlager* composer Peter Kreuder, one of the most popular songwriters of the 1930s and '40s, composed most of the film music, that is, the numbers and incidental music, the program announces that "the Italian opera composer Zandonai" provided the operatic music. Riccardo Zandonai, little known today, was one of the leading composers of opera in Italy in the 1920s and '30s. Best known for his opera *Francesca di Rimini*, Zandonai's style can be loosely characterized as a mix of Puccini and Richard Strauss; integrating musical innovations in terms of harmonic vocabulary and orchestration, Zandonai ultimately sought to retain the centrality of Italian opera by accepting moderate musical change.[42] Not only does this collaboration cement the "binational" character of this Italian/German coproduction, it also reflects the structure of the film's plot.

For our purposes, the key moments of the film are those that explicitly link opera and popular music, in particular by means of a simple musical motivic link: the film is constantly accompanied by the two versions of the basic musical material. On the one hand, an aria from Michele's opera, which he wrote especially for Carla, and on the other hand, "Traummusik," the title *Schlager* of the film, which uses the same motif in a "swing" version. Already in the opening credits, which visually insist on the "classical"—a marble background with "Roman" lettering for text—these two motives are placed side by side, staking out the two poles of the film's acoustic scope. This motivic link will reemerge often in the film to mark crucial moments in the plot: most importantly, the climax of the film in Budapest.

In an earlier scene in the film, the premiere of the new Mac Dynar revue is drawing dangerously close, but the final *Schlager* for the revue is still not yet composed. With the entire production team in a panic, Mac has to find a quick solution for his composer's block. Before we learn his solution, the visit of an eager young composer, piano concerto in hand, already clues us in on the possible sources for Dynar's new inspiration. Dynar/Michele glances briefly at the music, only to quickly dismiss it: "This is a pretty motif. But much too difficult. Why not turn it into a gay waltz?" The young composer, deeply shocked, offers a speech in praise of the life of the struggling, authentic artist, and leaves. The young composer is then replaced by Ronnie, who had previously picked up the now-completed final song. Coming to the piano in Dynar's office to play it, after a few measures he immediately recognizes the theme as that of the central aria from Michele's opera. Michele sits down at the piano: first playing (and speaking the words to) his aria, then: "This nobody wanted from me. But this way," now playing the *Schlager* version, at a quick tempo and with a marked, almost exaggerated syncopation, "Every boy will sing it on the street. This melody will be pressed on thousands of records, it will be danced to in all bars, and on the radio it will be heard ten times a day."

The sonic association which had already been planted in the spectator's mind by the opening credits is now given grounding in the plot, and will continue to serve to structure the rest of the film's acoustic material. Finally in Budapest, at the dress rehearsal, the comparison between the two pieces is repeated, this time in a more elaborate fashion. Carla has emerged at the dress rehearsal, only to discover what Donato has done to his aria. "You're opera, jazzed up *[verjazzt]*." After trying to convince "Michele Donato" to withdraw the revue, she receives the simple answer, "My name is Mac Dynar," and leaves. Dynar now sits in a chair in the audience, and we are offered a shot from his point of view (Figure 25) from the seats of the hall facing the stage, as the music returns to the refrain of "Traummusik."

On another cut, we are returned to Mac Dynar in the audience; as he leans forward, a shot of the earlier points-of-view (POV) image is

Figure 25. Traummusik *(Bolvary 1940).*

superimposed on the mid-range shot of Dynar. As the POV shot begins to zoom in, narrowing perspective, this second-layer image now dissolves, musically and visually, into a production of the opera, where Carla is, center-stage, singing the "original" aria. Now, instead of the background shot changing scope, the image of Dynar is replaced with a close-up, signaling a deeper level of interiority, increased by the movement of the camera in the second shot towards the figure of Carla. After five measures of the aria, incorporating both halves of the central motivic phrase, we move back to the revue: Waldmüller walking across the stage singing the verse, in approximately the same scale, the camera following her across the stage. Returning again after four measures to the opera, we see Carla walking in the same direction. The scene offers us one final comparison: now with both women walking towards "the camera." This double specular fantasy leads Dynar, now returning to the spectacle of the real production, to stand up, crying "Stop!"—and the revue is cancelled.

Despite the film's narrative insistence on the fundamental distinction between art and commerce, this scene, which in particular is supposed to underline this distinction, does in fact the opposite. By placing the two versions of the motive in the same acoustic space, and by insisting on a visual comparison between the two genres of stage performance, Carla and Odetta are far less emblematic of any kind of fundamental opposition than they are of the similar accessibility of both musical forms. Here the aria is valued more than anything because of its accessibility, the very accessibility that makes it available for commercial appropriation. Furthermore, the opera is not only inserted into the same acoustic space, but also the same visual frame: echoing the intense media linkages of other scenes of this film, where even television comes into one of the revue scenes to play a role. In the final scene (Figure 26), Odetta comforts the "frustrated" *Schlager* composer as they both sit in the box at the opera performance, "There have to be both. The Micheles, and the Ronnies."

When the film announces its close with the word "Ende" presented in an exaggeratedly classical type, the sound track repeats for one final moment the fundamental comparison which drives the film: giving the cinematic spectator a final confirmation of his own ability to consume both forms of musical practice with equal ability.

Witte has read this film as a "revue film, which refuses the temptation of decadent jazz with the promise of success for serious music"

(1995, 223). This is of course half-true: the serious composer does refuse the temptation of *Schlager*. But the film by no means pictures jazz as decadent: on the contrary. Only jazz produced at the expense of true art is a problem for this film. Despite the narrative drive of the opera plot, the film insists not so much on the superiority of opera over revue; instead it insists that while opera composers should dedicate themselves to their art, *Schlager* composers are equally welcome in the musical world. Indeed it is *Schlager* which by far dominate the plot and musical texture of this film. The structure of the film not only makes the opera "numbers" approximate revue scenes; the breaks in the narrative are either filled with an opera performance or a revue number.

Other roughly contemporary films, like *Wir machen Musik (We Make Music)* (Käutner 1942),[43] finally abandon any pretense of retaining a strict division between the "higher" world of art music and the commercial realm of *Schlager*; instead insisting on the equal need for both "entertainment" and seriousness. In this film, popular music, indeed so-called "German swing," serves not only as a relatively harmless consumerist attraction, as it appears in *Traummusik*, but is even positioned

Figure 26. Traummusik.

as the zone of "authentic," natural musical expression and artistic genius. In this film, Zimmerman, the substitute music lecturer at a Berlin music school, begins his opening lecture by explaining to his students a crucial distinction necessary to learn at the beginning of any "serious" musical study.

> Of course, there are musicians who do not make *Musik*, but rather *Musick*. There is a great difference between *Musick* and *Musik*. The difference is similar to the difference between *Kaffee* und *Kaffe*.

Zimmerman, played by Victor de Kowa, offers the second analogy to clarify his point by underlining the logics of class, which the first distinction, *Kaffee* and *Kaffe* (perhaps best translated for New York ears at least as *coffee* and *cawhfee)*, already mobilized. Needless to say, these distinctions are enormously difficult to translate: operating on a sociolinguistic grid of provincial dialect and class markers, the comparisons simply intend to show that certain forms of musical practice achieve levels of the sublime entirely alien from the banalities of a everyday life. While *Musik* is reserved to a plane of autonomy far from the world of labor and monetary exchange, the proletarian dialect of *Musick* places other forms of musical practice in direct contact with the contaminating effect of money.

But *We Make Music* is a musical comedy, and moreover a musical comedy to a large extent based on Hollywood models of film narrative. The fundamental binary opposition of this sociomusical cartography needs to be overturned in the film, and furthermore linked to the establishment of a married, heterosexual couple. But interestingly enough, while in the Hollywood version of this structure, the musical insists on the national component, here, the national component remains curiously bracketed: this is more interesting when we consider how *Wir machen Musik* is one of the exceptions of musical filmmaking during the Nazi period.[44]

This film depends on a cultural grid of distinctions that circumscribe a basic opposition between serious and popular music. The film's traffic in cultural capital speaks to multiple audiences in various ways, reproducing and denying the operation of class in its very address. This can only be described in broad outlines: on the one hand, for a cosmopolitan, bourgeois audience, the petit bourgeois rigidity of his orthodox explanation of cultural distinction—the accentual emphasis on the second syllable of *Musik*—is at best a cause of ridicule. At the same time, the comic aspects of de Kowa's performance obviously echo this and seem to open up the orthodoxy of class logics to lower-class audiences, while in fact, what to some audiences might seem like the ridicule of cultural capital is its reproduction in a real form. At the same time, the cultural capital circulating in a film like *Wir machen Musik* is invested in a strikingly familiar project: the structure of Käutner's film echoes an almost identical trope from American musicals of the same period, especially as developed around the figure of Judy Garland in the "Opera vs. Jazz" numbers of films in the late 1930s and early 1940s. In films like *Presenting Lily Mars*, with the number "Tom, Tom the Piper's Son," and *Babes in Arms* with the number "Opera vs. Jazz," the American musical sets up a strict opposition between authentically "American" forms of popular music and somehow alienating, elite forms of musical practice.

The irony here is of course that while the American character of jazz is central in the Hollywood musicals that make use of this opposition, here the "national" address of popular music remains strikingly insecure. But if the American version of this kind of film, popular at the same period, insists on the "foreignness" of classical music in contrast to the native qualities of swing, the German version of this plot obviously plays out quite differently. This is by no means a clear-cut question, however; while the compositional activity of the film's hero is repeatedly subject to ridicule, art music itself needs to be retained as a model. The nature of serious music as an arcane sphere is constantly played with in this film. Reminding the audience repeatedly that serious music is too complicated for them, at the same time, the "advanced harmonies" of the composer's opera allow the audience to laugh, imagining they indeed have access to the distinguishing power that cultural capital makes available. Indeed, the film will ultimately argue for a nostalgic reunification of "originally" unified spheres of musical practice. At the film's conclusion the marriage of the two main characters is saved by musical collaboration: the composer who has access to arcane musical knowledge is hired to "rescue" the work of the naively gifted, yet musically uneducated woman. In the key sequence to the first half of the film (Figure 27), which ultimately establishes the two couples of the film, this is illustrated dramatically by switching back and forth between the two narrative strands.

We are first shown a shot from the waist up of Sperling, conducting an "orchestra" in a symphonic jazz number. The camera pans right,

Figure 27. Wir machen Musik *(Käutner 1942).*

and we discover that the "orchestra" has no musicians: with a further pan to the right, now coming a complete 180 degrees, we see a tape playing what we can only presume to be the music we hear, and the woman sitting next to the apparatus, longingly looking up toward Sperling. On a cut, we return to the original shot, but this shot is now framed within the love narrative. Sperling, continuing to conduct, at some point gives a "cue" to some imagined instrument; with this cue, there is a cut, and we are now witnesses to the lonely spectacle of Zimmerman playing a Bach prelude on the organ alone in an empty hall. First announced by a fall of light at the other end of the room, Anni enters the shot from the right, and moves to the organ. On another cut, we return to the earlier couple, now seen from the perspective of the empty orchestra chairs, visually separated on opposite sides of the room. The positioning of this couple is mirrored in the next shot, a more close-up shot of Zimmerman and Anni, with Anni looking up to Zimmerman with the same admiring eyes as the other woman had gazed at Sperling. After this shot zooms in to focus on Zimmerman alone, he completes the prelude, and on completion, after a sigh, we hear Zimmerman proclaim:

> ZIMMERMAN: Johann . . . Sebastian. . . . Bach. That's where it starts, and that is the end. In comparison, everything else is small and pitiful. Can you feel that?
>
> ANNI: Only a poor soul couldn't. But wouldn't it be horrible if there were only music like that?
>
> ZIMMERMAN: Why?
>
> ANNI: Every day can't be a solemn holiday (*Feiertag*). There has to be music for all days, tender music, music in love, fun music.

Anni's description makes clear here what is at issue. She not only sees Bach as the composer of different forms of music applicable to particular social situations—that is, thoroughly divorced from any romantic conceptions of absolute music—she also sees the social situations that Bach's music is appropriate for not as public events, solemnities, but private emotions: solemnity, tenderness, love, and fun.

Coming back to Zimmerman and Anni, we come in on Zimmerman holding a diatribe:

> ZIMMERMAN: *Gebrauchsmusik Schlagermusik Hotmusik Jazzmusik* . . . Whatever you call it . . .

ANNI: Those are only slogans, slogans for misunderstood concepts . . .

ZIMMERMAN: Well, my art is at any event too valuable to me to
profane it as a humoristic or erotic background noise.

ANNI: Thank god the old masters were not so stubborn. Don't you
know the little love song which the great Johann Sebastian
Bach wrote for his little Bachess [Bachin], as "music for use"
[Gebrauchsmusik] for everyday romance [verliebten Alltag]? May I?

Anni turns towards the organ, and begins to sing Bach's "Willst du
Dein Herz mir schenken?" (BWV 518). Before arriving at the tonic,
Anni stops playing, and Zimmerman finally takes the initiative to kiss
her, a kiss that is then answered musically by a triumphant full-stop
major chord, which the two play together. The original establishment
of both couples is thus accomplished through music: the doubling of
the couples not only sutures the two romantic plot lines to one another,
but also links "popular" and "serious" music. Even in the singing style,
Ilse Werner insists on the identical character of *Schlager* and Bach, with
hints at mild slides between pitches, particularly on the last word, which
hint of Werner's swing background which otherwise dominates the film.
But the musical address of Werner's voice serves to produce a domestic
space: which is where the film is ultimately rooted. In the scene immediately following this one, we see the everyday life of a "modern" happy-
go-lucky couple in a Berlin apartment. Not yet married, but clearly
more than merely dating, Anni and Zimmerman have already established a regular home life, and this is first marked by Zimmerman in an
acoustic way when we hear him at the piano playing the same aria from
the prior scene. Thus ultimately rooting sociomusical experience to a
mass-mediated staging of privacy in the home, *Wir machen Musik* also
participates in the installation of an audiovisual imaginary that underscores the address of musical sound as being intended for a domestic
individual. Not the individual of the bourgeois public sphere, but the
subject of a shifting terrain of paradoxically mass-cultural privacy.

The Audiovisual Imaginary

As argued in the previous chapters, the nineteenth century's bourgeois
subject of the public sphere, firmly rooted in a heterosexual affectual
economy, and the private zone of individual experience required by
this structure had been perhaps threatened by the radically new modes

of public experience in acoustic culture represented by the *Schlager* and the radio. But as we have seen in this chapter, the *public* threat that *Schlager* and the radio presented to older modes of negotiating the contradictions of bourgeois social life was continually answered by a process that domesticated the force of these rearrangements of publicity by anchoring them firmly to a new mode of norming privatization. The claim of "truth" behind emotion witnessed in both the melodrama and in the revue film insists on the possibility of subjective musical expression in all forms of musical practice, provided they are inserted into the proper media apparatus, which makes the structure of their address properly intelligible as such. Sweeping up large sectors of the population in previously unimaginable ways, the emerging worlds of acoustic mass culture created zones of social experience that did not so much upset an older "balance" between public and private musical experience, but rather installed a different kind of zone of subjectivity, which in turn allowed the operation of new forms of hegemonic practice in the so-called "private" sphere.

Recalling the words of Fritz Brutz in 1924, his confused observations about the change in acoustic culture begin to seem savvier than we might have expected. Putting aside the value judgments Brutz laminates to his descriptions, we can recognize in his writing the outlines of a number of sociocultural shifts that would characterize the role of music in mass culture for the years to follow. As we have seen, however, what Brutz called the loss of "all immediacy" was in fact a transformation in acoustic mediacy itself particularly legible in the sphere of "serious music." This requires us to conceive of the use of "opus music" during both the Weimar and Nazi periods not simply as part of a nationalist antidote to cosmopolitan mass culture, but as implicated in the establishment of new structures of listening around the technologies of sound. Any mere focus on the ideological battles that seemed to have been fought over the role of serious and/or popular music in the period distracts from some of the fundamental changes that took place in the period. Enabled by an audiovisual media network, which included not only radio and the cinema but also the print media, the newly forming audiovisual imaginary produced "serious" music as a consumable good for a hitherto unreachable audience. Indeed, this audiovisual imaginary was a key element in molding that audience as a dispersed population of listening subjects.

Not only for those previously excluded from concert life, but for all participants in mass culture, music's mass cultural functionalization transformed the historical "essence" of music as it had developed within the context of earlier media networks. The ensemble of musical print culture, domestic musical consumption, and public concerts, which had served as the media apparatus supporting the idea of absolute music, was increasingly pushed to the background.[45] Just as earlier the consumption of piano transcriptions had molded practices of musical reception, and in so doing the very notion of music itself, the modern installation of acoustic sound technologies would also alter musical practices and the nature of musical texts far beyond any mere question of "increased" participation (Christensen 1999).

But this development should not be understood as a process determined merely by an abstractly conceived realm of "technological change." The installation of new sound technologies was only one component of larger processes of social transformation, ranging from shifts in the configuration of urban space to transformations of the domestic sphere, with a direct effect on the social constitution of both collectivity and subjectivity. This meant that the development of new sound technologies was inevitably caught up in the construction of new modes of interpellation, making for a radical revision of the basic structure of acoustic culture itself. The subjects addressed by the mass cultural use of serious music were installed in newly available zones of musical, familial privacy. The reconfiguration of the private sphere in modernity can only be understood as intersecting with the reconfiguration of the public sphere. A more proper term, however, might be the "installation" of privacy. As Antonie Prost suggests, only in the twentieth century did the strict division of privacy from publicity become a structuring element of everyday life on a mass scale. What Prost calls the "democratization of private life," however, should not be understood as a "fair" distribution of bourgeois privacy. In this sense, the term democratization is more than misleading. Instead, the privacies of modern life that emerged in new practices of housing and took form around new practices of media consumption were new zones of regulation that had only a formal similarity to early modes of privacy (Prost and Vincent 1987).

By way of conclusion, I would suggest that these developments are not only relevant for the history of acoustic culture in Germany, but also indicate some remaining dilemmas in thinking about the history of modern acoustic culture more generally. Obviously, these developments had a prehistory. Thomas Christensen has recently argued that the emergence of "absolute music" in the nineteenth century was fundamentally linked to the *privatization* of musical experience. In a very convincing look at the history of piano transcription, Christensen provocatively turns the tables on the usual narrative discussed in part in the prior chapter. While Bekker and later Habermas and their more recent interpreters Heister and Johnson each in different ways focus on the concert as the locus for intimately linked emergence of both the public sphere and the notion of "absolute music," Christensen radically changes the focus, and argues that the stabilization of "absolute music" required yet another cultural technology.

> Through the rise of both the piano transcription and the concert
> recital in the nineteenth century, musical genres became irrevocably
> untethered from their traditional geographies of performance . . .
> By extricating a piece of music from its physical presence in time
> and space, the piano transcription is implicated in the process of
> etherialization that became such a cornerstone of Romantic formalist
> music aesthetics. No longer dependent upon where it is heard, or,
> for that matter, the medium by which it is realized, the musical
> artwork becomes a disembodied notational trace. (1999, 289–90)

This is a vitally important move that makes the dialectic between publicity and privacy central. However, this reframing of music history, a welcome shift in focus to music's *mediacy*, is plagued by its own attempt to shift the focus of historicity: while rooting the emergence of "absolute music" in very specific social practices, Christensen defines these social practices by applying the seemingly universal opposition of public and private. This universal anthropology prevents us from coming to terms with its own historicity. The very terms "public" and "private," in Christensen's analysis, rapidly begin to reify as ahistorical constants.

> Transcription contributed to this destabilization of the generic
> contract by introducing new kinds of music into domestic settings;
> it served, that is, to break down the barriers of the musical landscape
> and thus to act as a conduit of nineteenth-century aesthetic values.
> To be sure, one of the immediate effects of transcription was the
> introduction of the public rhetoric of symphonic music into the
> domestic space of the parlor and the drawing room. But at the same
> time, this process may be said to have reciprocally helped tame and

domesticate the symphonic genre by opening it up to a more interiorized reception, one that had hitherto been associated with more private genres of music. (1999, 289)

This problem becomes especially clear when we attempt to study the linkage between music as a social practice in the nineteenth and twentieth centuries. Almost parenthetically, Christensen remarks, "The dislocation of musical genre from performing geography [was] a process whose profound aesthetic implications were only fully realized with the establishment of mechanical musical reproduction in the twentieth century" (1999, 290). This is of course in a way the central claim of Christensen's essay.

Crucially, this shift also involved a central transformation in notions of the public and the private previously central to the various forms of musical production and consumption. Instead of merely shifting forms of musical privacy and publicity—a process Christensen described as redefining "geographies of musical reception"—the emerging audiovisual imaginary was engaged in the construction of new forms of subjectivity which were thoroughly implicated in the media networks engaged. This is not "merely" a historical question, but a theoretical question as well, with implications that might lead our inquiries far beyond the emergence of the sound technologies of the first half of the twentieth century. If it is the case that this new arrangement far surpassed any simple renegotiation of the boundaries between public and private, we need to reexamine the validity of these categories as omnihistorical terms of empirical description. In other words, what Christensen describes as the introduction of "new kinds of music into domestic settings"—a process he explicitly extends into the twentieth century—we also have to think about the introduction of old kinds of music into new *domestic* settings, themselves reconfigured by transforming media networks and inhabited by historically specific modes of subjectivity. The construction of this audiovisual imaginary made the experience of musical privacy a thoroughly public phenomenon, dependent on the mediated experience of the private itself. But by trying to grasp this kind of interdependence in ways that call these matters into question, we can approach the issue of music's historically specific forms of mediacy in more precise ways.

4

"Songs the Gypsy Plays for Us": Racial Fantasy, Music, and the State

It might seem surprising that in a history of acoustic culture in Weimar and Nazi Germany the question of "race" has up to now played a relatively marginal role. This is, of course, not an accident, but has rather been a strategic move in trying to open up new perspectives on the period. The goal of this study has been to clear away a number of clichéd notions of the history of musical mass culture in this period. In order to engage in a properly critical investigation, it has been crucial to bracket those issues that automatically spring to mind when Germany of the 1920s, '30s, and '40s is discussed. One of these issues is the racialist basis of Nazi ideology and its link to mass culture. The previous chapters have shown that the link between music in mass culture and explicitly political ideology, in which race played a vital and explicit role, was more complexly articulated than has often been assumed. The blind spots in our understanding of the relationship between musical practice and ideology, as I suggested in chapter 2, result primarily from an undertheorized concept of the ideological. To briefly recap this argument: the key problem in investigations of ideology in this period is a stubborn reliance on a theory of the ideological that revolves around the epistemological question of representation. Not only is this representationalist paradigm completely inadequate for explaining ideology's social force, it is a particularly weak explanatory tool for examining the question of musical practice in this period. Contrary to what one might expect, direct reflections or representations

171

of otherwise elaborated ideological content in mass cultural musical practice were highly seldom. Instead, the ideological in musical practice in general should be located on a more fundamental, *productive* level. As apparatus theory long ago pointed out for the cinema, acoustic culture does not simply *represent* political ideology, but the various apparatuses of audition involved in acoustic culture enabled modes of subjectification and normativization which in turn serve as the historical basis for representation and reception. Far beyond any mere question of "musical representation," ideology structures the very materiality of all acoustic relations. It is here where the theory of ideology can offer a great deal to thinking about the history of acoustic culture, providing ways for moving beyond discourse "about music," or even "musical discourse," to learning to think about acoustic production and reception as a sphere of *social* productivity.[1] The case studies undertaken thus far—radio as a mode of musical publicity, the *Schlager* as an organ of experience, and art music and its relationship to modern forms of mediacy—have attempted to stake out particular approaches to grasping the social productivity of acoustic culture in order to develop a richer theory of "acoustic" ideology.

This "productivist" paradigm for studying the history of ideology is not only useful for going beyond any lingering textualist approach to musical life; it also holds great explanatory potential for other social questions particularly relevant to the Weimar and Nazi periods, in particular the study of "race." The productivist paradigm enables a more adequate grasp of this aspect of the social than the fundamentally liberal concept of "racism." While the latter ultimately assumes the ahistorical presence of the object of racial discourse, the former provides ways of conceptualizing the contingency of race itself, and thus offers fundamentally more powerful tools of critique. Furthermore, the productivist concept of ideology offers a theoretical approach to its material character by placing its operation firmly within "an apparatus, and its practice, or practices" (Althusser 1971, 166). Race should not only be understood as a component of political ideology, elaborated in textual means, it was in fact central in organizing the material production of personhood in Germany and the West in general in the twentieth century—that is, the very preconditions of any kind of textual production or reception. This becomes especially interesting when considered parallel to the modern notion of "music" in acoustic culture. As Philip Bohlman and Ronald Radano (2000) have pointed out, "the racial imagination" has particularly structured the intelligibility of "music," itself a more than wobbly construct, in the West, and thereby played a central role in determining the parameters of acoustic culture.[2] As they put it, dealing in particular with race and music as they emerged in the eighteenth century:

> Together the matrices of race and music occupied similar positions and shared the same spaces in the works of some of the most lasting texts of Enlightenment thought. A historical continuum emerges . . . so much so that, by the end of the eighteenth century music could embody differences and exhibit race. Once reified as a modern object or thing, it could undergo scientific observation because of its differences. Music's differences became as evident as those of color and the other human distinctions of a racialized world . . . As Europe looked outward, so does it position music at the foreground of its modern racialist perspective. (13–14)

Bohlman and Radano persuasively trace out the intimate linkage between these two profoundly historical complexes and the way this linkage continues to structure the operation of both. If there is a period when the two entangled post-Enlightenment configurations of race and music played a central role in historical process, then it is certainly Germany of the first half of the twentieth century. "Germany's" glance *inward* through the spectacles of race and music produced on the one hand a regime of national normativity and on the other various zones of supposed social crisis, manufacturing national and extra-national populations defined in racial terms. It is thus this conjunction that this chapter will address: How did "race" operate to configure the acoustics of publicity in Germany of the 1920s, '30s, and '40s; how did racializing operations mold acoustic culture? At the same time, how did acoustic culture structure the matrices of race as a technology of personhood? In order to begin to answer these questions let us first turn to a perhaps unlikely source.

In March 1939, the *Kurhessische Zeitung* reported that a gypsy band had made a guest appearance at a café in Kassel.[3] The author of this article, entitled "A Gypsy Band Played and 'Ladies' were Smitten," found this a cause for scandal. Not only did gypsy music continue to resonate in "the heart of the *Reich*" (Anonymous 1939, 2), it also seems to have attracted a very particular kind of audience in this Northern Hessian town. In this article, which was also reprinted a month later in *The German Podium*, a professional journal for German popular musicians, the author described the scene:

> There they hang on the lips of these deep singing gypsies, who gave away their gracious glances to everyone in order to ensure they get their fair share. Indeed one doesn't have the chance every day to pine after a seventeen or nineteen year old gypsy violinist *[primas]*. After closing time, however, violin and bow had barely been set down when the gypsy lover-boy *[Zigeunergalan]* hastened away from the scene of his effectiveness *[der Stätte seiner Wirksamkeit]*, in order to disappear into the darkness of night with his worshipper *[Anbeterin]*. (3)[4]

The author is not only scandalized by the possibility of actual sexual contact, but continues to depict a scene of audience depravity. According to the author's description, the music of the gypsies has brought this crowd to a frenzy, culminating in a spectacle of illicit exchange:

> We were subjected to the spectacle of this sort of "ladies" *["Damen"]* waiting on the street, until the sons of the puszta appeared. They just wanted to see [the gypsies] one more time, an autograph in exchange for a rendezvous, and, if chance allowed, to spend some amusing hours with one of these fellows. The letters and pictures they exchanged with one another, handled as generously as they were carelessly, are downright shameful evidence of such disgracefulness. (3)[5]

This description of misplaced feminine participation in this decadent musical public sphere echoes the anti-*Schlager* polemics from the late 1920s and early 1930s, restaging their linkage of modern forms of fan culture with seemingly primordial forms of feminine desire, reading the fetishistic, almost wild insistence on autographs to the uncontrolled character of a primeval force. But the author of this article was not content with describing the scandal of female fandom, but sought to link metonymically the uncontrollable desires of the women present to a form physical decay itself somehow implicated in racial difference.

> Let it also be mentioned incidentally that one of these "lovers" was afflicted with a horrible disease. Here was just about everything: the swearing of love from these teenagers *[Backfische]* who weren't slapped enough by their mothers, and the notorious adultery of so-called wives *[sogenannten Ehefrauen]*. Maybe they said at home that they were going out for a coffee; but now gypsy arms embraced the person who had said this. (3)[6]

This description of the scandalous female audience and the real or imagined illicit relations between members of this "German" audience and the gypsy *primas*, or lead violinist, traffics in a well-developed vocabulary of degeneracy. Race, gender, and sexuality are triangulated by the sound of a metonymically diseased music which, in this author's eyes, disrupts the "healthy" life of the German city. From teenage girls to housewives, illicit enthusiasm for these degenerate figures is itself feared as a sign of contagion. For the author, the "so-called wives" and *"Backfische"* attest to the ways this music and these musicians seem to have posed a threat to the security of the "healthy" patriarchal family order, presumably by attacking its weakest link.[7] To cure the problem, and to restore a national acoustics that renders inaudible any sonic threats to standards of decency and structures of familial propriety, these "sons of the *Puszta*" that have infected the German city with their plague of popularity must be excised. The author's editorial remark at the end of his rant makes this perfectly clear: "We do not want to see any more gypsy bands in Kassel."[8]

On first reading, this article seems symptomatic of the neat correlation in popular music between ideological discourse and actual state policy under the Nazi regime. In this light, the article is but part of a fully developed ideological system linking race, gender, and sexuality, where the combined specter of uncontrollable female sexuality and racial "impurity" threatens the German *Volksgemeinschaft*.[9] Indeed, this author's moral panic does operate quite clearly within the racial fantasies that drove the Nazi persecution of gypsies. Yet another Nazi attack on "degenerate music" *["entartete Musik"]* within Germany, the description of this spectacle merely serves to remind us of the systematicity of German racism in this period, the ultimate result of which was the brutal mass murder of up to 600,000 gypsies by the "Third Reich."[10] It is indeed most likely that the author's wish—not to "see any more gypsy bands in Kassel"—was, in some sense, ultimately fulfilled.[11]

But, as is the case with so many instances of seemingly transparent "ideological discourse" from the Nazi period, this interpretation merely scratches the surface. A look behind this highly structured example of national fantasy and racial panic reveals a much more complex ideological formation. In its reprinted version, this article appeared with a different title: *"Von der Pußta möchte ich träumen* [I'd Like to Dream of the *Puszta*]." Rather than, as we might expect, simply serving as a sarcastic reminder of the exotic longings of the female audience, this title refers to a *Schlager* from a film current at the time, *Der Blaufuchs [The Blue Fox]* (Tourjansky 1938). First shown in Düsseldorf on December 14, 1938 (Klaus 1996), this film featured some of the most popular stars of German film in this period: Zarah Leander, Willy Birgel, and Paul Hörbiger. Set in contemporary Hungary, the film tells the story of the failing marriage of Dr. Stephan Paulus (Paul Hörbiger) and the beautiful Ilona (Zarah Leander). The couple is mismatched: Stephan, a distracted, soon-to-be professor, has no time for anything but his work, and fails to pay enough attention to the increasingly restless Ilona. But Ilona's cousin, Lisi (Jane Tilden), does attract his attention: the film works out how to match Lisi with the professor, and Ilona with Tibor Váry (Willy Birgel), a dashing pilot and the professor's school buddy.

At the beginning of the film, Ilona is in the *puszta*, the Hungarian plains, about to return to Budapest after a stay with her husband's aunt. When Tibor first meets Ilona on her way to the train station, he is immediately smitten, and in order to pursue matters further, offers her a ride in his car. When she refuses, the pilot successfully engineers the situation to his own advantage by preventing her timely arrival for the train's departure, thereby leaving Ilona with no choice but to accompany him on his drive to Budapest. On their trip to the city, Tibor pulls yet another stunt: they pass through a small village holding a wine festival, and Tibor asks if they might stop. When Ilona informs him that she is in a hurry and has no time for such frivolities, Tibor fakes car trouble, and the pair are "forced" to stop off for a few drops of Hungarian wine, setting the stage for the first diegetic music in the film. Already as the car drives into the village, as the car rapidly passes by an otherwise undistinguished crowd, the first thing we see is a local band. A mere visual flash, but nonetheless clearly identifiable by the film's spectator, the band in this context is the first of a series of markers that label the village as authentically "country," in opposition to the shiny urbanity of Ilona and Tibor. The villagers are all dressed in what we are to presume is a form of local costume, in contrast to Leander in particular (Figure 28).

Indeed, the film redundantly emphasizes Ilona's cosmopolitan dress, as Birgel/Vary pointed out at their meeting that Leander/Ilona, dressed as she is, could only be on her way to Budapest. But sound is here the crucial element: the acoustic signal of the presence of "gypsies" in fact precedes the visual, inaugurating the immersion of the couple into the coherent world of a *Volk*.

The music the local band is playing at this wine festival utilizes a musical semiotics that marks it as recognizably "gypsy" for the film's audience. The first cue here is instrumentation, including most prominently the violin, bass, and cimbalom, a dulcimer that played a prominent role in "gyspy" music and its iconic representation. But the musical world is marked by more than the easily recognizable timbres and overly obvious visual contours of the "gypsy band": in terms of melodic material as well, the prominence of augmented seconds cues racial "otherness," and specifically the otherness of the gypsy. Finally, the rhythms of the *csardas*, one of the "typical" Hungarian gypsy dances that circulated in the late-nineteenth and early-twentieth centuries through the cosmopolitan centers of Europe, registered in the racial imaginary of the period as being attached to the essence of the gypsy.[12] But the film does not leave matters here: After having finished the wine, Tibor goes to check on the state of his car, which he had left in the hands of the village mechanic. Hearing the band strike up what Tibor has already called "an old folk song," Ilona/Leander begins to sing, beginning in a slow, melancholy vein:

Figure 28. Der Blaufuchs *(Tourjansky 1938).*

Von der Pußta will ich träumen bei Zigeunermusik.
Sehnsucht fühle ich im Geheimen,
Denn dort wartet mein Glück.
Wo der braune Csikose singt,
Wo vor Glück mein Herz zerspringt,
Von der Pußta will ich träumen, wenn der Csardas klingt.

When I hear gypsy music, I want to dream of the *puszta*.
I feel desire secretly,
For there waits my happiness.
Where the brown *csikos* sings,
Where my heart bursts with happiness,
I want to dream of the *puszta*, when the *czárdás* sounds.

Not only text and music, but the visual elements of this sequence also continue to emphasize the "gypsy" as central to the production of this rural idyll. While Ilona/Leander sings the song, the gypsy violinist comes to the foreground of the shot (Figure 29).

Even as the couple leaves the town, the violinist is prominently placed among the villagers, who cheer as the couple drives by on the

Figure 29. Der Blaufuchs.

way back to modernity. If this were not remarkable enough, the linkage between gypsy music and authentic emotion is strengthened later in the film. The song, composed by Lothar Brühne and with a text by Bruno Balz, two of the most successful figures in popular music of the "Third Reich," returns often in the film, playing a central role in the love story that drives the diegesis of this film.[13] Symbolically operative to the plot's depiction of "falling in love," and syntactically central to the cinematic development of narrative, this song comes to dominate the film, shifting between nondiegetic and diegetic moments of narration and plot.[14]

It might be objected that this was an isolated case. But on closer inspection of numerous sources from the period, this blatant contradiction between a discourse of gypsy racial degeneracy and the continuing fetishization of gypsy music cannot be dismissed as an isolated opposition between two different media contexts, and requires explanation. The contradiction manifested between the polemic tone of the article and the actual use of the song seems to have been endemic, and characterized the use of gypsy music during the Nazi period. Indeed, the journal in which this article was reprinted itself provides yet another example of the complicated nature of the discourse of gypsy music and musicality. In 1941, when gypsies were regularly subject to deportation, the journal, now renamed *Das Podium für Unterhaltungsmusik*, featured an advertisement announcing the new releases from the C. M. Roehr Verlag. This advertisement, which in its title, "Guide to the Entertainment Literature," seems to imitate the journalism that surrounds it, lists as one exoticizing musical fetish among others the song "Zigeunerfantasie," or "Gypsy Fantasy." The song, composed by Heinz Stahlberg, is described in the advertisement in a confusing vocabulary that through its excess of adjectives seeks to underscore the fetish character of gypsy musicality. Despite the advertisement's praise for the piece's combination of a broad "range of expression" *(Mitteilungsbreite)* and "dance vehemence" *(Tanzvehemenz)* typical of the "milieu," it would be safe to say that Stahlberg's piece (Berlin 1942) is a fairly appalling example of a more general phenomenon. Scored for a salon orchestra, the piece begins with a rubato semi-improvisatory section on the dominant, where the piano is intended to imitate the sound of the cimbalom. The second brief allegretto section is then followed by a second cadenza passage, and then a slower, rhythmic section. The alternation between "free" sections and rhythmic sections continues until the climactic *czárdás*, which also ultimately shifts to the major key. The final coda attaches the "standard" gypsy ending to the piece, not only in the three emphatic subdominant-dominant-tonic chords, but especially in the final chord, which is struck not once, but twice, in a succession of two sixteenth notes. In a way perhaps similar to some of the more clumsy "blues" written by Tin Pan Alley composers in the 1920s and 1930s, "Zigeunerfantasie" announces its "gypsy-character" far too clumsily and explicitly, and the composer tends to oversimplify the musical markers of style and structure to their lowest common denominator.[15] This is, for our purposes, in fact beside the point: the style of the piece, albeit in a fumbling manner, does mobilize most of the familiar musical markers of gypsy musicality.[16] In fact, the blatant stylistic redundancy of this case, its "insistence" on mobilizing the markers of gypsy musicality, and the scope of its possible dispersion after being advertised in this particular journal, are precisely what make it an interesting and informative example for the clarity of this musical semiotic in the period.[17]

Besides offering revealing advertisements for recent musical products and interesting examples of polemic criticism, *Das Podium* provides further indications of the more ephemeral details of musical everyday life in the Nazi years which give a sense of the scope of this contradictory field. Other reports in the journal provide a sense of the dispersion of this kind of musical practice in the 1940s. In the same year, the journal reported in one of its "Expeditions through Musical Establishments" of the Leipzig appearance in the summer of 1942 of the "Hungarian master violinist," Ferry Roy, along with, among others, a musician named Gyulua Forma as a cimbalom player. Here, at first glance, the term "Hungarian" might appear to mask the presumed gypsy semiotics of this band's performance. But seen in the context of other musical performances during the period, especially in films like *The Blue Fox*, it seems most unlikely that this music would have been consumed as anything else but "gypsy" music. Indeed, the terms "Hungarian" and "gypsy" were often simply used more or less synonymously; the long history of ideological battles about the definition of these two terms was simply irrelevant for the world of mass culture. This seems especially true considering the description of another performance, this time in Saarbrücken, where a band led by Willy Zäch played the numbers "Puszta Fairy Tale" and "Gypsy Love." It might be objected that this reflected a pragmatic relaxtion in cultural policy required by the harsh conditions of wartime life in the summer of 1942. While the cultural reins were certainly slackened to some extent in the 1940s, particularly when it came to antijazz polemicizing,[18] the explicitness and redundancy of these references to gypsy music and musicality, in instrumentation, iconicity, and musical style, is matched at the same time by the continuing negative use of now-familiar black and/or Jewish musical stereotypes. In other words, the racializing vocabulary of gypsy music was set in a positive light, while equally racializing tropes in jazz only served polemic critique, albeit with dubious effects of the actual practice of popular music itself. Again, in this same journal, the following cartoon was reprinted, entitled *Jazzkönig Isidore Moneymaker (Hollywood) macht einen neue Nigger-Song:* [Jazz King Isidore Moneymaker Makes a New Nigger Song]. It would have been unimaginable for a Yiddish-speaking klezmer musician to appear in a positive light in a German film, and a song entitled "Jew(ish) Fantasy" or "Jewish Love" would have been simply been unintelligible in the racial logics of the period.[19] Nevertheless, the romanticization of gypsy musicality and the demonization of Jewish musical degeneracy existed side by side, so much so that the wholesomeness of what went as "gypsy music" in the period is now considered by critics to be the typical "bland" style of popular music in the Third Reich.[20]

This does not mean that the brutal reality of state policy toward the gypsies was absent from this journal. In the very issue inhabited on the one hand by cimbalom players, "Hungarian" violinists, and dance hits like "Gyspy Love," anti-gypsy racial policy emerges in the form of a dry report on the "interesting results" of the work being done by a research post in the Imperial Health Ministry. The article, entitled "What about the Gypsies?," summarizes the results of this "interesting work" on the gypsies, "whose music, as is well-known, belongs to the sphere of entertainment."

> The most important result of the studies was . . . that almost all so-called gypsies are not true gypsies *[stammechte Zigeuner]*, but rather mixed-breeds *[Mischlinge]* in the most various combinations. Barely 100 families of the gypsies living in Germany are still somewhat "true" *[waschecht]* gypsies, while almost 90 percent are mixed breed. (Anonymous 1942, 260)

The pedantic racializing logic of this "finding" might seem relatively benign, and indeed easily able to accommodate the fetishization of gypsy music and musicality. But the remaining text leaves no room for "positive" interpretation.

> Now, these studies have also shown that the mixing of the gypsies—there are in Germany around 20000 gypsies and gypsies of mixed blood—largely took place with asocial and inferior [minderwertige] elements; the result was a dangerous Lumpenproletariat. (260)

Soon thereafter, this journal would publish official lists of musicians expelled from the Reichsmusikkammer, including, beginning in 1942, many names accompanied by the explanatory note, "gypsy." These two apparently incompatible images of "the gypsies" would continue to persist side by side in journals like this one and elsewhere until the end of the Nazi regime; indeed, it can be argued that there has still been no disruption in this racializing structure until the present day. Of course, the illogical character of this contradiction had little effect on the actual fate of the gypsies in Germany.

As these examples make abundantly clear, the ideological terrain of gypsy music and musicality was far more fragmented than the original journalist's easy use of the dialect of degeneracy might suggest. Able to generate both intense abjection and fetishization within economies of regulation, signification, and exchange, the figure of the gypsy was anything but a footnote to the development of modern German acoustic culture. How can we begin to understand the operation of "gypsy music" in the mass culture on the period? In the following pages, I will attempt to explore this powerful zone of social productivity. The linkage of race and music in gypsy music and musicality requires analysis in terms that go far beyond the realm of the exemplary. After a brief introduction to the general problematic of gypsy identity and persecution in Germany, I will return to this examination of the gypsy fetish by looking more closely at gypsy music and musicality as a site of social and textual productivity far beyond economies of regulation and repression.

Gypsy "Identity": The State and "the Gypsy"

Many commentators have tended to see the modern history of gypsy persecution in Germany as lying at the end of a long tradition, locating its roots in the early modern period, i.e., the 1500s and 1600s, if not even earlier.[21] When this critical approach emerged, it of course represented a welcome change, in light of the fact that postwar writing on "the gypsy problem" tended to retain the criminological discourse of the Third Reich well into the 1970s. More importantly, state policy towards the "gypsies" also continued to be based on prewar practices of gypsy persecution.[22] In this kind of historiography, the persecution of gypsies is presented as a kind of negative narrative of modernization; more or less chaotic outbreaks of prejudice in earlier periods against "the gypsies," a "people" which came "to Europe" around 1500, are replaced by the increasing "state control" of gypsy life. This narrative then culminates with the attempt at the deliberate, planned elimination of gypsies from European life under the "Third Reich." Despite the invaluable nature and clear critical thrust of this kind of work, much of which has transformed our picture of the treatment of gypsies in the modern period, the historical claims to long-term patterns of continuity in these accounts are based on extremely rocky foundations. Not only do they posit the object of racialist discourse as somehow independent of the discourse itself, an ahistorical given, they also fail to historicize not only the state, but also the nation, and ultimately reinscribe the oppositions they ostensibly seek to critique. As Foucault suggests, we need to be especially cautious about the circulation of seemingly "identical" ideological terms in an omnihistorical framework (1972, 21ff.). We first need to suspend the unity of the "discursive object" of the gypsy, before reconstructing it in a truly critical fashion; this kind of critical reconstruction can enable many more discursive linkages than a mere analysis of "racism" could ever allow.[23]

More recent approaches have attempted to produce this kind of critical reconstruction. Viewing "the gypsies" not as a historical constant, but rather as an identity that emerged in the disciplinary practices linked to the formation of the modern nation-state as part of the production of populations and the shift towards "governmentality."[24] Patterns of migration served as one of the primary objects around which the disciplinary practices of the police, and by extension other apparatuses of the modern state as well, were organized. Intimately linked to the economic conjuncture of rapidly expanding industrial capitalist production and the tremendous population shifts that industrialization entailed, the need to produce a national community or *Volk* at this stage required the production of ultimately unassailable populations.[25] As Klaus Bade has argued in his history of migration, the emergence of nation-states and the production of national populations was directly linked to the establishment of border control, although border control was in fact less a question than the control of space in and of itself, and more a part of the production and regulation of populations (2000, 186). In the context of welfare policies of developing state apparatuses, it became increasingly important to distinguish between those "belonging to the state" and those who "belonged" elsewhere. The ethnic dialectic of "us" and "them," Bade suggests, was always crucially linked to shifts in migration policy and the attempt of expanding state apparatuses to more precisely define their spheres of jurisdiction and intervention. In the course of state development, the lamination of "ethnic" identity onto the political entities that emerged in the spaces now produced created an "ethnic" conception of the practices of border control.

Social historians of migration like Leo Lucassen have radically historicized "gypsy identity" by rooting its development in the eighteenth and nineteenth centuries firmly in this context. Parallel to the increasing professionalization of the police,[26] and the concomitant refinement of modern social technologies of personhood such as the passport, the increasing interest of the police in gypsies in the nineteenth century was not a response to a predominance of criminal activity in a certain "ethnic group."[27] Instead, as Lucassen has shown, the treatment of gypsies in the nineteenth century primarily consisted in the criminalization of certain forms of unregulated migration and labor in ways that articulated with emerging forms of identity (1996). The historical shifts in the treatment of "the Gypsies" reflect shifts in definition; as Lucassen suggests, the groups termed "gypsy" in the mid-nineteenth century seem to have emerged from nowhere, indicating that the modern production of this category adhered to police practices of controlling particular forms of unwanted migration. "The exaggerated attention of the police for 'wanderers' in general and 'gypsies' especially proves to be a result of the praxis of excluding parts of the lower classes, from whom it was feared that they would require too much poor relief" (214). The relatively sudden emergence of the concept "gypsy" in the police reports and wanted lists *[Steckbriefe]* of the early nineteenth century indicates that the persecution of gypsies cannot be separated from the very formation of "the gypsies" as a modern tool of social description and a historically shifting conception of "ethnic identity." It was, Lucassen argues, precisely in this context that an emphatically modern, increasingly racial conception of gypsy personhood was cast. This is not to say that differences in language and multiple forms of social practice did not exist; it is, however, to argue that the organization of particular forms of difference into the opposition between national subjects and supposedly essentially "other" gypsies was part of the modern production of population. What now seems to us a clear ethnic category was in the nineteenth century a collection of various forms of "difference" under the collective title of "gypsy."

Shifting a discussion of "gypsy identity" from an ethnocultural perspective toward one rooted in multiple technologies of modern personhood and the state does not make the effects of persecution and/or fetishization any less real. Indeed, the historicization of identity as a result of specific practices and apparatuses of discipline says nothing about the *social* power of the category at any particular historical conjucture, either as a name for racial abjection or a source of fetishistic projection, just as the historicization of "the state" and national identity does not nullify the real effects of their operation. In other words, we do not only need to look at the way the history of gypsy identity is contingent, we also need to examine how this contingency played out over the course of the modern shifting relationship between the figure of "the gypsy" and state practice. In Germany, the formation of gypsies as an object of police surveillance was one of the central projects to the coordination of state activity along national lines. Already before the founding of the *Kaiserreich* in 1871, the gypsies had come to represent something of a nascent "social problem" in the ideological production of protonational populations (Lucassen 1997, 245–46).[28] Soon after the establishment of the *Kaiserreich* in 1871, each of the German states began to establish its own legal "struggles against the gypsy" (Hehemann 1987, 244). An essential element in this process was the discursive development of new terminologies in both the press and the law for the gypsy presence in the German state, from gypsy gangs *[Zigeunerbanden]* in the 1870s and '80s to the gypsy plague *[Zigeunerplage]* around the turn of the century (Hohmann 1990, 57–58; Hehemann 1987, 153ff.) The public circulation of these terms indicates the increasing sense of panic associated with the figure of both "foreign" and "German" gypsies within the newly established German borders. In addition, the move towards the notion of a "gypsy plague" in particular illustrates how the figure of the gypsy was understood as a potential threat to "national health," linking the racial discourse on gypsies to other emerging areas of social discipline.[29] By the turn of the century, the state, using new technologies of identity, began to compile lists of "gypsies" in order to keep this "social problem" under tight control. In 1899, the Munich *Nachrichtendienst in Bezug auf die Zigeuner* (Information Service Relating to Gypsies) was established; a predecessor of the later Berlin *Zigeunerzentralstelle* (Gypsy Central Office) in the "Third Reich," this office was charged with collecting the fingerprints, photos, criminal records, and family trees of all "gypsies" in Bavaria. Already in 1905, this office had begun to distribute a "gypsy book," an alphabetically organized listing of names of gypsies known to reside in German territory. By 1926, this office had collected information on approximately 14,000 gypsies (Hohmann 1990, 67–68).

The Weimar Republic inherited the modern technologies of state and personhood that characterized Imperial Germany; in the case of the gypsies, the operation of these technologies became increasingly invasive and brutal in their effects during the years of German "democracy." In 1926, the various German states began to work towards a codification of anti-gypsy laws for the entire Republic. Beginning in Bavaria with the "Law on Gypsies and the Work-Shy" and an agreement of the criminal police commission of the German states, "On the Struggle against the Gypsy Plague," a period of increasingly explicit and intrusive state involvement in the everyday lives of "gypsies" was inaugurated. This law required police permission to travel in caravan, and additionally stipulated that this permission could be withdrawn at any time. The logic behind this law was now profoundly racial. While earlier police measures might have classified the way of life of many gypsies as a *symptom* of crime, the traveling of gypsies in larger groups, increasingly characterized in the logic of these laws as not only nationally, but also "racially" alien, was now seen as a *source* of crime. This criminalization of the various aspects of what had become the gypsies' economic "way of life," or rather, those economic activities that seemed not to correspond to the increasingly regulative system of labor relations and which helped to define the "gypsy," would take a dramatic toll on this group's already precarious economic subsistence. In the eyes of "Germans," increasing poverty would come to fulfill many of the prophecies of "inferiority" that the developing racial logic of the period increasingly predicted.[30]

It should be clear that the case of the gypsies is radically distinct from that of other persecuted groups in the 1930s. Long before the radicalization of racial policies in the late years of the Nazi regime, the figure of the asocial gypsy had already been clearly established as key to the imagination of degeneracy and the production of its opposite, modern normality.[31] Unlike the case of the Jews, for example, by 1933 the apparatus that would later serve to "solve" the gypsy "problem" was by and large already in place on a local state level. More importantly, again unlike other groups, and despite its manifest contradictions, "the gypsies" seemed as a group both in legal and more vaguely "ideological" terms to present a much more coherent, essentially foreign element in the logics of the nation state. While the National Socialist state needed to work quite hard to (re)establish a clear, firm opposition between Jews and Germans articulated in modern racial terms, the consensus on "gypsies," similar to that of the "asocial," was firmly established long before the radicalization of anti-gypsy policy. Little or no extra effort was required to make the introduction of more radical anti-gypsy policies seem like a legitimate extension of previously existing forms of state practice. This was true not only on the political level—even the Social Democrats engaged in the discourse of the "gypsy problem"—but on the level of everyday common sense among all levels of society.

Within the increasing centralization of police authorities and population policy after 1933, gypsy "control" became a symbolically central issue to the nationalization of police functions. Already in the 1933 *Ländervereinbarung zur Bekämpfung der Zigeunerplage*, the state laws of the Weimar period were coordinated; laws similar to the pre-1933 Prussian and Bavarian laws, but more extreme in their extent, were rapidly established in the German states. By 1935, this "interim decentralized patchwork" (Milton 1994, 242) began to be replaced by codified national law. In the process, the two strands in the discursive production of the gypsy—racial and social—became increasingly intertwined, making gypsies a symbolic linchpin in the production of social abjection in general in Nazi Germany. On the one hand, the gypsy, now crafted by increasingly established discourses like that of "ethnology," became a largely racial figure. On the other, gypsies took their place in the series of abject populations known as the "asocial," difficult to separate from other groups like the "work shy." In two 1933 laws, the "Law for the Prevention of Offspring with Hereditary Defects" and the "Law against Habitual Criminals," gypsies were explicitly included as asocials (242–43). In turn, the gypsy was a central focus of Nazi social policy explicitly linked to racial policy, often mobilizing a language familiar from other cases in both Europe and North America in the same period.

In the 1935 Nuremberg Laws, the groundwork for Nazi racial policies, the gypsy "question" remained untouched. Soon afterwards, the infamous Globke and Stockart commentary on these laws would remedy this situation: this commentary declared the *Reichsbürgerschaft* (imperial citizenship) limited to *artverwandt* (related type) groups, and made clear that gypsies, along with Jews and blacks, were now officially classified as *artfremd* (alien type) groups (Hohmann 1990, 102–3). The marriage laws, issued a month after the Nuremberg laws, played an even more central role in the governmentalization of gypsy life. These marriage laws, less a break with the past than a fulfillment in the broad tradition of eugenics discourse that characterized many different political movements of the 1920s and 1930s, stipulated that all marriages would require permission from public health offices. Furthermore, this permission was dependent on the prior issuance of a certificate of "genetic soundness"; without such a certificate, the marriage license would not be granted (Milton 1994, 243). This policy made it all but impossible for gypsies to marry, and assisted the state in the further governmentalization of all aspects of gypsy life.

While the 1936 Olympics are often described as something of a "rest" period in the general radicalization of Nazi cultural and racial policy, for the case of the gypsy, the opposite was true. As part of an all-too-familiar campaign to "clean up Berlin" before the games, Berlin's gypsies were removed from their homes and deposited in a camp in Marzahn, at the outer edges of Greater Berlin. This camp became a permanent site of gypsy incarceration, and after years of being subjected to various forms of forced labor, most inmates were ultimately sent to Auschwitz (246). By 1938, new policies were crafted to keep the gypsy population increasingly separate from the rest of Germany. In addition, a distinction was enforced between gypsies of "pure" and mixed blood. But by 1939, gypsies were being deported to the newly conquered Polish territories, and by 1942, the status of the gypsies came to approximate that of the Jews in law and practice. Ironically, "pure" race gypsies, considered Aryan in some versions of the Nazi racial worldview, held a special status in the perverse logic of various officials until well into the 1940s, only to be eventually treated as one group, then systematically interned in concentration camps. By 1944, the gypsies in these camps were being quickly exterminated. In Birkenau IIE alone, the gypsy camp at Auschwitz, more than 80 percent (19,000) of the internees perished (Schenk 1994, 460).

The Racial Trope of Gypsy Music and Musicality

As we already saw at the beginning of the chapter, music and musicality were key in the popular notion of gypsy identity. This special role
for the figure of the gypsy musician marks the place of the gypsy in
the technologies of race and national identity as distinct from the operation of the perhaps less contradictory, more straightforward production and exclusion of other groups in and from the scene of national
fantasy in this period. The gypsy played a very different role in the
German national imaginary than Jews, "Bolsheviks," or blacks. These
three groups were the nexus of a very particular dynamic of the racialization of the political, and represented a quite effective, emphatically
modern production of otherness, beginning after World War I and
culminating at the start of the Nazi period. This was particularly the
case in discourse about musical style: as mentioned in the prior chapter, Eckhard John has shown that already during the Weimar Republic the concept of *Musikbolschewismus* or "music Bolshevism" was used
as a general category of disapprobation. Originally simply a term of
reaction against the avant-garde tendencies of post–World War I German art music, the term quickly came to operate in a wider context.
By 1927, the terms were applied most often to forms of popular music
in attacks on jazz (1994, 284). By this point, the concept of "music
Bolshevism" was a fully articulated racial epithet. No longer simply an
anti-Communist slogan, this term came to encompass all those forms
of musical practice that were anathema to the defenders of an "authentically German" musical culture because of their "racial" as well as their
political characteristics. Race was not the only term to operate as a
pseudopolitical category of threat; the attacks on jazz also characterized the "sexual obsession" that they found in this new popular music
(286–90). These attacks reached an apex in the debates surrounding
Krenek's *Jonny spielt auf*; now the simultaneously anti-Semitic, anti-
Communist, and anti-American trends in the musical public sphere
were integrated in a contradictory discourse about the symptomol-
ogy and source of cultural "degeneration." By the time of the "List
of Music Bolsheviks" was distributed by the *Kulturpolitisches Archiv
im Amt für Kunstpflege der NS-Kulturgemeinde*, the term had come to
operate primarily on "racial" grounds, as the composers listed on this
document were primarily Jewish (358). Although during the Third
Reich, this *Kampfbegriff* found its replacement in the term *"Entartung,"*

culminating in the "degenerate art" and "degenerate music" exhibitions of 1937 and 1938 (368), John illustrates how these terms represented a continuous development in the racialization of musical "taste." From a more or less politically centered, anti-Communist term of abuse to a primarily racial figure, the panics around various forms of modern art and popular musical practice arguably contributed directly toward the production of conceptions of normality and normalcy that both instigated and permitted industrialized mass murder.

External to this triangulation, gypsy music and musicality remained a positive source of fantasy in the Third Reich, even while the machinery of extermination was fully operative. As Katie Trumpener has argued,

> In a careful division of labor and an equally careful synchronization between the Third Reich's linked apparatuses of repression and representation, the two halves of the post-Enlightenment ideology of Gypsy alterity—feared as deviance, idealized as autonomy—are played out simultaneously but separately, making visible all its internal contradictions . . . In genocidal captivity, in the midst of a death camp, subject at will to medical experimentation, and prior to their own mass execution, Gypsies . . . found themselves compelled to live out German fantasies of autonomy in ways only more concrete, more perverse, and much more painful than usual. (1992, 853–55)

In short, while the vocabulary of degeneracy was certainly available for descriptions of gypsy music and musicality, the more general mass-cultural context of the period failed to reproduce this figure in any kind of consistent pattern, rather using gypsy music and musicality for different goals. This is by no means merely a question of the continuing circulation of "gypsy" musics in this period; the same was of course true for those forms of music linked to blackness in the racial imagination. But the operation of this linkage was much more vague, mixed as it was by the clashing notions of "America" and "Africa," and its seemingly more radical exoticism tended to disqualify it in the German context for successful mass consumption. The gypsy, in contrast, had now long become an established part of modern German acoustic culture, indeed one of its definitive components.

If on the one hand, the gypsy was seen as a source of danger, the same discourse could also see the gypsy in a "positive" light: In both sorts of textual production, gypsy identity is manufactured as a set of physical or quasi-physical characteristics. In Germany and across Central

Europe, the "image" of the gypsy has been intimately associated with various forms of music and musicality since the mid-nineteenth century. This conglomeration of musical practices and musical discourse was always accompanied by the simultaneous production of "the gypsy" as an object of social discipline and control. This link is more intimate than a simple connection in modes of representation. The very emergence of our modern understanding of musical expression and inherent, quasi-genetic musical talent around various forms of musical stardom in the first half of the nineteenth century coincides with the emergence of the gypsy in racializing discourse. First, the "gypsy" emerged as a fixture of both program and salon music: composers like Liszt and Brahms made the gypsy a centerpiece of the cultural fantasies of Central European art music.[32] At the same time, an urban, popular tradition based on gypsy musics and the figure of the gypsy began to develop (Bóvis 1965, 1282). Finally, a stock character in operettas like *Der Zigeunerprimás* (Emmerich Kalman 1912) and *Zigeunerliebe* (Franz Lehár 1908), the "gypsy musician"—and stylized versions of gypsy music—found ready popularity in the cosmopolitan audiences of the growing metropolises of Europe at the turn of the century, filling living rooms, concert halls, opera houses, and less reputable establishments of popular entertainment.[33] In literature as well, the figure of the gypsy was always associated with innate musicality: as but one example, *Friedemann Bach*, Brachvogel's historical novel on the "failed" Bach son, dedicates most of one chapter to his dealings with a gypsy "horde." The encounter with the gypsies is inaugurated by the sound of music, and the passage describing Bach's experience of this music is illustrative for the romanticizing investment in the gypsy sound.

> At this moment, a deep, wavering tone swelled up, as if a metallic basin had been struck, and a slow, earnest, almost plaintive song hurried down to him with many invisible voices . . . The deep pain, the secret, dark belief and a foreign, southern magic, which streamed through this melody, made an indescribable impression upon him . . . a deep, child-like emotion, which he had not felt for years, came over him, and a longing for love, for a holy something . . . hit him with increasing intensity. (1858, 357–58)

While the earliest versions of a modern sense of gypsy identity focused on a vague sense of the exotic and primeval, in the late-nineteenth and twentieth century version of gypsy discourse, traits that previously seemed "natural," rooted in a distant, exotic past, were now explained in biological terms. But the double tendency of gypsy discourse in the nineteenth century also characterized this more modern version of gypsy identity. In the more clearly racist mode of this discursive production, like a 1940 article published in the *Zeitschrift für Ethnologie*, the physical characteristics of "the gypsy" are produced through a complex apparatus of different forms of knowledge production—including photography—and enable claims not about the historical "backwardness" of the gypsies, but rather their inherent physical inferiority (Stein 1940).[34] This article, entitled "On the Psychology and Anthropology of the Gypsies in Germany," sees the "biological problem" (75) of the gypsies as an explanation for their essential cultural and psychological difference from not only Germans, but all Europeans.

> The essence of the gypsy is primitive and animal like, their thought and action is driven by instincts and natural feelings, while understanding and logical thought only play a subordinate role. Their emotional life can within the shortest span of time go through all phases of feeling. They live in their thoughts in a totally different world, which is why they remain for us difficult to understand. (1940, 109)[35]

Although the bulk of the article is dedicated to descriptions of "physical" or pseudophysical differences like "the smell which a gypsy spreads in his surroundings" (77), physiognomic considerations like the "nose index" (100), and general patterns of gypsy behavior—"the gypsy prefers sparkling wine" (82)—this "anthropology" of the gypsy also includes a brief musical characterization. In this case, however, musical performance is somehow seen, as in the later discussion of skull structure, as indicative of "the gypsy soul": even in this case, the musical side of gypsy identity is depicted in a surprisingly positive light:

> This primitive and animal like being is however to a large extent balanced out by a characteristic, which all gypsies of the earth, which particularly characterizes certain tribes among them and which has made these tribes famous, that is the great musical talent. There is no land on the planet in which gypsies are not known and treasured as musicians *[Musikanten]*. (89)

For the author, gypsy musicality was simply one more piece of the puzzle in compiling a complete psychological, anthropological, and physiological "understanding" of the gypsy. Indeed, gypsy music is here a key representation of the "essence" of "the gypsy soul": "It is typical that the already mentioned multifaceted character and variability of the gypsy soul is represented in his music most completely and clearly. Just as he plays, he is in reality" (89).

While Stein seems to be able to link this strange admiration for gypsy musicality to the eliminationist leanings of his physiological criminology, other writers of the period who took a more sympathetic position on the "gypsy problem" reproduced much of the racialist logic of the more eliminationist writings, and thus illustrated their own implication in the governmentalizing production of modern "gypsy identity." Martin Block's *The Gypsies: Their Life and Soul*, published in 1936, is a particularly rich example of this. Again, in this *Habilitationsschrift* gypsy musicality was key to the general picture.

> As properly dressed and clean musicians, they appear in cafes, messy and louse-infested, their relatives often listen to the violin sounds in a tent, in a wagon, or in a hut. And if a truly great skeptic is still doubtful, soon the external appearance changes. The gypsy who was just so unlikable becomes lovable as soon as he sets the bow to the strings and coaxes out of it tones that reach the borders of the possible, taking all listeners into a world where all is forgotten. It was not for nothing that boyars and magnates gave their riches for beautiful gypsy playing. It leads to the space and timelessness; it allows us to catch a glimpse of the harmony of the soul lost to us. Gypsy music makes human misery and strife forgotten. (1997 [1936], 185)[36]

Going much further than Stein, Block's fetishism becomes quite explicit when he claims that gypsy music has a unique power to return a "harmony of the soul" now lost to modern man.[37] The coexistence of these apparently positive and negative discourses in the Nazi period is by no means a unique product of scholarship under the Nazi regime, but rather symptomatic of modern forms of racializing knowledge production in general. At the same time, it did make the gypsy a uniquely powerful figure of contradiction in the Nazi state.

Gypsy Music and the Cosmopolitan

If there is one zone of seeming continuity in the history of modern Germany, it is the fraught relationship of the gypsy to the increasingly developed modern apparatus of the state.[38] At the same time, the relationship to the state apparatus was accompanied by a special role for the gypsy as the supplement to national identity, in particular linked to forms of musical style and "personality."[39] It is no accident that figures like Brachvogel and Liszt, linked in different ways to emerging forms of literary and musical nationalism in the mid-nineteenth century, also engaged in the production of "the gypsy" as a modern racial trope. The work of migration historians like Lucassen not only warns us to be cautious about ethnicizing the concept of "gypsy," but also implies that the very concept is intimately linked to its national complement. The operation of the figure of the gypsy was far more productive than simply playing a role in establishing the secure relationship between state, population, and territory. Like the nation itself, no functionalist explanation could account for the extreme affectual investment in gypsy music and musicality. These investments in the gypsy and gypsy music as social icons indicate that not only did it help to structure discourses of discipline and order, but that it also provided an affectual, ideological scaffolding for identity that had long achieved its own autonomous dynamic. If gypsy identity is recurrently the site of the production of both degeneracy and its complement, national normativity, and if music seems to adhere to the "essence" of the gypsy, how can we link the place of the gypsy to the figuration of "gypsy music" and musicality in German mass culture? What kind of specific forms of affect adhered to the figure of gypsy music and musicality, and how were these forms of affect continually reproduced?

Like the Jew in both anti-Semitic and philo-Semitic discourse, the gypsy was a definitionally transnational subject; this transnational character was, on the one hand subject to suspicion—in particular, gypsies were often suspected of espionage. On the other hand, the figuration of the gypsy as a sign of the foreign could be refunctioned in a seemingly "positive" way: the sound of gypsy music could serve as an icon of travel. This is made clear in an advertisement from a series published in the *Berliner Illustrirte Zeitung* between 1936 and 1937: "A World Full of Music!" (Figure 30).

The advertisement features a larger-than-life image of a gypsy violinist, emerging from the radio as he plays for the happy German couple at home. The text reads: "The true to nature play of the radio receiver from the new Telefunken year is wonderful. As if the *Zigeunerprimas* played in your room!" This image was part of a series of Telefunken ads that glamorized the exotic in radio listening. The series went still further in its Christmas ad, depicting a veritable ethnic potpourri not unlike the current marketing of world music in the Euro-American public sphere. The gypsy violinist in the earlier ad is depicted in a caricature that comes to inhabit the implicitly domestic space of the German living room through the technology of the radio. Serving as one more sign of the pleasures of commodity capitalism and reinforcing the glamour of this high-end radio receiver, the allure of "exotic" gypsy music in the home is comparable to that of other commodities that traffic in the exotic.

Although the media logic of the advertisement seems at first to model nineteenth century configurations of the domestic as an anchor for the subject in phantasmagorias of consumption, as I have shown in the previous chapter, the home in this media network is here no longer a "box in the world theater," as Benjamin suggested for the nineteenth century. The box in the "world theater" in the German 1930s is replaced by apparatuses of interpellation linked to the newer media formations, like the seat in the cinema balcony. On the screen in this particular cinema is a musical revue film depicting various modes

Figure 30. "A World Full of Music!" Berliner Illustrirte Zeitung, *1936–1937.*

of musical exoticism: even the title of this ad seems to echo the titles of revue films from the 1930s. Gypsy music and musicality is but one element in this elaborate production of "worldliness" within the media network cinema/radio/living room. The use of costume additionally produces this music as a would-be visual spectacle; a synaesthetic celebration of the cosmopolitan possibilities of the new mass media, the ad resolutely refuses the dialect of degeneracy, instead integrating the "true to nature" sound of gypsy music into the very production of domestic intimacy. The technology promises access to a commercial cosmopolitanism, and by placing the gypsy as one figure in an ethnically marked series, engages a fully articulated visual vocabulary of the exotic.

The production of gypsy music as an exotic commodity took place not only in the techniques of advertising, but in various zones of actual musical practice. If we assume that this advertising was at all intelligible to the audience of the period, we can already conclude that some familiarity with "gypsy music" is a common denominator of the audience addressed by this ad. Again, this advertisement indexes a media network around the figure of the gypsy: Everyday musical practice in the cities of Germany was dominated in the 1920s by the figure of the gypsy musician in various ways. Heribert Schröder describes "Hungarian bands or Gypsy bands, often called Hungarian 'ambience' bands ["Stimmungskapellen"]" as "a fixture in the band-landscape in Germany" during the Weimar Republic (1990, 91). These bands were most often small trios, quartets, or quintets. Led, like many other kinds of bands in urban Central Europe, by the "Stehgeiger" (standing violinist), the band would also include other string players, certainly a cellist or bassist, possibly a cimbalom and almost always a piano (91).

But by the coming of the Nazi period, this style of music also came to play a central role in the mass cultural scene. Barnabas von Géczy's big band arrangements of the 1930s, especially the very popular "Ungarnwein" of 1935 and "Pußta Fox" and "Zigeunerweisen" ["Gypsy Melodies"] of the same year, depended on a racial semiotics that clearly lies within this tradition. This kind of light music—which to modern ears seems to index less a cosmopolitan style than "German" kitsch—retained its popularity throughout the 1920s and '30s. But this kind of light music was only one of the styles of music linked to the figure of the gypsy: jazz music and jazzy renditions of popular song were intimately associated with the racial figure of the gypsy. Indeed, early performances of jazz on the radio were often described in terms that focused on the "gypsy blood" of their performers. In a 1927 review of a radio concert of the London Radio Jazz Band, the German commentator described the music of this "most frequently heard jazz band of Europe," broadcast by "twenty five radio stations daily . . . through the whole world" with the following racializing inventory:

> It is said about the leader of the band, the blonde Hun Sidney Firman, that he comes from a gypsy family. Sidney . . . won't say anything at all about this . . . Similarly with the banjo player, who, as an Argentine, is a true son of the Pampas. The saxophone is also cast according to style: Mr. Leslie is the real Yankee, like in a book. And that the man sitting behind the drum set has negro blood rolling through his veins almost goes without saying. (Anonymous 1927)[40]

The "gypsy" violinist is here placed as the racial starting point of this cosmopolitan inventory of sound and "blood." This trend towards a racial diagnosis of jazz virtuosity was by no means a purely German phenomenon, but rather played a role throughout Europe, linking German popular musics with a broader, cosmopolitan European vernacular.

By the late 1930s, a particular style of European jazz, focused around the role of the violin and guitar, came to take center stage in this phenomenon. Primarily due to the primacy of the violin—as well as the identity of some of its protagonists—this jazz style became known as *Zigeunerjazz*, and was most notably represented by the music of Stéphane Grappelli and Django Reinhardt's Quintet of the Hot Club of France.[41] Unlike those of some, and later most, American jazz bands, Reinhardt and Grappelli's records were readily available in Germany throughout the 1930s (Lange 1966, 86). Not only did Reinhardt and Grappelli's style become rather popular in the urban centers of Germany, "German" performers also imitated their music. The most prominent of these imitators was the violinist Helmut Zacharias. First discovered in 1940 by the record company Lindström, Zacharias played both in his own band and in some of the most popular large ensembles of the period (Lange 1966, 107).[42] One of Zacharias's most popular recordings, "Schönes Wetter heute," or "Fine Weather Today," was recorded in 1941. This recording illustrates quite clearly how Zacharias redeployed the *Zigeunerjazz* style: the guitars and violin familiar from Reinhardt and Grappelli are used here in a very similar way. Alternating solo passages, prominently displayed blues notes in both violin and guitar, and two rhythm guitars in the background make

Zacharias's music almost an exact homonym of the swing of Reinhardt and Grappelli.

Not only does Zacharias's music represent the popularity of *Zige-unerjazz* in the Third Reich, his beginnings also betray the intimate linkage between the cultural apparatus of cosmopolitan capitalism and the seemingly disparate site of social practice that the Nazi party itself represents.[43] Michael Kater has pointed out that at least one of Zacharias's first engagements was at a hotel frequented by travelers on the state-sponsored Kraft durch Freude ("Strength through Joy") sponsored vacations. This shows us that it is more than dubious to cast Zacharias as some kind of underground figure; instead, he seems far more to have been seen as a staple of "respectable" German society in the early 1940s. It might be suggested that Zacharias's music never approached the stylistic level of the more avant-garde recordings of Reinhardt and Grappelli, and that the playing of his band perhaps never quite approached the virtuosity of their French counterparts. But this qualitative judgment is in the end irrelevant to the question of this music's ideological function in the period. It remains crucial to remember the quite audible links of his performing style to forms of jazz that trade on the link between the "gypsy" and the cosmopolitan. Rather than merely arguing away Zacharias's popularity as part and parcel of the wartime apparatus of distraction, it seems that Zacharias's musical style must be seen in a longer history of fascination with supposedly *Zigeuner* styles of music, representative of the contradictory place of *Zigeuner* within various forms of German ideological fantasy.

While Zacharias certainly played a central role in the dissemination of the cosmopolitan style of "gypsy" music, one of the icons of this music, the guitar, came to play an even more visible role in the mass culture of the 1940s. The Johannes Heesters film *Karneval der Liebe [Carnival of Love]* (Paul Martin 1943) picks up on this guitar-dominated style of jazz in the number "Durch dich wird diese Welt so schön" ["Through You This World Becomes So Beautiful"]. Michael Jary's *Schlager*, at a much slower tempo, is certainly not played in as "hot" a style as that of Zacharias. Yet the song mobilizes the steady guitar strum familiar from more "jazzy" recordings like *"Schönes Wetter heute,"* and the film itself visualizes this exotic fetish. Indeed, at least one source suggests that "real gypsies" in Hungary were used as the musicians on this recording.[44] Whether or not this claim is true, the iconic production of gypsy identity is here quite clear, albeit in a more southern dialect. In this elaborate revue number, Heesters is depicted with a guitar, surrounded by a troupe of other male dancers with mock guitars. Heesters uses the guitar (and his "Spanish" costume) to mine the erotic potential of the exotic fetish, going so far as to insert that guitar as the mediation between male and female bodies, the substitute site of physical contact, in the duet with his female partner. Heesters's entire star text trades not only on his cosmopolitanism, but also crucially on his link with "swing." The scene makes clear that this star text also trafficked in the exoticism of the gypsy.[45]

But not only was this swing style of gypsy music popular in the Third Reich; "sweeter" forms of popular music continued to traffic in the exotic cosmopolitan sound of the gypsy violin up through the last days of the regime. One of the most famous "gypsy violinists" in particular, Georges Boulanger, a.k.a. Ghita Bulenca, was particularly popular in Berlin. Appearing at the Wintergarten and the Hotel Adlon, Boulanger was famous in the German context for his "temperamental Balkan sound combined with the technique of Paganini and a melodic elegance that is all French" (Antonietto 1993). In many ways combining the styles of Géczy and others with trends from *Zigeunerjazz,* gypsy violinists like Boulanger continued to be celebrated during the Third Reich, even in contexts generally wont to throw a critical eye on the "excesses" of popular music.[46] In a special issue of *Die Musik* dedicated to the "problem" of popular music, which begins with the "Obituary to Jazz," a list of "New Records" not only praises the "popularity of Barnabas von Géczy" but goes on to rhapsodize about "Georges Boulanger, a master on the fingerboard." Describing first Boulanger's recording of one of his own compositions, played to the piano accompaniment of Oskar Jeroschnik, the critic soon begins to thematize the gypsy issue explicitly:

> Boulanger plays "Mal so, mal so," his own composition, accompanied
> on the piano by Oskar Jeroschnik. Besides his eminent technique,
> his gypsy-like rubato style is full of individuality. One is pleasantly
> surprised by his spicatto technique and left-handed pizzicato. The
> same is true of his charmingly played "Aber warum gnädige Frau."
> (Schlüter 1936)[47]

Boulanger is thus by no means praised in a "race-neutral" vocabulary of taste, but the "gypsy character" of his music is explicitly emphasized as part of his musical quality. This happens not only once, but twice:

A happy union of beautiful sound and sensational technique is offered by Georges Boulanger, discretely accompanied by a Hungarian gypsy orchestra, with the Russian Gypsy Romance, the Puszta Fox and the slow foxtrot "Liebe."[48]

Boulanger's most popular recording was the song, "Avant de Mourir." Re-recorded by the American group The Platters as "My Prayer," the song reached a worldwide audience in the late 1930s. Boulanger recorded this song with Michael Danzi in 1939 for Lindström (Danzi and Lotz 1986). But as late as 1944, one of the last recordings of the "Third Reich" was a remake of this 1930s hit. The song was this time switched in its exotic repertoire: Gino Bordin played the hit on the "Hawaii-Gitarre," or slide guitar.[49] The song remains part of a network of racially coded musical practice, which during this period was pivotally linked to gypsy music and musicality.

These multiple forms of popular musical practice insistently returned to the locus of "gypsy musicality." Even if the linkage to gypsy racial identity was not explicitly mentioned, the context made it clear that the implicit linkage was more than readily understood by the audience. Not only did these forms of practice traffic in a given set of recognizable musical traits, but these musical traits themselves were seen as icons of cosmopolitan, urban, modern life. The figure of gypsy music and musicality, detached from the specific linkage of place to personhood that determined the operation of the modern, capitalist nation-state by the gypsies' mythologized wanderings to and through Europe, remained in this period the locus of cosmopolitan capitalist fantasy, even while the forced removal of gypsies from Germany increasingly became state policy. While the practice of migration was in policy to be limited to cases of the search for work, this music served as the space in which the glamour of a work-free life of travel and decadent pleasure could be enjoyed by the nonmigrant population of "Germans."[50] This form of popular music, often divorced from its producers, became in fact a sonic emblem of an increasingly impossible outside to the increasingly regimented division of labor that marked 1930s Germany. In other words, the "fatherlandlessness" of the gypsy musician, the "cause" for his persecution under the intensified production of national populations that characterized the Third Reich, remained an auratic device in mass culture, even during the time of the gypsies' mass murder.

The Gypsy and "Heimat": Hot Blood

Like *Carnival of Love, Heißes Blut [Hot Blood]* (Jacoby 1936)[51] invokes gypsy music and musicality as part of a broader jargon of the cosmopolitan. In a scene near the close of the film, each of the main characters in the film has been narratively located in the same place: a newly opened "Wonderbar" in Budapest. During this opening night, Marika Sarössy (Marika Rökk) attempts to attract the attention of her would-be lover, Lieutenant Tibor von Denes (Hans Stüwe), by singing a song. Choosing a song that was "familiar" to both, she sings "*Lieder, die uns der Zigeuner spielt* [Songs that the Gypsy Plays for Us]" (M: Franz Doelle, L: Charles Amberg). Using the typical musical stereotypes of "gypsy" music, especially in its long, "emotional" verse ("*Ziga primas, spiel!*" or "Gypsy primas, play!"), the song shifts into a major key, but in a slow tempo, evoking in melodic lines and in text an affect of nostalgia.

The song ultimately fails to achieve its intended goal: to recapture the lieutenant's affections. But as Sarössy concludes her song, and she and Denes begin to dance, the music shifts from one dialect of exoticism to another. The gypsy song becomes a tango, and thus links these two modes of exoticism in the display of "high society" and glamour that this scene is intended to represent. Like Gino Bordin's Hawaiian-guitar version of Boulanger's hit, this musical manifestation of an ideology of the exotic positions the figure of gypsy musicality—symbolized by the violin—as a central point of mediation through which multiple "versions" of ethnicity can be consumed in the cosmopolitan sphere.

But this song has a history in the logic of the film: this is a *Schlager* that refuses the claims to the hyper-present tense that the cosmopolitan dance club might otherwise suggest. This is, in other words, a hit song with a quite distinct past. Like the characters inhabiting the "wonder bar," this "gypsy" music appears here in costume: earlier in the film, this musical jargon of the cosmopolitan is crowded out by a different use of gypsy music and musicality. More than a mere style of urban music, gypsy music makes a more ontological kind of claim for the "sound" of an ersatz *Heimat* in this fantasy version of Hungary. The gypsy violin, in other words, is not limited to serving as a medium of cosmopolitan affect; the same instrument is also capable of mediating modern personhood to the locus of a "timeless" sense of homeland.

This song first emerges in the diegesis of the film in a much earlier scene: after stealing back her own horse (which had been auctioned along with the rest of her property), the Baroness Marika eats supper with the lieutenant. As this sequence begins, the film fades in on the scene of the restaurant, the camera following the movements of a waiter from left to right in an establishing shot of the restaurant's dance hall. The band is playing a fairly nondescript waltz, and the room is full of dancing couples. The film's main couple have ensconced themselves in a more intimate side room, separated from the dance floor by a curtain. While Tibor attempts to flirt with Marika, the hungry baroness cannot be distracted from her food. The scene begins to alternate between two sound regimes: the first dominated by the sound of music, and the second, dialogue.

The smaller room where the couple has decided to eat is established as visually opposite the original location of the musicians in the larger dance hall. Mediated by the waiter, whose movements between the smaller and larger rooms are consistently the uniting syntactical unit between shots, these two spaces are ultimately united by the figure of the gypsy violinist (Figure 31). In a false point-of-view shot from the position of the gypsy, we see the gypsy violin set at the break in

Figure 31. Heisses Blut (Jacoby 1936).

the curtain, literally indexing the pair for whom this song is intended by pointing into the smaller space.

This interruption of the couple's solitude is quickly absorbed into a new level of diegetic action, when Marika begins to sing, picking up her wineglass. Both song and sequence come to a climax as Tibor swoops down, carried away by the moment, and kisses Marika.

This moment of romantic love, accompanied by the sounds of the country gypsy, will soon be disrupted by the annoying, stereotyped voice of Ilonka, the city girl who represents Marika's polar opposite, and who also vies for the lieutenant's affections.[52] But the moment of song, and its depiction, at least at this moment, successfully deploys the sounds of the countryside to mark "true" heterosexual love. Thus, if one side of the gypsy fetish circulated as an icon of the "worldly," gypsy music also exhibited an uneasy relationship to the production of *Heimat* in German mass culture.[53] Always positioned in complex ways in relation to this formation, gypsy music provides insight into how contradictory the musical production of *Heimat* in the cosmopolitan capitalism of Germany in the Weimar and Nazi periods in fact was.

As Celia Applegate has shown, the ideological production of *Heimat* has always been a contradictory field of the social. Shuttling between strictly local and national conceptions of identity and its relationship to place and everyday life, the concept of *Heimat* was particularly subject to the ideological problems that determined the history of German national affect in the Weimar and Nazi periods (1990). During the Weimar period, the concept of *Heimat* was mobilized both as an emphatically local, potentially democratizing validation of popular traditions in opposition to aristocratic models of the production of history and place (169), and a more national tool for "cultural renewal" and translocal collectivity (170ff.). In the Nazi period, these conflicts remained, if in a quite different register: as Applegate has remarked, the role of *Heimat* in the Nazi period is emblematic of larger ideological divides in the production of the German nation in the particularly modern conjuncture that the Nazi state represented.

> Somewhere in between the two extremes—*Heimat* as, on the one hand, necessary to Nazism and, on the other, irrelevant to it—lies the real history of the appropriation and exploitation of *Heimat* symbols, ideas, and people by the confused and self-contradictory political culture of Nazism. (198)

Not only was the affect of *Heimat* an unstable ideological ground for the new state, in popular music the *Heimat* came to be intimately associated with forms of ethnic fetishism that recall the exotic. Far from being opposites of one other, the idea of "Germanness" as something lived locally was continually reinvented in mass culture by techniques similar to exoticism, mining signs of ethnic difference and distinction for something both lost and unattainable. The simultaneous development of the notion of "authentic" folk culture and commercial exoticism, which itself depended—and still depends—on the affect of authenticity, presented the constant threat of conflict.

Popular music in the "folk" idiom represented a domain of the social where this ideological problem was especially clear. This was true both of *Trachtenmusik*, or "folk" music played as entertainment by musicians in seemingly traditional costumes, as well as newly composed popular music in the "folk" style. Throughout the Weimar period, the growing entertainment industry used *Trachtenmusik*, literally "costume music," to accompany the other pleasures of city life (Schröder 1990, 80–90). Kracauer's description of *Haus Vaterland* (Fatherland House) points out the intimate relationship between the commodification of the exotic and the production of national or protonational icons of *"Heimat."* In this "asylum for the homeless" *[Asyl für Obdachlose]*, the monotony of the employee's everyday life is distracted by the presentation of a wild fantasy world, commodified through and through, serial in its presentation. At the time of Kracauer's writing, *Haus Vaterland* aimed its attractions "more for the provincial" (1971 [1930], 97) than the metropolitan. It offered a series of thoroughly saturated panoramas, mockingly reproducing the "experience" of travel.

> The room in which the new wine is enjoyed offers a splendid view of Vienna by night. St. Stephens' tower is darkly contrasted with the starry sky, and an illuminated streetcar slides away over the Danube bridge. In other rooms . . . the Rhine flows, the Golden Horn glows, beautiful Spain stretches out far in the south. From Löwenbräu, "Bavarian landscape: Zugspitze and Lake Eib—Alpine glows—entrance and dance of the Bavarian *Bua'm. Schuhplattlerpaare* . . ." or from the Wild West bar: "Prairie landscape on the big lakes . . . negro cowboy jazz band . . ." The fatherland encompasses the entire globe. (97)[54]

Far from isolating *Heimat* from the experience of commodity capitalism, its musical production is intimately associated with the apparatus of distraction that Kracauer here seeks to describe. He links the global fantasy of mass culture to the increasing banality of everyday life:

> The exact pendant to the office machine is the colorful world. Not the world as it is, but the world as it is created in hit songs *[Schlagern]*. A world that into the last corner has been cleaned of the dust of the everyday with a vacuum cleaner. The geography of the homeless asylums is born of the hit song. (97)

Despite claims to the contrary, "folk music" in musical mass culture could only serve as a weak support for any kind of attempted onto-logical linkage with the collective ethnic or racial "essence" of the audi-ence; instead, "folk music" functioned as one possible form of exotica among many. In other words, contrary to the ideological terms of its own discursive production, and its obvious attractions for nationalist and conservative politics, the actual use of mass cultural "folk music" was always tainted by the folkloristic, and the accompanying problem of inauthenticity. Always suspect of kitsch, *Trachtenmusik* failed to be disciplined, subjecting the "authenticity" of *Heimat* in popular music to the disruptive dangers presented by commodity capitalism. Published in the professional journal *Der Artist*, the following "public warning" illustrates this problem in a dramatic fashion:

> Public warning! In the interests of both parties, we ask all Hamburg [Hansestadt Hamburg] directors, restaurateurs, and concert agents to exercise caution in engaging Otto Gips' so-called *Oberlander-Kapelle* [Bavarian Highlands Band] from Berlin. The advertisement of this man in the February 2, 1924 edition of *The Artist* is not accurate. The members of this band are in fact almost exclusively Berliners. They thus have neither the right to travel with a Bavarian name, nor to wear shorts during their musical performances.—Group III of the Nuremberg Local of the German Musician's Association. (cited in Schröder 1990, 90)[55]

The problem of "authenticity" was exacerbated in later years, when the ideological investments in *Heimat* became more explicit and—perhaps necessarily—less tenuous. On June 30, 1939, as the culmination of a long obsession with the authenticity of *Trachtenmusiker*, the afore-mentioned trade journal *The German Podium* went so far as to publish a list of those musicians who were allowed to appear in Bavarian cos-tumes. These "sanctioned *Trachtenmusiker*," the list tells us, could claim authenticity. The claims of both of these examples are not merely musical, but suggest a particular proper arrangement of person, place, and music that is appropriate to the commodification of *Heimat*. In a strange mirroring of the state's listing of the gypsies as nonnational subjects, in particular the later listing of gypsy musicians in this professional journal, these attempts to ameliorate the problem of an implicitly "inauthentic" practice of costume and masquerade through the rigorous policing of person and place illustrate the risk to which this domain of social reproduction was subject.

Not only was the specter of Berliners in Bavarian drag a problem in the musical production of *Heimat*, the musical tradition of folk-like music in the popular vein was also suspect of the taint of what was seen in the Nazi period as Jewish kitsch. In an article also appearing in *The German Podium* in the same year, Hans Brückner complains about the continued presence of "Jewishisms" in music: choosing the music of Leon Jessel as the object of his scorn, Brückner (1939) worries about those orchestra leaders who continue to play this "Jewish" music at vacation spots in the "Third Reich." That Jessel, the composer of *Schwarzwaldmädel (Black Forest Girl)*, was subject to the accusation of Jewish kitsch makes clear that the entire tradition of *"heimatliche Musik"* in the popular vein was itself marked by a racial panic.[56] The popular vein under suspicion here is specifically cinematic: *Black Forest Girl*—which would later serve as the basis for Hans Deppe's film (1950)—was already a popular subject for film. Already filmed three times, in 1920, 1929, and 1933, both story and music had already achieved a special status as a signifier of *Heimat*. The fact that this author chooses Jessel's work for special scorn points to the particular danger that the film operetta/musical represented. As an article in *Deutsche Film und Funkwacht* makes clear, the integration of *Schlager* in *Heimat* situations in particular was seen as productive of disruption. After dismissing *Schwarzwaldmädel* (Zoch 1933), which "did not understand how to find the right mix of the elements music, plot, landscape, and *Volkstum*," the author, Otto Bertram, complains of the "tastelessness" in *Hochzeit am Wolfgangsee [Marriage on Lake Wolfgang]* (Behrendt 1933) when "the young barman sings a *Schlager"*(1934, 11). While he attempts to find examples of proper execution of *Heimat* representation in mass culture, it is ultimately clear that the specific national fantasy of the local that the author wanted the folkloric film to engender was ultimately at odds with the profoundly delocalized and commodified version of the popular that mass culture represented. Content and form fail to coalesce in a properly national medium of representation.

This concern about the authenticity of folk music would soon extend to those territories later incorporated into the Reich. In an article entitled the "Aryanization of the Emotions," published during the year of the *"Anschluß,"* an Austrian "political satirist," took "Viennese music" to task.

> We don't need to mourn the Jewish *Schlager,* arranged for zither, violin, and accordion . . . And by the way, none of these songs were themselves set to text and music in Vienna; it always happened on the spa promenade in Ischl, where the librettists, with their crooked legs in short *Lederhosen,* strolled together [zu zweit lustwandelten] and cobbled together chansons, in which Viennese dolls *(Pupperln)* acted before the background of the giant Ferris wheel or good old St. Stephen's *["guatn at'n Steffl"].* We can easily do without most Viennese operettas without being embarrassed about the fact that without Jews there would be no Viennese operetta. The Jews raced the operetta to its death . . .
>
> They didn't earn so badly from our soul *[Gemüt]* and our sentimentality. Some . . . Jewish vagabond could plunder the works of Schubert and serve us "the Dreimädlerhaus," which became a world success, and the Jew who called himself Berte shoveled (scheffelte) money and allowed himself to be celebrated as if there had never been a Franz Schubert, with whose laurels he dressed himself and sold throughout the world.
>
> But this is bar music *[Heurigenmusik]* and certainly not culture *[Kulturgüter].* Culture can be enjoyed sober without having its impression weakened by this normal human condition . . . Not only do we need to Aryanize businesses, we also need to Aryanize our emotions. (Mungo 1938)[57]

The music of the *Heimat*—be it Vienna, Bavaria, or the Black Forest— was thus by no means secure as an ideological apparatus for the production of national affect. Instead, it was always subject to the threat represented by mass culture more generally. Either suspect of Jewish contamination, or simply linked to the urban distractions which dominated acoustic culture in the 1920s and '30s, there was no musical practice that could both claim a "down-to-earth" quality and retain and foster the "purity" of the German *Heimat.*

One more secure way of mobilizing the idea of *Heimat* in popular music was displacement. Hungary—as the most clearly nationally grounded political unit associated in the German imagination with "gypsy" music—provided a powerful locus for this displacement.[58] To return to *Heißes Blut*, the scene immediately following Rökk's initial performance of the "gypsy" song is set in the city. The now-dispossessed aristocrat, the Baroness, who has lost her home in the *Puszta* and the idyll which it represents, has been forced by her officious aunt to come live and work with her as a schoolteacher in Budapest. As the scene begins, she is seen in her new role, in front of a classroom. When Marika's friend and former servant, Josci (Paul Kemp), arrives, the couple meets on the other side of the classroom's large picture window, the schoolchildren left on their own. Outside, gypsy music begins to sound. In an elaborately orchestrated scene, the music becomes almost a character, positioned between Marika and Josci and the classroom window. As the young primas begins to sing, the film opposes his song to a shot of the classroom window, where the children look out longingly to hear the music. This window serves as a rather unsubtle metaphor for the "prison" of modernity, outside of which the gypsy's sound of a lost *Heimat* resonates. This becomes even more explicit when the gypsy child drops out of view; hidden by the icons of reminiscence. The film suggests that the music serves as a sound track to a flood of nostalgic images in Marika's mind. With a close-up on Marika, a series of shots from earlier in the film—superimposed on her face and organized by a series of dissolves—depict her memory of life on the *puszta* and the romance with the lieutenant. The music actually removes us from the space and time of the city, as Marika's face itself dissolves into the image of the lieutenant, upon which scenes of his army regiment are projected. Returning to a shot of Marika, now crying, the gypsy child is shown again, concluding his song.

The gypsy child is explicitly positioned here as the iconic mediation between modernity and the lost *Heimat*; not only does his music accompany Marika's memories, but the syntactic use of the figure separates Marika's reverie from the rest of this scene. On returning to the "reality" of modern life, Josci encourages the primas to play something "fun," and a czárdás begins. The children inside are also swept up by the happy sounds of a would-be *Heimat*, as the window becomes now narratively transparent. This scene suggests that the Baroness and the gypsy child are both mourning the loss of their homes, their *Heimat*, in the space of the city. The gypsies in the city serve to musicalize and authenticate urban experience, enabling the Baroness to transform modern space into the memories of her "premodern" countryside existence.

The irony to be grasped here, of course, is that gypsies were increasingly unwelcome in German cities. Already during the Weimar Republic, it was everyday police practice to keep groups of gypsies that tried to enter the city under constant control (Fings and Sparing 1992, 17). Gypsies caught without permission to do itinerant trading—the *Wandergewerbschein*—were subject to imprisonment for begging (20). In addition, public performance of any sort, including music, required permission from the police (20). If anything, gypsy musical practice in urban spaces in Central Europe was precisely the location where the modern state made its most visible impression. During the Nazi period, musicians and other traveling performers (circus employees, for example) were hit particularly hard by the increasing regulation of itinerant trade. In Düsseldorf, musical street performance by gypsies was effectively banned by 1936, the year of the film's premiere (41). Performing in bars and restaurants was also made increasingly difficult; by 1940, the Düsseldorf welfare office bragged that the now-illegal music-making of gypsies had come to an end (42). It is clear that many of the now-unemployed gypsies ultimately were subject to internment. For example, already in 1938, a 36-year-old musician from Magdeburg was sent to Buchenwald with the following explanation: "In 1937 and this year he was denied a permit for itinerant trade. Since this time he has been without work. According to these observations he is to be seen as a work-shy person. He has not as of yet engaged in criminal activity" (cited in Zimmermann 1996, 116).

But this scene is even more complicated by its focus on children: childhood and schooling served in the entire early twentieth century as one of the densest sites of governmentality, powerful tools of the state as they began to "solve" the "gypsy problem." As Hohmann points out, the authorities used children as a primary means for claiming greater regulatory authority over the lives of the gypsies in general (1990, 75). Already in the 1920s, many cities in Germany began to establish special education for gypsy children; these special schools and classes were usually structured under the assumption that "gypsy" children were subject to racially based learning disabilities. Even when these children were sent to general *"Hilfschulen,"* they tended to be singled out for special forms of mistreatment. Since the turn of the century, gypsy children had also been subject to being separated from their parents, usually with the thinly disguised excuse of violations of the school duty or "moral decay" *(sittliche Verwahrlosung)* (Fings and Sparing 1992, 40–41).

The figure of the gypsy child musician was by no means unique to this film, but rather a stock figure in mass cultural depictions of "musicality."[59] As late as 1938, the *Berliner Illustrirte Zeitung* published a photo-reportage entitled "Of the Gypsy Violinist School." Like the scene in *Heißes Blut*, the musical genius gypsy child is here the source of fantasy, although in this case the fantasy is given a double edge:

> Born to be a musician. Fiery temperament, delicate pull of the bow, wonderful ear . . . that distinguishes the small gypsy boys, ages 4 through 10, who go to the Gypsy Violinist School in Budapest. The goal of this school: to make large bands out of these young first violinists *[Prim-Geiger]*, who travel through the whole world and with the intoxication *[Rausch]* of their music play for the audience of the big cities.

The figure of the lost gypsy child mourning the loss of *Heimat* places this racial formation at the center of the ideological configuration of the desire for "wholeness" that the *Heimat* concept seeks to engage. The musical gypsy child, forbidden from actually singing in the German city, but displayed in this cinematic version of an alternative, Hungarian national modernity, represents the gap between the modern German city and the *Volk* that the concept of *Heimat* seeks to bridge.[60]

Ironically, the sound of "gypsy music" in the acoustics of German national publicity then not only came to represent the exotic, but was also mobilized to produce the affect of *Heimat* in popular music. Thoroughly attached to fantasies of land and place, this displaced experience of "homeland" offered the affect that *Blut und Boden*, translated into the realm of popular music, could not. Gypsy music ironically provided the popular musical embodiment not only of authenticity, but more crucially of complete identity. When fantasized as part of a provincial Hungarian landscape, the "gypsy" was able to produce an ideologically "consistent" image of patriarchally structured national community *[Volksgemeinschaft]*.[61]

"Race" and "Racism" in Musical Mass Culture

The acoustics of publicity in German mass culture during this period did require fantasy "others" for their formation. While some of these fantasy others simply operated as the constitutive outside to German national identity, one fantasy other, the gypsy musician, was not excluded, but used to occupy a deeply "internal" space of the German nation, the national fantasy of wholeness that remained an unattainable desire. Gypsy music was not merely "tolerated" by the fascist state; instead, the contradictory role of gypsy music and musicality in the 1930s and 1940s was symptomatic of its functioning. Gypsy music and musicality linked a number of related ideological fantasies and served as a double supplement to the production of national affect within modern capitalist structures. On the one hand, it served to preserve the "cosmopolitan" air of modern capitalism despite the increasing regulation of place and subjectivity which early twentieth century forms of governmentality and Fordist industrial production increasingly required. On the other hand, it engaged in a quite clearly demarcated, yet strangely dislocated racial logic of place and subjectivity, which seemed to ameliorate the everyday experience of capitalism for "German" subjects, calling up an ersatz *Heimat*. As Ron Radano has argued for the figure of black music in American national fantasy, gypsy music in the German—and wider European—context played a dual role: a stand-in for "rootedness," while at the same time serving as a screen on which the fears of instable "German" national identity could be projected. Like black music in America, "gypsy music" in Germany also represented "less a formal continuity grounded in the vernacular than a series of socially constituted expressive practices emerging in the complex discursive matrices of . . . public culture" (Radano 1996, 508), and represented the "supplement or missing link of . . . national identity" (522). At the same time, like black music in the American context, gypsy music served to index a cosmopolitan modernity, making available otherwise unavailable fantasies of approaching the "worldly" character of the commodity itself.

Decadent and wholesome, indescribably foreign and, in a complex way, essentially domestic, gypsy music presents a particularly interesting case for understanding the role of the racial imagination in the acoustics of publicity during this period. As Žižek suggests for "the Jew" in anti-Semitic ideology, the gypsy is "a point at which social negativity as such assumes positive existence" (1989, 127). The gypsy serves as a site of displacement, whereby the fundamental antagonism of the social is transferred to an opposition between "the gypsies" and "the Germans." But the work of the gypsy is double: the gypsy also serves as a screen on which ideological fantasies of social rootedness and "authentic" subjectivity are projected. In this case, the gypsy—and in particular gypsy music—serves as an object of desire which embodies a sense of the "wholeness" and authenticity which ironically in its other manifestation the gypsy is supposed to disrupt. Shuttling between two ideological poles in the production of an acoustics of national publicity, gypsy music and musicality were a central point of contradiction between fantasies of the national and the cosmopolitan in the Weimar and Nazi periods. Racial and ethnic "difference" was not merely excised from the public sphere. While it is certainly the case that the idea of "jazz" (if not the musical practice) served as a powerful visual icon of racial and political threat, combining "Bolshevism," Jewishness, and blackness in one, other modes of racial and ethnic difference not only survived the coming of fascism, but in the increasingly mass cultural environment of 1930s Germany, these differences were integrated into a highly developed system of racial and ethnic exoticism.

But the case of this form of musical exoticism, paired with the brutality of the Nazi's extermination of the gypsy population, is instructive in a broader sense. If generally mass culture in the Third Reich continues to be imagined in more or less "black-and-white" hues, it certainly plays a dominant role in the historical imagination of the Third Reich's mobilization of race in musical mass culture. The German national imaginary under fascism is usually understood as being structured by a particularly pathological kind of racism: in this dominant conception of the history of German popular music, race and ethnicity structured the interpellative operations of the fascist state in a unique way. On a quite different front of sociocultural research, Daniel Goldhagen's work, as well as his work's popularity inside and outside Germany, seem indicative of this more general problem. Goldhagen argues that the kind of "eliminationist" anti-Semitism that existed in Germany was unique and uniquely culpable for a kind of unique crime in kind and scale.

> Germans' anti-Semitic beliefs about Jews were the central causal agent of the Holocaust. They were the central causal agent not only

of Hitler's decision to annihilate European Jewry. . . but also of the perpetrator's willingness to kill and to brutalize Jews. (1996, 9)

Putting aside the many theoretical difficulties of Goldhagen's fundamentally idealist conception of historical process, as well as the methodological issues of evidence that have been more than adequately handled by other critics, we might want to approach his thesis by way of comparison to the treatment and ideological function of the gypsy under Nazi rule.

The mass murder of the gypsies by the Nazis, though often understood as a footnote to Nazi history, was in many ways central to their conception of norms and normalization and the linkage of these to the production of the nation within capitalism. The pivot point between discourses of racial identity and social policy, the gypsy's embodiment of degeneracy would serve as a model for the production of other forms of biologically coded inferiority. But in this case, we have a mass murder of terrifying scale, carried out in many of the "hands-on" methods that Goldhagen privileges as the locus of ideational expression, but with a far more complex image of the murdered in the minds of the perpetrators. To summarize a racial hate, in other words, as the causal moment in the production of mass death fails to investigate the intimate relationship between the mass murders of the Nazi regime and the production of industrial, capitalist modernity.[62] Instead, Goldhagen's ultimately circular explanation of "racial hate" underwrites an understanding of the relationship of race to industrialized mass murder in fascism as resulting from a particularly pathological formation with deep historical roots, a formation approaching the apparent ontological stability and dubiousness nature of "national character." But if we consider the popular culture of the Third Reich and Weimar, the racial ideology that is the key to Goldhagen's argument begins to appear far less unique and certainly more complex. The racial worldview often seen as the key to a National Socialist ideology was matched by kinds of racial fetishization quite clearly related to exoticisms in other forms of capitalist state. Parallel to this conception of the racial imaginary of Nazi Germany is a conception of the ways the fascist state used the concepts of *Heimat* and *Volk* to structure the national imaginary. Nazi Germany, it is suggested, was able to produce an emphatic equivalence between race, *Volk*, and nation, seemingly premodern in its persistence. But this conception of the German national imaginary also needs to be elaborated. Not only does the way race operated in mass cultural formations fail to correspond to our ideas about the essential difference of Nazi or German racism, but the ideas of *Volk* and *Heimat* operated in very tenuous ways within the contradictory terrain of mass culture.

Musically, one of the trends often seen as corresponding to a general change in political direction at the end of the 1920s is the "end" of jazz. The popularity of marches and waltzes is said to correspond to a certain kind of national sentiment in popular music absent during the "stable" years of the Weimar Republic. Robinson, for example, argues that German popular music, in contrast to American jazz, "regress[es] . . . to the military march." What Robinson diagnoses as an increasingly parochial musical style ultimately seems homologous to the degree of "totalitarian" state practice. The musical public sphere, in other words, was increasingly purified of "racial" difference in the late years of the Weimar Republic, both symptomatic of and contributing to a progressive racialization of the national affect of the public of German mass cultural musics.

While we might want to think that fascism was somehow marked by a constitutively different configuration of racial otherness and mass cultural pleasure, the material from the period exhibits startlingly familiar organizations of the investment in otherness. What makes of course the appearance of these investments in mass culture before and during German fascism specific is the clear connection between these forms of exoticism and mass murder. This is nowhere clearer than in the case of the gypsy during and prior to the "Third Reich." This connection is as clear as it is complex. By reframing our understanding of the ideological mechanisms by which mass death on ethnic or racial lines was produced, departing from a more or less monolithic conception of the German culture of race to a more relational model, we can avoid the dangerous oversimplifications present in arguments like Goldhagen's, and refuse the comforting pathologization of another historical other—the "ordinary German"—that they offer.

By way of a conclusion, we can trace out the continuity of this problematic in German popular culture by looking at one additional example, this time from fifty years later:

> Budapest, November 1942 . . . At any event the composer [Michael Jary] attempted to get as many gypsies as possible in his film orchestra. He did this, all the same, not only for noble reasons, in order to

protect these people from persecution, but also for purely artistic reasons, since Sinti and Roma are in our experience highly musical. Indeed many of them could not read a single note, but after one played a piece on the piano just once for them, they mastered without problem every measure. That had recently become especially clear in the recording of the Johannes Heesters' Schlager "Durch dich wird diese Welt erst schön," when Jary engaged a gypsy violinist who was only fourteen. (Jary 1993, 211)[63]

This passage from Micaela Jary's novelistic account of the love affair between her father Michael Jary and Zarah Leander illustrates the problematic continuity of this regime of fascination in the "mastering" of German popular music's pasts.[64] A mere footnote to her biographical attempt to claim Leander and Jary for the "inner resistance," the appearance of the racial fetish once more reminds us of the clear difference between the Third Reich's mobilization of gypsy musicality to other forms of musical engagement with variously constructed racial and ethnic others. But it also reminds us of its similarity: the exoticism that Jary continues to mobilize in her ostensibly liberal description of difference was one that was not submerged, but fully operative in the Nazi period itself.

While the thoroughly modern apparatus of extermination that represented the other side of fascism's division of ideological labor might remain unmatched in scale in other modern capitalist social formations, the striking familiarity of the figure of the gypsy should also serve as a warning paradigm for the dangers of seemingly more innocuous forms of symbolic appropriation. It is certainly worth asking about Jary's motives: other "artists" were also wont to use the "musical gypsy" for their work. The humanist adoption of the "correct" term for the "gypsy" fails to disturb the continuing operation of the deeply problematic racializing figure of gypsy music and musicality in the present.

Notes

Introduction

1. One critical take on the consumption of the Weimar and Nazi periods as historical fantasy, which focuses especially on the figure of decadence, is provided by Mizejewski (1992).

2. For one of the classic functionalist accounts, see Broszat (1981). For a recent study of German "national character," see in particular Goldhagen (1996).

3. See Schäfer (1983). Of course, Schoenbaum's (1966) work was also important in this light, despite his reliance on the problematic language of "modernization." The approach rooted in *Alltagsgeschichte*, or the history of everyday life, is best represented by the work of Lutz Niethammer (1983).

4. I also share Schulte-Sasse's sympathy with the work of earlier film scholars, such as Leiser (1974) and Hull (1969), but at the same time I believe it is crucial to undertake rigorous critique in order to understand why their readings of Nazi cinema in fact were at all persuasive.

5. For example, Schulte-Sasse and Rentschler (1996) use the term "Nazi cinema" prominently, though I would suggest that their readings belie its usefulness as a description.

6. Even Schulte-Sasse's reading of the narrative and visual elements of *Swing Kids* is marred by the following footnote, which combines all the typical elements of a certain "repressive hypothesis" on popular music: "*Swing Kids* does have one redeeming feature: its focus on unharnessed music (the 'racially suspect' jazz that Nazism objected to) and sensual, frenetic dance as a form of bodily liberation from the lockstep synchronized by the Nazi drill machine" (1996, 2). The notion that jazz or swing is "unharnessed" is precisely what needs to be critiqued: here, the standard and so often misunderstood work of Adorno on the ideology of jazz is right on target.

7. Other works on the nation that have been crucial to my thinking about the problem are Mosse (1975), Bhabha (1990), and Berlant (1991).

217

8. See also Hobsbawm (1983).

9. See Hansen (1991), Buck-Morss (1989), and Petro (1989) for various attempts to complicate mass culture's historical emergence and specificity.

10. See, among others, Berlant (1993; 1997) and Kruger (1992). On the problem of the translating *Öffentlichkeit*, see Warner (2002).

11. In the 1970s, the currency of the debates on fascism and the public sphere led a number of left-liberal scholars to mobilize the concept of publicity for discussions of fascist mass culture. But often the use of this concept has been limited to locating the specific distortions of "fascist ideology" in the fascist public sphere. See Storek (1972) for a classic liberal account of "directed" publicity. The debates in the 1970s among leftist scholars about the usefulness of the concept of publicity for discussing fascism also inform my own thinking on the subject. See especially the debate in *Ästhetik und Kommunikation*, (Brückner et al. 1976).

12. See also Hansen (1995).

13. Hanns-Werner Heister's work (1983) on the concert has been crucial to my thinking on this subject. See especially 100–189.

14. Here I am thinking primarily of the work done by Levi (1994), Kater (1997), and Potter (1998).

15. On the centrality of cinema as a zone of modern public experience, see Hansen (1995).

1. Radio, Mass Publicity, and National Fantasy

1. The relationship of "classical" to popular musics in this period will be discussed in chapter 3.

2. For detailed statistics on broadcast times, see Schumacher (1997a).

3. For exceptions to this, see Stapper (2001) as well as the work of Nanny Drechsler (1988), discussed below.

4. "Von den Massenmedien Presse, Film, und Rundfunk ließ sich die 'achte Großmacht' des 20. Jahrhunderts am leichtesten von den nationalsozialistischen Machthabern für ihre Ziele einspannen. Durch den Rundfunk konnten die Massen unmittelbar geführt und der nationalsozialistischen Propaganda ausgeliefert werden . . . die Technik dieser Lenkungsmethoden . . . bestanden aus stundenlangen Reden, nationalsozialistischer Partei- und Staatsführer, Reportagen von Reichs- und Gauparteitagen, von Staatsakten und Ausstellungseröffnungen." [All translations from the German, unless otherwise noted in the bibliography, are my own.]

5. Goebbels used this term in a speech in August 1933 at the Berlin Radio Exhibition (Diller 1980, 9).

6. This has been particularly true of cinema studies.

7. The recent excellent collective research on radio in a project led by

Adelheid von Saldern and Inge Marßolek is a prominent exception, in that they attempt to adopt a "cultural studies" approach to the problem. They explicitly question the dominant "propaganda" approach to Nazi radio familiar from the standard account. "Mit einer apriorischen Betonung von Massensuggestion und Manipulation verstellt man sich aber die Möglichkeit, dem Radiopublikum mit seinen unterschiedlichen Aneignungsweisen, seinen differierenden sozialen, regionalen, geschlechts- und altersspezifischen Erfahrungen, die sich auf das Radiohören auswirkten, näherzukommen" (Marßolek and Saldern 1998). In many ways, this chapter should be seen as a further contribution in some of the directions of thinking the authors began. But in their attempt to mold a "cultural studies" approach into a paradigm of "dictatorship comparison," the perspective offered in this research ultimately returns to the framework of the standard account. "Die Kämpfe um Einfluß auf die Massenkultur können im Kontext der schon erwähnten cultural studies mit einer Art gesellschaftlicher Arena verglichen werden, in der um kulturelle Dominanz gerungen wird. Allerdings waren und sind die Einfluß und Machtchancen höchst ungleichmäßig unter den gesellschaftlichen Gruppen verteilt. In Diktaturen, wie die in folgender Studie zu behandelnden, trifft dieses Bild von der Arena allerdings nicht mehr den zu analysierenden Sachverhalt. Statdessen ist das Arena-Bild für die Zeit des NS-Regimes vorranging durch den polykratischen Charatker seiner Herrschaftspraxis konturiert." (1998, 23–24). The "polycratic" character of rule here in the National Socialist period mixes two moments of the social: the "state," understood now as the ensemble of repressive state apparatuses, in the Nazi period was polycratic, but this says little about the structure of everyday life, or culture that these authors are interested in. The authors fail to mobilize the full critical potential of their research, which in fact precisely points out that "dictatorship" is a tremendously un-useful theoretical tool. Ultimately, my own work on radio builds on and undertakes a theoretical discussion with this research, mobilizing the Althusserian theory of the state and the concept of hegemony that I see as a corrective to the liberal democratic paradigm of "dicatorship comparison." In particular, Schmidt's (1998) approach to the question of *Radioaneigung* is very productive, and has been useful for my thinking in this chapter, linking in a productive way to the discussions in the following chapters as well.

    8. Pohle (1955) takes issue with this standard account of the technical problems of the Volksempfänger, but he simultaneously insists on the direct effectiveness of the receiver as a propaganda tool. Schmidt's critique of this account is particularly useful—see Schmidt (1998).

    9. See Peters (1999) for a history of the idea of communication.

    10. The literature is vast here: see the introduction for a brief overview.

    11. See Saldern et al. (1998, 368).

    12. For a thorough description of the *Wunschkonzert für die Wehrmacht*, and

an explanation of its origins in earlier broadcasting (like the *Wunschkonzert für das Winterhilfswerk*, which began broadcasting in 1932) see especially Pater (1998:224ff.). See also Drechsler (1988, 131–34) and Bathrick (1997).

13. The film was one of the most popular films of the Nazi period.

14. See Berlant's (1991) development of these concepts. "By '[national] fantasy' I mean to designate how national culture becomes local—through the images, narratives, monuments, and sites that circulate through personal/collective consciousness" (5). "The National Symbolic . . . seeks to produce a fantasy of national integration, although the content of this fantasy is a matter of cultural debate and historical transformation" (22–23).

15. Gute Nacht, Mutter, gute Nacht.
   Du hast an mich jede Stunde gedacht.
   Du hast gesorgt, gequält um deinen Jungen.
   Jeden Abend ein Schlaflied gesungen.

   Gute Nacht, Mutter, gute Nacht
   Ich hab' dir Kummer und Sorgen gemacht.
   Du hast verziehen mir, du hast gewacht.
   Gute Nacht, Mutter, gute Nacht.

This song is probably more familiar to present day readers from Spielberg's *Schindler's List* (1993), where it is appears as semi-diegetic background music during a mass killing.

16. I am well aware that the term "revisionist" is obviously quite loaded when talking about the Nazi period. It should, however, be clear from this context that I am referring to a quite specific revision of a certain dominant historical narrative. It also behooves us to think about why the term has become so loaded: do we think to possess the "final" version of a history of this period?

17. This is arguably also due to the remaining visual bias of film studies. For a powerful antidote to this, see especially Lastra (2000).

18. This is made particularly clear by the magazine *Der Deutsche Sender.* The weekly organ of the *Reichsverband Deutscher Rundfunkteilnehmer,* this magazine began in 1930 as the "only national(ist) radio magazine." By 1931 the organization and its magazine came under the almost exclusive control of the National Socialists, in particular, the radio propagandist Eugen Hadamovsky. See Pohle (1955, 162–68).

19. See Pohle (1955, 165–67).

20. Hans Bredow, the so-called father of German radio, was the most prominent of these figures to suffer at the hands of the Nazis. These leading figures were tried in a show-trial that lasted from November 1934 to June 1935. The main charge was corruption; at the conclusion of the trial they were sentenced to a total of 24 months in prison (some had already been held

for weeks in concentration camps and months in *Untersuchungshaft*). Bredow's sentence would be later reversed by a higher court in 1937, and by 1939, the now embarrassingly failed campaign against the radio officials of the Weimar republic, indeed against Weimar Radio generally, was called off by Goebbels. On the radio trials, see Pohle (1955, 179–81), and Diller (1980).

21. "Mit kleineren Apparaten könne man seit längere Zeit kaum einen deutschen Sender bekommen, doch seien auf den deutschen Wellen ununterbrochen und mit ziemlicher Lautstärke ausländischer Sender zu hören . . . Es werde immer wieder die Feststellung gemacht, daß nach Beendigung des 22 Uhr Nachrichtendienstes auf Wellenanlagen deutscher Reichssender zahlreiche Auslandssender durchschlagen." For more on foreign listening and its interesting figuration as "resistance" in the context of postwar (auto)biographical narrative, see Schmidt (1998, 319).

Yet another *Meldung aus dem Reich*, this time from 1939, emphasizes the difficulties of radio reception during the Nazi period. In this case, we witness again the technical difficulties to which the fascist National Symbolic was subjected, but this time with a surprisingly frank discussion of the forms of political agency that were engaged by these failures. "From different parts of the *Reich* it is reported that in the affected segments of the population who have no electricity in their home for their radios the wish is expressed for a bigger supply of anode batteries. Since the ordering of anode batteries at the moment needs to be done through the regional administration [*Kreisleitung*] . . . unpleasant disagreements, it is said, are sometimes thereby unavoidable" (Boberach 1984, 605). Ironically, here, the local representatives of Nazi power in the *Kreisleitung* are seen as somehow banally disruptive of the pleasures of national fantasy supposedly guaranteed by radio participation.

22. As Inge Marßolek has recently argued, "the apriori emphasis on mass suggestion and manipulation blocks the possibility of coming closer to the audience, with its different forms of appropriation, its differing social, regional, gender and age-specific experiences, which in turn affected radio listening" (Marßolek and Saldern 1998, 19).

23. Lerg comments: "Brecht's call for radio as an apparatus for communication is one of the clearest utopic formulations of a different kind of radio— as well as a critical account of the role of radio in relation to older forms of publicity. "*Sollten Sie dies für utopisch halten, so bitte ich Sie, darüber nachzudenken, warum es utopisch ist*" (130).

24. See Marßolek and Saldern (1998) on the problematic notion of the "passive listener."

25. "Die Zahl geheimer Funkanlagen ist in steter Zunahme begriffen. Das Bestehen solcher Anlagen gefährdet ernstlich die Sicherheit des Staates und der öffentlichen Ordnung, da sie für staatsumstürzlerische Kreise die Möglichkeit

bieten, sich ein umfassendes geheimes Nachrichtennetz zu schaffen, das in Fällen von Gefahr die Durchführung von Maßnahmen der verfassungsmäßigen Regierung ernstlich gefährden kann."

26. This was established by the *Funknotverordnung* of March 8, 1924. On this, see Lerg (1965, 165–70). Interesting in this context is the film *Rundunk einst und jetzt*, part of the permanent exhibit at the Radio Museum in Berlin. This film, made by the UFA and the *Reichs-Rundfunk-Gesellschaft* in 1932, and edited (Jewish actors removed, Nazis inserted) by the Nazis in 1933, is based on a narrative structure that makes this subculture both familiar and archaic. The espoused "modernity" of temporally subsequent forms of controlled, disciplined listening is certainly one of the central ways in which other kinds of publics were eliminated.

27. Or, to be precise: "25 RM Grundwert, vervielfacht mit der am Zahlungstag gültigen Verhältniszahl für die Berechnung der Telegraphengebühren im Verkehr mit dem Ausland" (Bausch 1956, 28). This regulation was made necessary by the excessive inflation of the early Weimar years. See also Pohle (1955, 46).

28. See Halefeldt (1990). "Die publizistische Dimension der technischen Möglichkeit des 'Sprechfunks an alle' spielte erst von 1922 an eine nennenswerte Rolle beim Zustandekommen der schließlich 1926 fixierten Weimarer Rundfunkordnung . . . Indem [die Funkindustrie und die verschiedene staatliche Instanzen] verstanden, ihre Auseinandersetzungen intern auszutragen, verhinderten sie erfolgreich ein Eingreifen der Parlamente, die allein verfassungsrechtlich legitimiert gewesen wären, rundfunkpolitisch Ordnung zu schaffen und dem Hörfunk einen gesellschaftlichen Auftrag zu geben. Da diese Art demokratischer Legitimation in Deutschland bis Ende der 40er Jahre erfolgreich umgangen wurde, sind die offiziellen Funktionszuweisungen an den Weimarer Rundfunk nur als staatliche, nicht als gesellschaftliche Aufträge anzusprechen." (46). On these issues, see below. See Lerg (1965) on the shift from Bastler to listener (270).

29. For the full text of the 1924 emergency decree, see Lerg (1980, 101–03). The choice of radio devices that were now to be allowed was by no means a purely technical decision. This was ultimately part of a comprimise with the larger radio manufacturers, who at the beginning were quite unwilling to cooperate with this form of state regulation. Telefunken, Lorenz, and Huth, now built the officially allowed receivers, and smaller producers, whose devices often did not meet the standards required by the government, were now virtually excluded from the market. See Lerg (1965, 167–68).

30. The ultimate success of these measures should be considered, however, only in relation to the continued development of various forms of radio subculture in Weimar, for example, the Workers Radio Club. See Dahl (1978).

31. The German State held *Funkhoheit*, or radio sovereignty. While this somewhat odd notion—especially in terms of radio reception—seems inexplicable

to modern readers, it was based on the early military uses of radio technology and derived ultimately from the early linkages between transportation services and modes of communication: the sovereignty over radio was always simultaneously *Telegrafenhoheit*. A complex legal model however had to be developed to retain the state's power over the radio—both broadcasting and reception—while at the same time making the commercial production of radio receivers and the commercial use of the airwaves possible. In other words, the state needed to finagle a compromise that allowed them to maintain control and at the same time not lose too much money.

32. See also Kracauer's "Boredom" (1995a), written in the first month of regular German broadcasting.

33. On the association of the spectral with broadcasting, see Peters (1999).

34. On the dialectics of embodiment and disembodiment in the public sphere, see Berlant (1993) and Warner (1992).

35. "Das Publikum des Rundfunks hat eine nahezu gespenstische Eigentümlichkeit Es ist zu gleicher Zeit eine ungeheure Zahl, aber eine ungeheure Zahl von ganz getrennten Einzelnen oder kleineren Gruppen. Ihm fehlt das Erlebnis des Massenhaften vollständig, das dem Publikum der Theater, Konzerte, und Versammlungen den charakteristischen Gefühlsfaktor gibt. Die Rundfunkhörer ergeben von allen Arten des Publikums die größte Menge, aber sie haben nichts davon. Sie bleiben in Zustimmung und Ablehnung vor der ihnen übermittelten Produktion so einsam wie ein Leser vor seinem Buch, oder wie eine Gruppe, der etwas vorgelesen wird. Der Rundfunk hat das Paradoxon des lautlosen Hörers geschaffen. Das Publikum ist eine Masse von Einsamen . . ."

36. See Kracauer's essays on "The Cult of Distraction" and "The Mass Ornament" (1995b, 75–88, 323–29). See also the secondary literature on Kracauer, among others: Hake and Hansen (1991). See also the exchange between Martha Maria Gehrke and Rudolf Arnheim originally published in *Die Weltbühne* in 1930 (Arnheim 1984; Gehrke 1984).

37. Also relevant in this context is Brutz's (1925) polemic on radio's tendency towards distraction, which begins with the provocative words: "Radio, you monster!" For more on this text, see chapter 3.

38. "Die explosionsartige Ausbreitung des Rundfunks macht es dem auf der Beobachtungsstelle sitzenden Rundfunkleiter schwer, sein Publikum zu überschauen."

39. "Als aber die große Masse dahinter kam, dass der Rundfunk ihnen auch fuer ganz wenig Geld mit Hilfe eines kleinen Detektor-Apparates Anregung und Freude ins Haus trug, veraenderte sich die Zusammensetzung des Publikums vollkommen, und bald stellte der Arbeiter und der kleine Beamte das Hauptkontingent der Zuhörer. Aber auch andere Schichten blieben nicht aus, und so erschein es bald schwierig, diese Riesenmasse geschmacklich unter eine Hut zu bringen."

40. There is already a rich literature of the association of femininity with the mass; for more on the specific role of this figuration of crisis in the Weimar period, see Lacey (1996).

41. See Matthew Biro's account of the gendering of the relationship to technology in Lang's *Metropolis*. "As a whole, *Metropolis* sets up a . . . type of ambivalence which is created by the contradiction between a good or useful technology, identified with the controlling gazes of the film's leading men, and a dangerous form of technology, which the film naturalizes and identifies with female sexuality" (1994, 85–86). See also Michael Mackenzie's (n.d.) forthcoming dissertation on technology and the body, especially his chapter on Weimar. Finally, see Schmidt's treatment of the problem of gender and *Radioaneigung* (1998, 334) and most importantly the extensive treatment of radio, gender and the public sphere in Germany in the work of Lacey (1996).

42. Fritz Brutz, writing in 1924, explicitly makes this comparison. See chapter 3.

43. "Ob dem Empfänger der Sendung die Wiedergabe des Gesendeten durch Lautsprecher auch an Dritte ohne weiteres gestattet sei, weil die einmal erteilte Sendererlaubnis dies mit umfasse und es gerade so sei, als ob in einem Konzertsaal die Türen aufgemacht würden, ist eine stark umstrittene Frage."

44. For more on publishing around the "radio" and its usefulness as a source, see Lacey (1996, 11).

45. See also Bausch (1956, 28–39), Lerg (1965, 138–53).

46. On this subject, see Bausch (1956, 40–54), Lerg (1965, 252–64), Lerg (1980), and Halefeldt (1997).

47. This set of conflicts would eventually be put aside by the *Rundfunkordnung* of 1926. One key area of conflict was the interpretation of nonpartisanship, or "Überparteilichkeit." Weimar radio was officially supposed to be politically neutral. This neutrality tended, however, to be guaranteed far more at the expense of left-wing than right-wing views. While center-right politicians considered nationalism as somehow "apolitical," and therefore more than permissible, left-leaning radio policymakers repeatedly attempted to thematize the politics of certain "national" broadcasts, but ultimately without much success. For an informative analysis of these issues, see Schumacher (1997b, 475–86).

48. I am here using Laclau's productive notion of "suture." See Laclau (1990); Laclau and Mouffe (1985).

49. Pringsheim (1883–1972) was a conductor, composer, and music critic (*Vorwärts, Weltbühne*), and served as music director for Reinhardt's theaters in Berlin.

50. "Mehr Rücksicht—auf die Arbeiter-Hörerschaft—Rücksicht bei der Aufstellung des Musikprogramms . . . Nachmittags Unterhaltungsmusik, abends seriöse Musik . . . so ungefähr lautet das Programmschema der Berliner Funkstunde. Es ist der typische Stundenplan des mondänen Zeitgenossen, der immer

Zeit hat, immer ausgeruht ist; es ist das tägliche Musikpensum der sogenannten guten Gesellschaft. 'Man' geht nachmittags zum Tee, abends ins Theater oder ins Konzert, nachts wird getanzt . . . Wer nicht 'ausgehen' will, bekommt seinen musikalischen Fünfuhrtee ins Haus geliefert; zur gewohnten Nachtstunde hat er seine Tanzkapelle im Lautsprecher . . . Die [Stunden von 8 bis 10 Uhr abends] müssen dem Arbeiter gehören. Das heißt nicht, daß in dieser Zeit 'Arbeiter-musik' gemacht werden soll, wir erwarten von der Funkstunde keine 'prole-tarischen Feierstunden' aber es soll nur Musik gemacht werden die—auch—für Arbeiter geeignet ist . . ."

51. For more on the structure of radio broadcasting across the day, see Schumacher (1997a).

52. On the welfare state during the Weimar Republic, see Peukert (1989, 129–46). See also Soppe (1993, 58–59) on the installation of radio systems in Frankfurt housing projects.

53. "Bei seinem kurz nach 22.00 Uhr beginnenden Rundfunkdebüt verlas er den vom Kabinett gebilligten Aufruf an das deutsche Volk vor einem in der Reichskanzlei aufgestellten Mikrophon und gab damit den Startschuß für den Wahlkampf. Goebbels fand die Rede 'sehr schlagend und wundervoll in den Argumenten.' Die sozialdemokratische Rundfunkzeitschrift Volksfunk war da völlig anderer Ansicht. Von geringem Gehalt sei die Ansprache gewesen, Hitlers Stimme habe kasernenhofartig, unsympathisch und gar nicht deutsch geklungen. Aus Österreich sei sogar ein Telegramm gekommen, daß seine Landsleute ihn nicht verstanden hätten."

54. *Rufer und Hörer* existed before 1933, but was able to adjust relatively quickly to the new publishing situation after the Nazi takeover. During the early years of the Nazi regime, the journal was dedicated primarily to a strange form of seemingly Heidegger-influenced theories of radio broadcasting and radio listening.

55. "Ich höre gern lustige Musik. Aber die Musik ist meist für 11 Uhr nachts angesetzt, dann muß ich immer ins Bett und kann kein Radio hören. Das ist dann immer schade. Wenn die Leute aus unserem Haus diesen Aufsatz schreiben müßten, würden sie sagen, daß ihre Männer des Abends müde von der Arbeit nach Hause kommen, dann können sie nicht noch bis 11 Uhr auf lustige Musik warten, welche sie auf andere Gedanken bringen kann . . . Jedenfalls wünsche ich nach der Schulzeit von 2 bis 7 lustige Musik . . ."

56. On this dynamic, see Lüdtke (1991).

57. On the early elimination of federalism in German radio, see Diller (1980, 76ff.)

58. In this way, radio seems quite similar to the Internet. While at first prom-ising a global communication utopia, it seems plausible to suggest that in many instances the Internet is being used to invent new forms of media community which model the nation-state. Arguably, this is also what took place around the

radio. It would be interesting to compare the way hegemonization around the nation-state congealed to these two different technological formations.

59. "In die Erinnerung vieler Generationen hat sich die beleuchtete Senderskala als imaginäre Weltkarte zutiefst eingeschrieben. Auch wenn die meisten der verzeichneten Sender nur mit erheblichen Antennenaufwand 'hereingeholt' werden konnten—die Stationen verhießen eine Welt, die außerhalb der leiblich erfahrbaren Möglichkeiten stand, luden zu phantastischen Reisen und zu Reisen der Phantasie ein" (Schmidt 1998, 317).

60. "Die Welt ist klein geworden . . . und trotzdem sitzt, irgendwo hinter den Bergen, in der weiten Ebene des ostdeutschen Tieflandes, in einem einsamen Fischerdorf auf der Friesischen Küste ein Mensch, für den ist—auch heute noch—die Welt genau so groß, genau so grenzenlos geblieben wie seinen Vätern. Er tut seine Arbeit und leidet an der uralten Krankheit aller Deutschen: dem Fernweh . . . Eines Tages steht in der Wohnung des Fernwehkranken ein kleiner, unscheinbarer Apparat, und über das Dach seines Hauses spannt sich schwankend eine Antenne. Der Einsame stellt einen Schalter, dreht an einem Knopf—und dann hält er atemlos ein: aus dem Apparat kommt klar und tönend die Stimme eines Mannes, der von den fernen Erdteilen spricht, von fremden Menschen, von abenteuerlichen Fahrten und wilden Erlebnissen . . . Die Welt mag unendlich groß sein, unerreichbar und fern für uns. Das Mikrophon der Sender hat sie uns nahe gerückt, und plötzlich stehen auch wir mitten im Geschehen, mithörend, miterlebend . . ."

61. "Fast in alle deutschen Hörerkreisen werden seit der Septemberkrise nach wie vor regelmäßig deutschsprachige Nachrichten und Sendungen ausländischer Sender gehört." Listening to foreign radio is often reported in the *Reports*. For another example, see Boberach (1984, 1013).

62. See Pohle (1955, 268–72), Diller (1980), Dahl (1978).

63. The author of this article, Wolfgang Koeppen, was a novelist and journalist; his name is now most well-known for his postwar novels, most importantly *The Greenhouse* (*Das Treibhaus*).

64. "Über der Pflege des Gemeinschaftsempfangs darf jedoch der häusliche Empfang, die Urform und die einzig funkgemäße Empfangsform, nicht vernachlässigt werden. Gerade auch der häusliche Empfang ist für den neuen, nationalsozialistischen Rundfunk von allergrößter Bedeutung und bedarf einer gründlichen Reform im nationalsozialistischen Sinne. Auch der häusliche Empfang ist in weitaus den meisten Fällen Gemeinschaftsempfang. Und zwar ist es die natürliche, festgefügte Gemeinschaft der Familie, die hier den Hörakt vollzieht und durch den geistigen Rundfunk ständig gefordert wird . . . Eine Stimme, ein Klang, ein Geräusch ist, anders als bei der Schallplatte, von draußen eingedrungen und erfüllt den Raum mit unmittelbarem Leben . . . das Haus wird plötzlich zur Stätte eines großen Geschehens, der engste Wohnraum wird zum weitesten Mitraum . . . Der größte Palast und die ärmste

Hütte nähern sich auf einer gemeinsamen Raumebene und fallen schließlich im Erlebnis, das kein illusionistisches wie beim Film ist, sondern die reale Grundlage hat, zusammen."

65. "Durch welche Medien der Gefühlsaustausch gesteuert wird, gibt Heesters singend zu erkennen: 'Mein Herz müßte ein Rundfunksender sein, dann könntest du mich hören.' Der Gegenschuß zeigt ein auffallend junges, vorwiegend weibliches Publikum, in dem die Zuschauer von 1944 sich selbst erblicken durften. In diesem Revuebild 'Die Welt gehört mir' tanzen die Girls nicht mehr auf den Klaviertasten, sondern auf der Radiotastatur, während der aufgezogene Vorhang enthüllt, daß in den Röhren: Musiker sitzen. Eine naive Übersetzungsarbeit der ansonsten unüberschaubaren Technik des Massenmediums Rundfunk, witzig zur Not: aber auch die Sehnsucht der Nazis ansprechend, Kunst an allen Orten, wo sie dekadent scheint, in schöpferische Natur zurückzuverwandeln. Vom Musiker in der Radioröhre ist es nur ein Schritt zum Kirchenfenster, das aus Sonnenlicht, zum Haus, das aus dem deutschen Wald gebaut wird . . . Die Kunst, in welchem Medium der Revuefilm sie auch thematisiert, unterliegt stets der Metamorphose in den Ursprungsmythos."

66. See Anderson (1983).

67. "Ich bin leider ach so schüchtern, und das Reden fällt mir schwer,
was ich sage klingt so nüchtern, als ob ich kalt und herzlos wär."
Dabei bin ich so romantisch und ein heimlicher Poet
der, erfüllt von bunten Träumen, unerkannt durchs Leben geht.
Was mich gerade jetzt so sehr betrübt,
denn ich bin doch so in dich verliebt.

Mein Herz müßte ein Rundfunksender sein,
Dann könntest Du was hören.
Es tönte in die weite Welt hinein:
"Ich liebe Dich allein, o stell dich auf mich ein."
Dann könnte ich von früh bis Mitternacht
dir brav was treues schwören.
Und hätte ein Programm für dich gewagt
mit Liebe ausgedacht, das wäre eine Pracht.
Als Symphonie,
als Tanzmusik,
erklänge dann mein Lied vom Glück.
Mein Herz müßte ein Rundfunksender sein,
Dann könntest Du was hören.
Es tönte in die weite Welt hinein:
"Ich liebe Dich, wann bist du endlich mein."

68. The *Illustrierter Film Kurier* to *Wunschkonzert* has been reprinted in the collection edited by Mertens (1995). The original German text runs as

follows: "Eine Stimme schwingt durch den Äther. 'Hier ist der Großdeu-
tsche Rundfunk! Wir beginnen das Wunschkonzert für die Wehrmacht.' Ein
magisches Band umschlingt Front und Heimat. Im Unterstand in Frank-
reich, im U-Boot auf Feindfahrt, im Fliegerhorst an der Küste, im stillen
Zimmer einer Mutter, in Tausenden, Hunderttausenden von Wohnungen,
überall klingt und schwingt der Strom von Wort und Lied und Musik. 'Wir
rufen Hauptmann Herbert Koch . . .' spricht Heinz Goedeckes vertraute
Stimme aus dem Lautsprecher bei Wagners, 'er wünscht sich zur Erinnerung
an die Olympiade in Berlin die Olympia-Fanfare!' Über Inges Gesicht zuckt
ein freudiges Erschrecken. Ihre Augen werden feucht. Ein Lebenszeichen
von Herbert—jetzt muß alles gut werden! Es gelingt ihr tatsächlich, Herberts
Anschrift zu ermitteln. Ein eiliger, glücklicher Briefwechsel vereinbart ein Tref-
fen in Hamburg. Und wieder verbindet das Wunschkonzert alle Deutschen.
Leid und Freude des einzelnen, Unbekannten, Namenslosen wird Leid und
Freude der ganzen Nation. Alle Herzen schlagen im gleichen Rhythmus des
Empfindens . . ."

69. I intend this of course in the almost overly literal sense of "hailing," as
elaborated in the mise-en-scène of Althusser. "The existence of ideology and
the hailing or interpellation of individuals are one and the same thing" (1971,
175).

70. See Silberman (1995, 77).

71. See Bracher's account of the "problems of the democratic idea." "[P]olit-
ical modernization intensifies and exacerbates the claim to political participation
and codetermination by the citizen. This demand for 'participation,' likewise,
has not been a militant slogan only since the sixties. In fact it was, for the old
and new democracies of the twenties, a central element of the urge for political movement and change, an urge born in the trials of the First World War
and the disappointments of its aftermath. It was mainly the radical movements of the Left and Right which turned that democratic principle against
democracy itself" (1984, 170). If there is anything useful about Bracher's
account of the "age of ideologies," it is his obvious Cold War politics: "militant" calls for participatory democracy and the spectacle of extra-parliamentary
activism are identified explicitly with fascism as an "enemy of democracy." In
this quite rabid polemic against the Left, and specifically the Greens, which
"operate . . . in the boundary zone between democracy and dictatorship" and
who thus "might provide a nutrient for the incubation of totalitarian ideologies" (xii), ideology, used by "demagogues," operates by "seduction" (6). The
"masses," for Bracher, are particularly subject to being "irrationally" manipulated (21). What I am suggesting here is commentators who do not share
Bracher's explicit polemic unwittingly endorse his reading of the political
more generally if they fail to think about the complexity of ideology, and for-
get the relationship of ideology to domination.

72. "Effectivity" should not be understood as synonym for "effectiveness"; it is here used in the specific Althusserian sense (1990), in which the notion of specific effectivity and "degrees of effectivity" was intended to rethink the usual topological model of the social.

73. While this chapter seeks to rethink the way the history of radio is conceived in the development of fascism, it is not within the scope of this project to adjudicate among the plethora of theories on fascism. I will maintain throughout this book that the Marxist tradition(s) of historiography and theory (with all its problems) offers the most cogent and productively radical critical interpretation of this history, and continues to offer the most powerful way of theorizing the relationship between fascism and other kinds of capitalist social formation.

For a lucid explanation of the debates around the coming of fascism and its relation to capital see Eley (1986). Eley wants to rescue the critical potential of the critical historiographical project, while complicating its operation. "Fascism was not just a particular style of politics, it was also inscribed in a specific combination of political conditions . . ." (273). "Older attempts to take the relationship between fascism and capitalism as the primary causal nexus were indeed inadequate. But that is no excuse for evading the challenge of more recent discussions of fascism or more general theories of the state, forms of domination, and so on" (276–77). The classic text on the economic interpretation of fascism is Sohn-Rethel (1973).

74. This point of view is specifically complicated in Diller's account of political in-fighting between party and state officials during the Nazi regime, as well as conflicts between different parts of the Nazi state apparatus. One example: the propaganda ministry and the armed forces struggled over control of the dissemination of radio propaganda to foreign audiences. But, while describing these conflicts in some detail, the overall picture that congeals in Diller's account is radio's successful instrumentalization by the Nazi regime. Intentionalism remains the dominant account of agency in radio, accompanied by an antimodern fear of "the masses."

75. This is recognized, if not critiqued, by Soppe (1993, 11). See also Mizejewski (1992, 3–36) for a related argument about the use of fascism as a spectacle and a tool for normative politics in the present.

76. Another recent response to the emergence of the discourse of "totalitarianism" in the 1990s is provided by Michael Hardt and Antonio Negri (2000). Reading Hardt and Negri also makes clear the very high political stakes of combating this reemergence. See especially 421, FN9.

77. On this, see especially Dahl (1978). See also Pohle (1955) and Bausch (1956).

78. See as an example Pohle's account of the "politicization" of the radio in the Nazi period (1955, 341). Pohle's account as a whole is useful as a kind

of paradigmatic version of the liberal view of Nazi radio practice. See especially his account of the *"irreale Welt des Nationalsozialismus"* (345) and the plebiscite (346).

79. "[A]ll obviousnesses, including those that make a word 'name a thing' or 'have a meaning' (therefore including the obviousness of the 'transparency' of language) . . . [are] ideological effect(s) . . . It is indeed a peculiarity of ideology that it imposes (without appearing to do so, since these are 'obviousnesses') obviousnesses as obviousnesses, which we cannot fail to recognize and before which we have the inevitable and natural reaction of crying out (aloud or in the 'still, small voice of conscience'): 'That's obvious! That's true!'" (Althusser 1971, 172). The use of the term "ideology" to describe the public sphere in National Socialism often refuses any engagement with a theory of ideology, and thereby pretends itself not to operate within terms that are themselves profoundly ideological, and invested in the reproduction of a very particular set of conditions of production, those of liberal capitalist democracy.

80. For a brief but strongly argued polemic on the use of "totalitarian" as a tool of historical description, in this case as applied to Stalinism, see Resch (1992, 14–17). The point that Resch makes is germane to the discussion of fascism, in so far as totalitarian theories of fascism rest on the assumption that fascism is not capitalist, and because he makes clear the ideological and political stakes involved in totalitarian "theory." "Totalitarianism," Resch argues, "projects onto the history of the Soviet Union a dystopian fable of an even harsher oppression stemming from the absence of capitalism . . ." and elsewhere: "No social system, in short, is more 'totalitarian' than capitalism." Certainly one of the most comprehensive theorizations of the relationship between fascism and capitalism is Poulantzas (1974). See especially on the issue of "totalitarianism" (314–18). ". . . the difference between the fascist State (the exceptional State) and the other forms of capitalist State do not lie in the fact that in the one case the institutions belong to the State system while in the other they are independent or 'autonomous.' In fact, contrary to the all too obvious apologias of the ideologists of totalitarianism, the fascist State is akin to the other forms of capitalist state because it is itself *a capitalist State*" (315).

81. The emergence of the "uniqueness" of the Nazi regime and its crimes can only be understood properly within German politics of the 1980s. In answer to right-wing attempts to relativize the crimes of the Nazis by "explaining" them as a response to Stalinism, the German Left, most prominently Habermas, took a forceful, if logically untenable (or banal) position: that the mass murder of the Jews, and by extension Nazi rule as a whole, was inherently unique in history. Although it was certainly effective in the debate at the time, rightfully warning against the attempt to exculpate German history by pointing to the crimes of Stalinism, the "singularity" of the Holocaust and the Nazi period has now become something of an embarrassing logical problem for serious

scholars of the question, despite its firm place in the popular imagination. For a lucid dismantling of this "concept," see Novick (1999): "The . . . talk of uniqueness and incomparability surrounding the Holocaust in the United States performs the opposite function: it promotes *evasion* of moral and historical responsibility" (15). An unfortunately less lucid, theoretically flawed, but certainly passionate polemic about these issues is Finkelstein (2000).

82. See Laclau (1990).

2. The *Schlager* and the Singer Film

1. I have chosen in this chapter to retain the German term *Schlager*, since the English "hit song" is not only an inadequate translation of the term, but more importantly, the genre meaning of the German term (see below) does not hold in the same way for "hits." Interestingly, now in Germany the term *Schlager* tends to refer only to specifically German songs, or to those songs that date to the heyday of a specifically "German" musical mass culture, that is, after "Americanization" in the late 1950s.

2. For more on the question of "genre," see Jameson (1981).

3. See Schär (1991) for a discussion of the various dance crazes of the Weimar Republic. See also Robinson (1994).

4. For an interesting contrast, see Kracauer's symptomatic reading of early sound film. "Since the Germans opposed Hitler on the political plane, their strange preparedness for the Nazi creed must have originated in psychological dispositions stronger than any ideological scruples. The films of the pre-Hitler period shed no small light on the psychological situation" (1947, 204).

5. See chapter 1.

6. Two good examples of this kind of music are the Evelyn Künneke hit "Sing, Nachtigall, Sing [Sing, Nightingale, Sing]" (1941, M: Michael Jary, L: Bruno Balz), and Lale Andersen's "Es geht alles vorüber [Everything Passes]" (1942, M: Fred Raymond, L: Michael Wallner and Kurt Feltz).

7. See Hansen (1995) for a discussion of this problem.

8. In fact, if we wanted to explore this question with a director-as-author focus, we might even suggest that the makers of *Kuhle Wampe* were quite aware of this problem. It is no accident that many techniques used in Dudov's film are also familiar from early commercial forms of musical film.

9. Useful in this context is Negt and Kluge's earlier discussion of fantasy and experience, and their own attempt to disengage (as well as analyze) what Žižek terms the "representationalist problematic." "It is . . . wrong to contrast the unreality of proletarian fantasy to the reality of the bourgeoisie" (1972, 29).

10. For a detailed, critical debate on the specific effectivity of "the state" that suspends the liberal democratic notion, see Poulantzas (1974, 1978) and Laclau (1977).

11. It is also important to note that the reified national audience of the *Schlager* in this account is at least as problematic as "the radio audience": these models operate implicitly within a national narrative, without thinking of the conditions of that narrative's production or the effects of its productivity. See the introduction and chapter 1 for a discussion of this problem.

12. Bie's works varied in their levels of "seriousness," but almost all are fascinating for their frank desciption of surprising details of everyday musical life, from concert behavior and dress to domestic musical practice. Particularly interesting is a feuilletonistic illustrated account of concert life, which registers many of the shifts of the time. See also his book on opera, as well as a brief volume on *Intime Musik*.

13. Exposés on *Schlager* composers were a common appearance in German magazines of the late 1920s and early 1930s. For another example, see Nantonek (1929).

14. This should of course also be seen in a transnational, especially pan-European context. Bie's description of "musicalization" is very reminiscent, for example, of Rene Clair's cinematic "depiction" of the hit song in *"Sous les toits de Paris" ["Under the Roofs of Paris"]* (1930). For a sense of the role of this film in Europe more generally, see Kracauer's review of the film (1974).

15. Kollo, or rather Kollo's music, was hijacked as the anchor for a pseudo-biopic (with all Kollo music), *Leichte Muse [Light Muse]* (Rabenalt 1940), starring Willy Fritsch as the operetta (and later, *Schlager*) composer P. P. Müller. This film begins with the following title, suggestive for its investment in the relationship between "folk" song and the *Schlager:* "The music of this film is by Walter Kollo, whose melodies already during his lifetime went so deep into the *Volk*, that some who sing them have already forgotten their creator. At the same time, this story isn't about his destiny, but the destiny of the city in which he lived—Berlin."

16. Meisel composed the music and wrote the texts for a number of "evergreen" *Schlager*, including "Ilona" (1926) and "Fräulein, Pardon" (1929). The latter has been re-popularized by Max Raabe in the sound track to the film *Der bewegte Mann* (Wortman 1994).

17. On Joost, see Lange (1966) and Polster (1989, 47–48, 95–98).

18. Wenn man heut als Mann irgendwo und wann gute Laune braucht
weiß man wie man's macht daß das Herz uns lacht 'Alva' wird geraucht
Auch die Frau raucht gern 'Alva' wie die Herrn, weil sie mild und schön
Aroma und das Format sind eine wahre Tat
Rauch! Und du wirst sehn!

Es gibt ein neues Zauberwort das zaubert alle Sorgen fort:
Alva! Nur Alva!
Du warst vielleicht schon oft verliebt! Wer zeigt dir daß es Treue gibt?

Alva! Nur Alva!

Du träumst am Kamin von süßer Harmonie, die Zigarette Alva, die
    enttäuscht Dich nie!

Es gibt ein neues Zauberwort, das zaubert alle Sorgen fort:

Alva! Nur Alva!

Alva! Nur Alva!

Von Alva geht man niemals wieder fort!

19. "Der Umschlagspunkt zum eigentlichen Konzert ist dann erreicht, wenn
man sich funktional, temporal, und lokal . . . um der Musik selbst willen ver-
sammelt, als Musikpublikum; es ist 'harmonische Gemeinschaft' mindestens
insoweit, als deren Erlebnis in der Realisierung autonomer Musik einge-
schlossen ist. 'Öffentlichkeit' als wesentliches Kriterium des Konzerts ist dabei,
mit Ausnahme des Hofkonzerts, weitgehend schon gegeben und nicht erst
faktisch herzustellen wie bei der bürgerlichen Vereinigung. Nach außen
erscheint der Umschlag dann in der Formalisierung von Öffentlichkeit als
'Zugänglichkeit gegen Eintrittsgeld,' in der Verwandlung des Konzerts in
selbständiger Ware, in der ökonomisches Interesse des Musikers und ökono-
misch materialisiertes Interesse des Publikums an eigenständiger Musik kon-
vergieren" (Heister 1983, 193).

20. On the Comedian Harmonists, see Czada and Große (1993). This book
is particularly useful for both its discography and filmography of the group.

21. Also interesting in this light is the film, *Sag' Mir, Wer Du Bist* (Georg
Jacoby, 1933). The *Schlager* "*Madonna, wo bist du?,*" comes from this film. As
Hasse describes in his plot summary, the song arises in the plot as the spon-
taneous words of the song's composer. An interesting recording of this song
stages a radio show in which "the composer" interrupts the normal radio broadcast to "advertise" his *Schlager.*

22. Altman describes the "backstage musical" as a subset of one of the sub-
genres he locates in the musical as a whole—the "show musical." See Altman
(1987, 200–249). While it might be too easy to adapt these terms to the German case, I would suggest that the similarities between Hollywood film style
and the musicals of the UFA make comparison instructive. For three different takes on the complex relationship between "Hollywood" and the UFA
style, see the recent works by Schulte-Sasse (1996), Rentschler (1996), and
Witte (1995).

23. The comparison between *Schlager* and *Volkslieder* often served to normalize this new mode of publicity. One example of this appeared in the *BIZ*:
see Anonymous (1934). For more on the problem of the *Volk* and popular culture, see chapter 4.

24. Bie's terminology suggests his familiarity with work on folk song that
develops the concept of *"Kunstlied im Volksmund."* See Meier (1906) and Bohlman (1996).

25. See also Friedrich (1936). The image of the *Schlagerspekulant* is not unrelated to other mass cultural links between the stereotyped image of "the Jew" and money: see Schulte-Sasse (1996, 231–73). Earlier *Schlager* of the Weimar period were often demonized in the early Nazi period, in order to justify the mass culture of the "new order." One interesting example of this appeared in the *BIZ*. Itself attempting to "adapt" to the new order, this formerly Jewish-owned periodical published an article entitled "Tanzlied statt Song und Gassenhauer": the article featured a reprint of an earlier *BIZ* article from 1927, entitled *"Unsinn, du siegst!,"* which documented the "crazy" song texts of the mid-1920s. The 1933 article laments the "excesses" of Weimar culture, and celebrates the inauguration of a new era of "German" *Tanzlieder*. This kind of practice underscores again the centrality of *Schlager* in Weimar and Nazi Germany's configurations of modernity and the discourses of crisis that characterize modernity. See Anonymous (1933).

26. See Negt and Kluge (1972).

27. Habermas, like Sennett, of course sees this deprivatization as linked to the loss of an emphatic sense of publicity. This will be discussed further in the following chapter.

28. What I have somewhat flippantly called here the "Althusserian penchant for ahistoricity" requires further comment. This does not mean to hold on to the historicism Althusser criticizes when he asserts that "Ideology has no history" (1971, 160). Althusser's "history" here is a very particular one indeed: the historical materialist notion of history propagated by a certain form of Stalinist "theory." "Ideology has no history" means then that ideology is not rooted in the history of class struggle in its teleological conception. On this, see Jameson (1981, 27–58). Furthermore, Althusser's remark is a link to Freudian discourse, and refers to the omnipresence of "ideology" as a structure determining the formation of subjects, "omnipresent in its immutable form throughout history." The crucial point is that according to Althusser, there will *always* be ideology, a useful reminder in the age of "post-ideology." All the same, despite the immense value of Althusser's work—and its incredibly seductive elegance—we should obviously be wary of hagiographic defenses of "the theory," if only for the reason that this tendency among "Althusserians" is something that has left this kind of theorization far too open to sometimes facile critique.

29. ". . . vom rhythmisch Sprühenden, klangsinnreich Berauschenden, bis zum Entnervenden, Dekandenten, gemein Aufreizenden, bis zum ödesten, sinnlosen Kitsch."

30. "So fliegt der Schlager, die Sinne ergreifend, mühelos ins Ohr und fließt ebenso leicht wieder von der Lippen—kein Wunder, daß er sich so blitzschnell verbreitet und im Nu eine ganze Stadt zu beherrschen mag."

31. "Wie würde sich Lilian Harvey freuen, wenn sie hier nicht nur viele

'Doubles' sähe, sondern auch ihr Wiener Freudenliedlein 'Das gibt's nur einmal, das kommt nicht wieder' als Höhepunkt dieser famosen Modeschau hörte. Sollen wir solche Entgleisungen wirklich nur als harmlose Kinderei auffassen? Oder glaubte eine nicht unbedeutenden Bildungsanstalt, ihr Niveau in derart zeitgemässerweise unterstreichen zu müssen??! Wenn Deutschlands künftige Jugendführerinnen und Mütter in Schlager-Singen und Filmstar Nachäfferei ihre Note mit '1' bestehen, so dürften wir nicht allzu viel von ihnen erwarten."

32. Both the text and the filming of this song, it could be argued, echo the new temporality of musical mass publicity in this period. "Das gibt's nur einmal" is filmed as a long sequence moving from town to country, where the song moves "through" the people, a people that is constituted by the passage of the song itself. It should be noted that the concept of experience I am using here is indebted to Negt and Kluge (1972, 3–8).

33. See also Döblin 1961 [1929] (188, 208–9, 394). For more on Döblin's use of montage, see Dollenmayer (1988, 65–80).

34. "Weißt du, wo? Wos mir gerade paßt. Ich hab jetzt grade kein Engagement, weißt du. Ich geh in Lokale, wos schön ist, dann frag ich. Und dann: mein Schlager. Ich hab einen Schlager."

35. "'Du, nicht kitzeln.' 'Laß doch, Mensch.' 'Nee, Hände weg, das versaut mir das Geschäft. Mein Schlager, sei lieb, Süßer, ich mache Auktion im Lokal, keine Tellersammlung: Wers dazu hat, kann mich küssen. Wahnsinnig, was.'"

36. See Huyssen (1986, 44–53) on the overall problematic of the "identification of woman with mass" (52).

37. "Sie setzt sich einen Herrenzylinder auf, kräht ihm ins Gesicht, wackelt die Hüften, die Arme eingestemmt . . ."

38. "Sie trällert, streckt sich auf das Kanapee. Sie pafft, streichelt ihm die Haare, trällert, lacht."

39. The commodity references continue throughout this passage: not only does she offer Biberkopf a drink, "ein Mampe," a bitters (Mampe's Halb und Halb) named after a chain of "liqueur bars" in Berlin at the time, she later sings a local Berlin spoof on a famous optician advertisement: "Sinds die Augen, geh zu Mampe, gieß dir ein auf die Lampe," a takeoff on the opticians' slogan "Sind's die Augen, geh zu Ruhnke." The weekly columns by "Rumpelstilzchen" are very useful for details like this: See http://home.t-online.de/home/0222478110-0001/rmp22-28.htm#t29-8.

40. "Sie entlassen mir nich. Ick bin noch immer nich raus [. . .] 'Ich bin kein Mensch mehr.'"

41. "Testifortan, geschütztes Warenzeichen Nr. 365695, Sexualtherapeutikum nach Sanitätsrat Dr. Magnus Hirschfeld und Dr. Bernhard Shapiro, Institut für Sexualwissenschaft. Berlin. Die Hauptursachen der Impotenz sind: A. ungenügende Ladung durch Funktionsstörung der innersekretorischen Drüsen; B. zu

großer Widerstand durch überstarke psychische Hemmungen, Erschöfpung des Erektionszentrums. Wann der Impotente die Versuche wieder aufnehmen soll, kann nur individuell aus dem Verlauf des Falls bestimmt werden. Eine Pause ist oft wertvoll."

42. "Jedenfalls kann mir Jonny Klotz heute abend den neuen Tango beibringen, damit ich in jeder Beziehung auf der Höhe bleibe. Ich bin ganz kribbelig—den ganzen Tag ohne was zu tun und habe Hunger auf Dunkelwerden—und habe in meinen Ohren immer die Melodie: ich hab dich lieb, braune Madonna—in deine Augen glüht der Sonnenschein . . . Und der Geiger in der Palastdiele singt wie sanftes Mehl—Gott mir wird so—und muß so eine Nacht mit Musik und Lichtern und Tanzen und so ganz auffressen, bis ich nicht mehr kann—als wenn ich am Morgen sterben müßte und bekäme dann nie mehr was. Ich möchte ein Kleid haben aus blaßrosa Tüll mit silbernen Spitzen und einer dunkelroten Rose an der Schulter—ich werde versuchen, daß ich eine Stelle kriege als Mannequin, ich bin ein Gelbstern—und silberne Schuhe— . . . ja so ein Tangomärchen . . . was es doch für wunderbare Musik gibt—wenn man betrunken ist, ist sie wie eine Rutschbahn, auf der man heruntersaust."

43. See Adorno (1990 [1941]).

44. Although his work would later develop in different directions, at this point Mersmann's work seems to have been concentrated on both "new music" and folk music. He was, among other things, one of the coeditors of *Jahrbuch für Volksliedforschung*, under John Meier, and the author of a number of books on the issue, including *Grundlagen einer musikalischen Volksliedforschung* (1930).

45. Davis (2000) explores similar phenomena in the American context.

46. In the film *Ich bei Tag und du bei Nacht [I By Day and You By Night]* (Ludwig Berger 1932), the *Sängerfilm* was the subject of "self-referential" comedy. Included in this film—which also interestingly features the Comedian Harmonists thematizing mass culture and modern experience in the *Schlager "Wenn ich Sonntags in mein Kino geh* [When I Go to the Movies on Sunday]" (M: W. Heymann, L: Robert Gilbert and W. Heymann)—is a sequence that depicts spectatorship in sound film: the film in the film has the typical kind of plot from one of these films, with a clear excess of singing. See Ritzel (1995, 178).

47. The singer films attempt to obliterate any distinction between "classical" forms and *Schlager*; this problem will be discussed in the following chapter. For our present purposes, *Ein Lied geht um die Welt* is particularly interesting for its use of popular song.

48. As far as I know, the only extant copies of this film, which was banned by the Nazis in 1937 as part of their attempt to rid "German" culture of Jews like Joseph Schmidt, have English subtitles and intertitles. While I cannot be sure of the original German intertitles, it seems safe to assume that these were more or less identical in meaning to the English ones.

49. For example, *Heute abend bei mir* (Carl Boese 1934), starring Paul Hör-biger and Jenny Jugo.

50. The plots of the following *Sängerfilme* also revolve around mistaken iden-tity and the voice: *Abenteuer am Lido* (Oswald 1933), *Das Lied der Sonne* (Neu-feld 1933).

51. "Dieser Film ist für Joseph Schmidt gemacht worden, und um Joseph Schmidt gemacht worden. Er wird durch den Gesang getragen . . . Wenn er singt, füllt er die Leinwand aus . . . Auf Grund der Stimme des Rundfunk-tenors Joseph Schmidt hofft man, daß große Massen neugierige Radiohörer diesen Film sehen wollen. Es waren viele parfüm-duftende Frauen anwesend, die durch ihre frenetisches Klatschen beweisen, daß sie bestimmt nicht so gehandelt haben würden, wie Fräulein Nina—Charlotte Ander . . ."

52. See McCracken's (2001) recent account of the crooner, a phenomenon in the United States during the same period, which bears comparison to the radio tenor and the forms of fan culture that developed around it.

53. "Der Hörer, der einen Schlager behält und wiedererkennt, wird dadurch, in einem imaginären, aber psychologisch sehr besetzten Bereich, zu dem Sub-jekt, für das idealiter der Schlager spricht. Als eine der vielen, die mit jenem fiktiven Subjekt, dem musikalischen Ich, sich identifizieren, fühlt er zugleich seine Isolierung gemildert, sich eingegliedert in die Gemeinde von fans."

54. Sonnen's (1931) critical account of recognition is also pertinent in this context.

55. "Ich gedenke eines Mädchens, das von seinen Freundinnen 'Heimchen' genannt wird. Heimchen ist ein am Gesundbrunnen wohnhaftes Prolatarier-kind und arbeitet in der Registratur einer Fabrik. Der Zauber des bürgerlichen Lebens erreicht sie gerade noch in seiner schäbigsten Gestalt, und gedanken-los nimmt sie alle Segnungen auf, die von oben herabträufeln. Bezeichnend für sie ist, daß sie, im Tanzsaal oder im Vorstadtcafé, kein Musikstück anhören kann, ohne sofort den ihm zubestimmten Schlager mitzuzirpen. Aber nicht sie ist es, die jeden Schlager kennt, sondern die Schlager kennen sie, holen sie ein und erschlagen sie sanft. In einem Zustand völliger Betäubung bleibt sie zurück."

56. Some commentators based on this and other writings have accused Kra-cauer's taking a misogynist view. To a certain extent, of course, this accusation is true: "twittering" certainly resonates with dominant images of the nervous woman, etc., from the early twentieth century, subject to involuntary convul-sions and not capable of sovereign choice. But while this observation is in a cer-tain sense true—especially in light of other writings like "The Little Shopgirls Go to the Cinema," it is true in a banal way. The accusation of misogyny is bet-ter directed at the reality that Kracauer was seeking to describe. In other words, this kind of critique is ultimately liberal in its foundations, in that it presumes as its ideal the notion of free will familiar to capitalist social formations.

57. In many ways, these early sound films should be considered in relation to the later "woman's film" of the 1930s and 1940s and its addressing and production of a "female audience." Particularly fascinating is the way the singer films seem to celebrate the female gaze to such an extent that the pretty male characters (or pretty male voices) that surround them seem flat surfaces of desiring projection in comparison to the identificatory roles of the women. In my interpretation, however, it should be clear that the overly psychological interpretation of "female spectatorship" is not sufficient for a properly historical approach to cinematic publics. For the classic attempt to link a psychoanalytic approach to a social history approach in the study of the Hollywood woman's film, see Doane (1987). The next chapter will also treat the problem of the "woman's film" in Germany in some more detail.

58. "Die Erfahrungen, die in Bewegung setzen, müssen nicht nur durch den Kopf hindurch, sondern durch Körper, die Nerven, die Sinne, die Gefühle; sie müssen am Geschichtsverhältnis als einem faßlichen Gegenstand arbeiten können."

59. "Auf der einen Seite hat der Lohnarbeiter, der dem Kapitalisten gegenübertritt, im Verhältnis zum mittelalterlichen Fronarbeiter einen Erfahrungsverlust in der Durchschaubarkeit dessen, was mit ihm geschieht, erlitten. Auf der anderen Seite gewinnt er aber auch neue Organe der Erfahrung hinzu. Die Form, in der im Arbeitsprozeß vergesellschaftet wird, zeigt ihm eine Vielzahl andere Individuen in der gleichen Situation. Die Herrschaft, von der er betroffen ist, wird nicht als willkürliche oder zufällige Bedrückung erlebt, sondern also produzierte, als künstliche."

60. See Foucault's (1984) development of this concept in relation to sexuality.

61. The extent to which this film makes use of Gründgens's unique theatricality begs an interpretation of this film within his star text. Gründgens is most famously associated now with Klaus Mann's *Mephisto* and the controversy around this book. See also Mühr (1984).

3. "Musik" and "Musick"

1. See Weber (1975) on the social makeup of concert audiences in the nineteenth century.

2. Here Dahlhaus's comments on the "religion of art" and absolute music are instructive (1978, 91ff.). See also Adorno (1973) for a still-challenging analysis of the distinction between "light" and "serious" music.

3. See Schröder (1990).

4. See Stapper (2001, 67ff.) for a detailed discussion of the "field" of "entertainment music."

5. See also Adorno (1984 [1968]). For more on both Adorno's earlier and later writings on music in mass culture, see Levin (1990).

6. "The classifying subjects who classify the properties and practices of others, or their own, are also classifiable objects which classify themselves (in the eyes of others) by appropriating practices and properties that are already classified . . . according to their probable distribution between groups that are themselves classified. . . A class is defined as much by its being—perceived as by its being, by its consumption—which need not be conspicuous in order to be symbolic—as much as by its position in the relations of production (even if it is true that the latter governs the former) . . . The individual or collective classification struggles aimed at transforming the categories of perception and appreciation of the social world and, through this, the social world itself, are indeed a forgotten dimension of the class struggle" (Bourdieu 1984, 482–83).

7. The collection of essays edited by Pamela Potter and Celia Applegate (2002) on this subject, which appeared during the last phases of writing this book, provides an interesting spectrum of approaches to the problem of the national imaginary in "German" musical history.

8. Potter in particular sketches out the long history of this process of invention, even going so far as saying that the question of German particularities can be "traced at least to the end of the Thirty Years' War." Potter's claim is provocative, but stands on rocky epistemological and empirical foundations; her time line tautologically produces the very object that this kind of historical study attempts to explain, i.e., the German national imaginary. In other words, she seems briefly to ally her own research with the musicologists she is investigating, herself implicitly mobilizing certainly an ahistorical sense of "Germanness," if not German music.

9. This is not to argue that other nationalisms were more "natural" than the German case, but rather to point out that other nationalisms in Europe had more secure foundations in other historical aspects of the social. The massive centralization of authority and insistence on linguistic uniformity that took place in France at the end of the eighteenth and beginning of the nineteenth century, for example, did not take place in the German states. See especially Hobsbawm (1990, 19–24).

10. See the following chapter for a more detailed discussion of the problem of "race" and music in this period.

11. On the male chorus, see also Bohlman and Currid (2002).

12. On national pastness, see Wallerstein (1991, 78).

13. "Das Deutschlandlied. Josef Haydn, der geniale Vorläufer Mozarts, eröffnete die Reihe der großen österreichischen Komponisten. So lebendig seine formvollendeten, klassischen Kompositionen auch heute noch wirken, durch keine hat er solche Volkstümlichkeit erreicht, wie durch die österreichische Volkshymne, deren schlichte und ergreifend edle Melodie ("Deutschlandlied") Gemeingut des ganzen Deutschen Volkes geworden ist.

Ebenso alt wie die österreichische Volkshymne ist auch das österreichische Tabakmonopol . . ."

14. Of course, the obviousness of this advertisement's "map" character serves rather to enforce the class limitations of cultural capital than to allow access to previously unavailable zones of social practice.

15. The titles of the Weber and Schubert films derive from specific, highly popular pieces of the two composers, readily recognizable to the German audience of the 1920s and 1930s. While these composer-as-hero films simply reproduce the structure of other historical film genres in a musical setting, a more complicated later biopic is Traugott Müller's 1942 film *Friedemann Bach*, based on Brachvogel's historical novel on the tragic life of this Bach son.

16. For more on the Germanification of Händel, see Potter (1998).

17. Here the most clear example is so-called German swing. For more detailed discussions of this phenomenon, see Kater (1992).

18. "Musik ist aber auch eine Generationenfrage. Während unseren Großeltern und Eltern und Polka als moderne Unterhaltung und Tanzmusik lieb geworden sind, auch der Walzer war einmal neu und mußte sich gegen ältere Tanzformen erst durchsetzen—verlangt die junge Generation nach einem straffen, modern Rhythmus."

19. See chapter 1.

20. On this, see Stoffels (1997, 656–57).

21. "Das 58. Wehrmachtswunschkonzerrt hat allgemien sehr angesprochen. Besonders genannt wurden die 'Träumerei' von Schumann, die Lieder, die der Mozart Chor der Berliner HJ gesungen hat, und die humorvollen Darbietungen wie das ABC des Films."

22. In the context of the 1930s and '40s, however, the similarity to the English "swing" was unavoidable—and intentional.

23. "Aber niemand soll glauben, daß die Musik unsere großen Meister immer von dieser Art sei (schwer). Nein, auch sie wußten zu scherzen, zu unterhalten und den Krampf, den sie so oft in des Menschen Brust erregten, wieder in sanfte Heiterkeit zu lösen. Und solche Musik ist es, nach der wir uns in dieser großen Zeit sehnen. Sie sucht der Schaffende, wenn das Rattern der Machinen in seinem Ohr verklingt, und der Verwundete, wenn er aus der Stille de Krankenzimmers wieder in das Leben hinaustritt. Alle haben sie den einen Wusnch: den nach beschwingter Musik."

24. The concerts clearly paralleled similar attempts elsewhere: At the same time in the United States, Toscanini had already become a household name, and the BBC pursued an active broadcasting policy of popularized classics, indicating that the shift to a star culture of "popular" classics reflect a general trend in mass culture of the period.

25. "Musikverständige Kreisen äußerten dankbar daß sie [mit der Matthäus

Passion] auch einmal auf ihre Rechnung gekommen seien . . . gerade die Stimmen der Kritik am Osterprogramm auf dieser Veranstatlungen beziehen von Arbeiterkeisen und zum Teil von Urlauber mit dem Argument vorgebracht wurde, daß sie an den Sonntagen zur Enspannung von ihren Arbeit am liebsten möglichst viel Operetten und Tanzmusik hören."

26. On Gerigk, see Potter (1998, 143–45).

27. "Auf ausdrückliche Anordnung der obersten Führung im deutschen Rundunk ist dem Hörer unbedingt eine zentrale Stellung bei der Gestaltung der Programme einzuräumen. Da erheben sich die Fragen, wie weit darf man dem Hgörer nachgeben, und wo setzt die Aufgabe unsere Zeit ein?"

28. "Wie in der Loge des Opernhauses—so musikgetreu hören Sie Gesang und Spiel aus dem Rundfunkempfangsgeräten des neuen Telefunken-Jahrgangs."

29. Lynn Spigel discusses a similar phenomenon in television advertising in America in the 1950s. See Spigel (1992).

30. Here intended as a translation of the problematic term *Vergesellschaftung*. On the history of this concept, see among others Postone (1996).

31. For opera and operetta in the silent film period, see Traubner (1998, 9–15).

32. For more on *Romanze in Moll*, see Silberman (1995, 81–96).

33. In the case of the Sierck film, the link to Hollywood and the woman's film is certainly intensely overdetermined by the question of directorial authorship: Detlef Sierck, of course, would in Hollywood serve as "Douglas Sirk," and become one of the central icons of later critical production and consumption. For more on the problem Sierck/Sirk, see especially Trumpener (1994), Hake (1997), and Koch (1988).

34. The status of these films as melodrama is in fact telling. On melodrama and the cinema, see Doane (1987) and Gledhill (1991).

35. The use of Händel in the Nazi period, and particularly an oratorio with a Jewish biblical theme like *Judas Maccabeus*, in the Nazi period requires comment. One of the reasons why *Judas Maccabeus* might appear here is due to the happenstance of timing: The year before the premiere of *Final Chord*, 1935, was a key triple anniversary year, marking the 250th anniversary of both Händel's and Bach's birth, and the 350th anniversary of the birth of Schütz. Not only then was Händel's music well-placed in the ears of the German audience, musicologists had also used the year to discover elements of a romantic conception of German identity in Händel's biography and elements of German musical character in Händel's works, despite the fact that the composer spent most of his life in "non-German" territories, and that furthermore, *Judas Maccabeus* was an oratorio based on an Old Testament narrative of Jewish uprising against the Romans. In Germany, it was argued that the use of the "Jewish people" was merely allegorical, and that Händel's oratorios were particularly

well suited for motivating the "German people." The Imperial Music Chamber allowed works like *Judas Maccabeus* to be performed in their original setting. The Germanification of Händel would intensify during the war. For more on this, see Potter (1998, 221–28).

36. This shot is particularly interesting: the spinning image in fact resembles more than anything a spinning swastika, and seems easily legible in the Sier(ck)ian paradigm of excess.

37. "Tausend glückliche Stunden erkaufen Sie für Ihre Familie, Ihre Freunde, und sich selbst . . . Wohltuende Enstpannung von der Mühe und Last des Tages bedeutet der Bestiz eines dieser herrlichen Instrumente. Der Rhythmus, mit dem jedes Modell den lustigen Schlager, die harmonische Schönheit der ernsten Musik tonrein und naturwahr überträgt, erweckt den Eindruck der unmittelbarern Anwesenheit des Künstlers."

38. "In dem Dirigentfilme *Schlußakkord* ferner geht es natürlich nicht ohne die 9. Symphonie ab—als wenn Beethoven nicht auch andere recht gute Werke geschaffenhätte. Aber beim Film (377) luasst man sich nicht lumpen . . . 9. Symphonie, h-noll Messe, Mattheus Passion. N die ale dieser Profanierung und Verschleisung ist nur das eine Gute, dass dei Filme so kurzlebig sind. Man hat damit die Gewähr, daß dergelichen Attentaten auf den Gescmahck und den Kunstsinn wenigstens nicht von Dauerwirkung bleiben."

39. The premiere of *Dream Music* was in December 1940.

40. This theme will end up doubling the course of Michele's development in the film. The Italian title of the film echoed this: *Rittorno*.

41. Television broadcasting was begun briefly in 1938.

42. There is astonishingly little work on Riccardo Zandonai available in English. A somewhat chatty biography appeared in 1999: see Dryden (1999). Very useful is Cescotti (1999), which includes Zandonai's film work as well.

43. *We Make Music* is one of the exceptions of musical filmmaking during the Nazi period, being set in the present, and thematizing at least marginally the issue of wartime life. In particular, this is done through a framing device at the beginning and end of the film, which includes a reference to the "lights out" of a bomb alarm. Furthermore, the virtually all-female band featured in the film reflects a trend necessitated by mobilization, a trend equally present in the United States and Germany during this period. Made in 1942, at the height of Nazi military power, this Helmut Käutner film can, like *Die große Liebe*, deal with war as if still a minor "inconvenience."

44. Framed at beginning and end by direct address, each of these bookends places the film emphatically in the present tense of the war, referring among other things in a jocular tone to the "lights out" required for civilian air defense in war time.

45. On absolute music, see especially Dahlhaus (1978).

4. "Songs the Gypsy Plays for Us"

1. See especially chapter 2 for a more elaborate discussion of these issues.

2. See also the essays collected in Born and Hesmondhalgh (2000).

3. The issue of terminology is in this case quite complex and manifestly political, and requires comment. I have elected to use the word "gypsy" throughout this chapter. I have done this for two reasons: first, the racial fetish of the "gypsy" under discussion here was precisely *not* bound by the specificity implied by terms like Sinti and Roma (Germany), Vlax (the Balkans), or Traveler (UK and Ireland); see Hehemann (1987, 9). But there is also a more important problem here: the mobilization of this kind of ethnic discourse, as can be witnessed in contemporary Romani activism, can achieve something over the short term in the context of sheer mobilization and political debate. At the same time, in ways similar to the history of "African-American," I believe that, like this term, the ultimate effect is a normative one. As a political concept, the ethnic model of identity currently serves more as mode of "entry" than as critique of the relations of racial production. Furthermore, for my purposes, the study of "race" in German acoustic culture of the 1920s, '30s, and '40s, a change in terminology from "gypsy" to "Roma and Sinti" would, more than anything, serve to *cloak* the operation of racial fantasy under a liberal humanist mantra. When "gypsy music" becomes the "music of the Roma," then the investigation implicitly participates in the racializing processes under investigation, albeit with a positive valence, and could scarcely have the maneuvering room to comment on these processes. Furthermore, the use of the term "Roma and Sinti" almost seems to willingly accept what Hardt and Negri have recently called the "Empire's" current attempts at normalization through "racial management," by transforming "the gypsy" into part of a multicultural fabric, or worse still, yet another group in the series of "true" Holocaust victims whose music can be purchased in the world music lists at amazon.com (Hardt and Negri 2000, 190–95). This is a dangerous game, and one that ultimately condemns critique to failure. For more on this, see Žižek's (1989) critique of the concept of anti-Semitism, discussed later in the chapter: any effective critique of those practices that we know as "racism" cannot succeed if it fails to consider the production of the object. See also the conclusion of this chapter for an example of how "Sinti and Roma" operates equally effectively in the same racial apparatus as the more "obvious" term, "Gypsy." For more on the problem of terminology, see Trumpener (1992, 846) and the earlier comments of Acton (1974).

4. "Da hängen sie an den Lippen dieser Zigeuner, die ihre gnadenerweisenden Blicke massenweise verschenkten, um nur ja nicht zu kurz zu kommen. Man hat ja auch nicht alle Tage Gelegenheit, einen 17-oder 19jährigen Zigeunerprimas anzuschmachten. Kaum aber waren Geige und Bogen nach

Ladenschluß aus der Hand gelegt, da enteilte der Zigeunergalen der Stätte seiner Wirksamkeit, um draußen mit seiner Anbeterin im Dunkel der Nacht zu verschwinden."

5. "Wir haben es erleben müssen, daß solche 'Damen' auf der Straße warteten, bis die Söhne der Pußta erschienen. Man wollte sie nur noch einmal sehen, ein Autogramm gegen ein Stelldichein austauschen und, sofern der Zufall günstig, mit einem dieser Gesellen einige amüsante Stunden zu pflegen. Die Briefe und Bilder die man miteinander tauschte und mit denen man, ebenso spendabel wie leichtfertig umging, sind ein geradezu beschämender Beweis solcher Würdelosigkeit."

6. "Daß eine von diesen 'Liebhabern' mit einer ekelhaften Krankheit behaftet war, sei nebenbei erwähnt. Hier war nur alles darin: Liebesschwüre von ihren Müttern zu wenig geohrfeigten Backfische und notorische Ehebruch sogenannte Ehefrauen. Vielleicht hat man zu Hause erklärt, auf Kaffeejagd zu gehen; nun waren es Zigeunerarme die einen gefangen hielten."

7. For one of the clearest descriptions of this kind of triangulation in the modern Central European context, see Gilman (1988).

8. Indeed, Kassel was a city with a very low gypsy population. See Engbring-Romang (2001, 107).

9. Marc Weiner (1993) sketches out this ideological configuration and the role it played in the literature of the period.

10. See Hohmann (1981, 177–78) for a discussion of the many different victim counts of the Nazi persecution of gypsies in Europe. One writer claims that up to 70 percent of the European gypsy population was murdered during this period (Wolf in der Maur, cited in Hohmann 1981, 178).

11. For more on Nazi policy in the Hessian states during this period, see Engbring-Romang (2001).

12. Sárosi (1978) describes elements of this "Gypsy style." It should, however, be noted that the question of the "gypsy style" is thorny, and, like the general question of terminology, has been an eminently political question at least since Bartók. For more on this, see Brown (2000) and Trumpener (2000). All descriptions of "the gypsy style" can thus only be used with reservation. At the same time, a certain set of musical markers did function as a set in the racial imagination of early twentieth century Europe. One of the key markers of the "gypsy style" is the two-part structure of the czárdás: *lassu* and *friss*. In the German popular reception of the czárdás, the *lassu* is most often used for the song, which is then followed by an instrumental czárdás, as is the case in this film.

13. The central song in this film, and a song still familiar to German audiences today, is Balz and Brühne's hit, "Kann denn Liebe Sünde sein?"

14. Interestingly, while the specter of musical degeneracy does circulate in this film, it by no means adheres to the sound of gypsy music or the figure of

a gypsy violinist. The degenerate Viennese accent of the urban womanizer (and tenor) Trill (Karl Schönböck), serves as this film's iconic representation of the disturbing musical "other" of sexual excess to the production of a rooted, ultimately familial regime.

15. Here Adorno's (1973a) (in)famous arguments are more than appropriate.

16. Strangely enough, Stahlberg avoids the augmented second, carefully replacing it with its inversion in the allegretto section.

17. Also interesting here is "Hoch Ungarn!" which appears beneath the song's title. Most likely intended as a salute to Hungary as a fellow axis power, this "salute" also makes clear the association in Germany between "gypsies" and Hungary—an association that the Hungarian fascist government itself, in the tradition of Hungarian nationalism, certainly did not share.

18. In fact, what might seem like a "loosening" in cultural policy indicated more a shift toward more entertainment at any cost. But "jazz" was never forbidden in the Third Reich, despite the prevalence of rabidly antijazz discourse.

19. Of course, the question of klezmer music here is particularly provocative, considering the intimate linkage between klezmer and "gypsy" musics. But in Germany of the 1930s and '40s, the sounds that might be associated with both klezmer and gypsy music were coded for the vast majority of the audience as gypsy, since "klezmer" had not yet emerged as the dangerously philosemitic racial fetish familiar from modern Germany. On klezmer music's multiple ethnic implications, see Bohlman and Radano (2000, 41–44).

20. See Robinson's description of Barnabas von Gézcy's hit song of 1935, "Ungarnwein," for example. Robinson describes music like "Ungarnwein" as a symptom of the "decline" of jazz in the Third Reich, in tones that incidentally echo Bartók's condemnation of gypsy music. See Robinson (1994).

21. For the German context, the most important texts here are Hohmann (1980, 1981, 1990) and Wippermann (1986). A recent reproduction of this narrative can be found in Lewy (2000). Lewy's reading of this history ultimately returns to an approach that strangely echoes the criminological texts of the 1950s and '60s, when he suggests that there were "reasons" that the mainstream population reacted so negatively to the gypsies, including things like their supposed poor hygiene and seminatural tendency to trickery. This slip back into older discourses is a good illustration of the limits of a "cultural" approach to "gypsy difference."

22. For a useful summary of the older literature, see Zimmermann (1996, 23–26).

23. "Die These, es existiere eine kostante, gleichsam überhistorische Identiät der Zigeuner läßt sich . . . nicht verifizieren . . . [Die] Bezeichung, ob nun 'Zigeuner', 'Sinti' oder 'Roma' sagt als solche nichts Eindeutiges über den Begriffsinhalt aus. Wenn das Spezifische der nationalsozialistischen im Verhältnis zur vorhergehenden und nachfolgenden deutschen Zigeunerpolitik

herausgearbeitet werden soll, ist es deshalb von besonderer Wichtigkeit, die unterschiedlichen Diskurse über 'Zigeuner', 'Sinti' oder 'Roma' in ihrem historischen Entstehungs- und Wirkungszusammenhang zu analysieren und dabei nach dem Kontinuitäten und Brüchen zu fragen, die sich vor allem in Deutschland in diesen Diskursen abzeichneten" (Zimmermann 1996, 18).

Zimmermann's overview of the historiography is particularly useful, although here as well the problem remains that critique implicitly relies on the concept of "racism"—a concept that is ultimately based on the underlying assumption of an inherent ontological distinction between racial groups and other forms of population. As a "political aside": it should be stressed that this argument also understands the mobilization of "Roma" identity in the modern case as partially productive. It has secured the interpellative operation of the notion of a "people" for "the Roma," which has made it possible to establish active political communities and coalitions around very real social conditions that produce "the Roma" as a potential political subject. We need, however, to be clear that the discursive traps and slippages that this chapter discusses also apply to this ostensibly resistant usage. I would suggest that a more powerful political counter-imaginary, which can mobilize constellations that perhaps take into account the discursive history of "gypsy"—the criminal, the asocial, and the migrant—might be necessary to achieve the desired goals even of the Romani movement.

24. See Foucault (1991).

25. See Wallerstein's discussion of "peoplehood" and its relationship to capitalism (1991). For an explicit discussion of this linkage regarding the role of the "gypsy" in the Western imagination, see Streck (1979).

26. On the police in the nineteenth century, see especially Lüdtke (1992).

27. For the continuing prevalence of this kind of view, see, as one particularly shocking example, the recent work of Guenter Lewy (2000), who in his seemingly "sympathetic" portrayal of the persecution of the gypsies astonishingly argues that "prejudices alone are not a sufficient explanation for the animosity, with which the gypsies have been met over the centuries. Certain aspects of their way of life . . . are disposed to cause animosity among their fellow men."(!)

28. See Foucault (1991) on "population" and governmentality. See also Lucassen (1996).

29. The gypsy is linked as an identity structure to the other forms of degeneration produced most famously in the work of Cesar Lombroso. For more on his attempt to locate the social in the body, see Seitler (2000).

30. See also Schenk (1994, 347ff.).

31. The ideological terrain of race, sexuality, and degeneracy has been explored in Germany and elsewhere by many scholars. For a sampling of this work, see Mosse (1985) on the linkage between the historical development of

German national fantasy and a vocabulary of degeneracy. On *entartete Musik*, see Dümling (1993) and John (1994). On the general enforcement of regimes of capitalist normality in National Socialism through the racial/sexual relay, see Peukert (1987). My thinking on the subject of degeneracy has been influenced by discussions with Dana Seitler. See her work on degenerationist discourse in the U.S. context at the beginning of the twentieth century (Seitler, 2000).

32. See Liszt (1910). For a detailed discussion of this, see Baumann (1996).

33. See Sárosi (1978) on the relationship between Hungarian and gypsy musics, and an introduction to what we know as "gypsy" style.

34. On the various techniques used to define "the gypsy," see Lucassen (1996).

35. The discursive need to produce the "gypsy" as radically other came to take on particularly sinister effects when the problems of gypsy internment were discussed. Stein is particularly good example of this: "Ganz besonders empfindlich ist der Zigeuner gegen jegliche Einschränkung der persönlichen Freiheit. Er leidet und spricht von Freiheitsberaubung, wenn man nur einen Lagerplatz mit Stacheldraht einzäunt, und der Kontrolle halber von jedem verlangt, daß er sich abmeldet, bevor er den Platz verläßt" (1940, 88).

36. "Als befrackte und geleckte Musiker treten sie in den Cafés auf, zerlumpt und verlaust lauschen häufig daheim ihre Angehörigen den Geigentönen im Zelt, im Wagen oder in der Hütte. Und wenn ein noch so großer Skeptiker nichts Rechtes im Spiel zutraut, so wandelt sich sehr bald ein äußerer Eindruck. Der eben noch unsympatische Zigeuner wird liebenswert, sobald er den Bogen an die Geige setzt und ihr bis an die Grenze des Möglichen reichende Tönen entlöckt, die jeden Zuhörer mit sich in eine Welt nehmen, wo man alles vergißt. Nicht umsonst haben Bojaren und Magnaten Reichtümer gegeben für ein schönes Zigeunerspiel. Es führt in das Raum und Zeitlose, es läßt die uns verlorengegangene Harmonie der Seele ahnen. Zigeunermusik macht Menschenelend und Menschengehässigkeit vergessen."

37. Although some have seen Block's writing as an exception to more general practices of Nazi racial ideology, it is more accurate to point out that despite Block's somewhat more "benign" intentions, the racializing effect of his writing is practically indistinguishable from that of other texts of the period.

38. See Hehemann (1987); Schenk (1994).

39. This notion is partially indebted to Ronald Radano's (1996, 2000) work on black music in the United States.

40. "Vom Leiter der Kapelle, dem blonden Hünen Sidney Firman, geht die Sage, daß er der Sproß einer Zigeunerfamilie sei. Sidney . . . schweigt sich über diesen Punkt konsequent aus . . . Ähnlich geht es seinem Banjospieler, der als Argentinier ein absolut waschechter Sohn der Pampas ist. Auch das Saxophon ist stilgerecht besetzt: Mr. Leslie ist der echte Yankee, wie er im

Buch steht. Und daß hinter dem Schlagzeug ein Mann sitzt, in dessen Adern Negerblut rollt, ist eigentlich schon selbstverständlich . . ."

41. Hemetek's recent ethnography of Roma and Sinti in Austria discusses the complicated relationship exhibited in the music of the Roma and Sinti towards the outside world and the cliché of *Zigeunermusik* (1993, 106). That Grappelli himself was not a gypsy does not exclude his music from this discussion.

42. Lange's clearly partisan account of Zacharias's status as a jazz innovator is relevant here: "An der Modernität der damaligen Zacharias-Gruppen ist nicht zu zweifeln, da die alten Schallplattenaufnahmen aus den Jahren von 1941 bis 1943 auch heute noch eine Musik präsentieren, die zeitlos ist. Genauso zeitlos wie die Musik des berühmten Quintette du Hot Club de France. Die Zacharias Aufnahmen sind heute fast vergessen und den meisten deutschen Jazzfans kein Begriff mehr, dennoch zählen sie zu den Meilensteinen der deutschen Jazz-(Swing)Geschichte und verdienen mehr Beachtung" (107–8).

43. See Kater (1992, 69) for an anecdotal account of Zacharias's beginnings.

44. This claim is made by Micaela Jary in her book on Zarah Leander and Michael Jary. See Jary (1993, 211). Of course, this kind of source can only be treated with a great deal of skepticism; nonetheless, it might point in an interesting direction for further research, considering the abundant evidence of continuing musical performance by gypsies in the Third Reich in numerous contexts. Jary's text is further discussed at the end of the chapter.

45. The link in films between gypsy exoticism and vaguely Spanish forms of the exotic is made most clearly in a film like *La Habanera*. While this linkage is in some ways distinct from the Hungarian version of the gypsy stereotype, its function as a racial icon of the exotic is similar. See Trumpener's (1994) discussion of the use of music in that film. For more on *Karneval der Liebe*, see Witte (1995, 232).

46. A recent CD collects a number of Boulanger recordings from the period. *Georges Boulanger: L'exceptionnel Virtuose du violon tzigane. Engristrements Originaux 1932–1942.* (Inter Loisirs Discs SARL, IRL 642146).

47. "George Boulanger, ein Meister auf dem Griffbrett der Geige, spielt das von ihm komponierte "Mal so, mal so" [A. 1775—Telefunken] auf dem Flügel begleitet von Oskar Jeroschnik. Neben seiner eminenten Spieltechnik wirkt seine zigeunerhaft anmutende Rubato-Manier voll Eigenart. Verblüffend ist seine Springbogen-Technik und seine Pizzicato mit der linken Land. Das gleiche gilt auch für sein geigerisch hinreißend gespieltes 'Aber warum, gnädige Frau."

48. "Eine glückliche Vereinigung von schönem Ton und sensationeller Technik bietet Georges Boulanger, diskret begleitet von einem ungarischen Zigeunerorchester, mit der russischen Zigeuner Romanze (28 447 Odeon), dem Pußta-Fox (25 589-Odeon) und dem langsamen Fox-trot 'Liebe'" (Schlüter 1936).

49. Compare Boulanger's recording (included on the set *Tziganes: Paris/Berlin/Budapest 1910–1935*. Frémeaux & Associés S.A., FA 006) of his song with the 1944 recording by Gino Bordin, this time on slide guitar (or Hawaiian guitar) (Polydor LC 0309, included in the collection *Tanzmusik aus Deutschlands dunkelsten Jahren 1942–1948)*.

50. See Hohmann (1990, 79–82) on the relationship between work and migration in the Nazi period.

51. *Heißes Blut* was also released in a French version, *Les Deux Favoirs*, starring Lisette Lanvin in the role of Marika. See Klaus (1996, 90).

52. Ilonka's annoying repetition of the phrase *"es ist ja auch gleichgültig"* is a running gag in the film. The formulaic, implicitly hypercorrect speech of Ilonka marks her as *arriviste*, in contrast to the baroness's natural, easy-going form of speech.

53. In fact, as Julie Brown has recently pointed out, authors like Bartók explicitly thematized the links between "gypsy music," the complex relationship of urban/countryside, and registers of cultural capital (aristocrats and fallen aristocrats). This of course makes the role of the Baronness Marika even more intriguing. See Brown (2000).

54. "Der Raum, in dem der Heurige genossen wird, bietet einen herrlichen Fernblick auf das nächtliche Wien. Matt hebt sich der Stephansturm vom gestirnten Himmel ab, und eine innerlich beleuchtete Elektrische entgleitet über die Donaubrücke. In anderen Räumen . . . fließt der Rhein, glüht das goldene Horn, dehnt sich fern im Süden das schöne Spanien . . . Dort heißt es von Löwenbräu, 'Bayerische Landschaft: Zugspitze mit Eibsee—Alpenglühen—Einzug und Tanz der bayerischen Bua'm. Schuhplattlerpaare . . .' oder von der Wildwest-Bar: 'Prärielandschaften an der großen Seen . . . Neger-Cowboy Jazzband . . .' Das Vaterland umfaßt den ganzen Erdball."

55. "Oeffentliche Warnung! Im beiderseitigen Interesse ersuchen wir die H.H. Direktoren, Restauranteure, und Konzertagenten um Vorsicht bei evtl. Engagement der "sogenannten" Oberlander-Kapelle Otto Gips aus Berlin. Das Inserat des genannten Herrn in der Nummer vom 22.2.24 des 'Artist' entspricht nicht die Tatsachen. Die Mitglieder dieser Kapelle sind nämlich fast durchweg Berliner Herren, und haben infolgedessen weder Berechtigung auf bayrischen Namen zu reisen, noch bei musikalischen Darbietungen kurze Hosen zu tragen. Gruppe III der Ortsgruppe Nürnberg des Deutschen Musiker-Verbandes."

56. On Jessel and *Schwarzwaldmädel*, see Dümling (1992).

57. "Wir brauchen den jüdischen Schlager, für Zither, Geige und Ziehharmonika instrumentiert, nicht nachzutrauern . . . Und im übrigen wurde keines dieser Lieder selbst in Wien in Text und Ton gesetzt, sondern es geschah immer auf der Kurpromenade in Ischl, dort die Herren Librettisten, die krummen Beine in den kurzen Lederhosen, zu zweit lustwandelten und Chansons

zusammenstoppelten, in denen Wiener Pupperln vor der Kulisse des Riesen-rades oder dem 'guatn alt'n Steffl' agierten. Wir können ruhig die meisten Wiener Operetten vom Spielplan streichen, ohne über den hämischen Hin-weis erröten zu müssen, ohne Juden gäbe es keine Wiener Operetten. Die Juden haben die Operette zu Tode gehetzt . . . Sie haben nicht wenig verdi-ent an unserem Gemüt und unserer Gefühlsduselei. Irgendein dahergelaufe-ner jüdische Vagabund konnte die Werke Schuberts plündern und servierte uns das 'Dreimädlhaus,' das ein Welterfolg wurde, und der Jude der sich Berte nannte, scheffelte Geld und ließ sich feiern, als ob es nie einen Franz Schubert gegeben hätte, mit dessen Lorbeeren er geschmückt in der Welt herumhausierte . . . Es handelt sich bei der Heurigenmusik beileibe um keine Kulturgüter. Kulturgüter muß man auch nüchtern genießen könne, ohne das durch diesen Normalzustand des Menschen deren Eindruck abgeschwächt wird. Das frohe bodenständige Lied ist nun einmal kein Produkt, das nur im Kaffee 'Museum' gedeiht, woselbst zwischen zwei und sechs die Muse kom-ponierend Juden zu küssen pflegte. Die Wiener Gemütlichkeit war für die Juden nichts als ein gutgehendes Geschäft, und die jüdischen Operetten und Filmen haben dem Ansehen des Österreichers mehr geschadet, als es auf den ersten Blick den Anschein hat . . . Wir müssen nicht nur an die Arisierung der Geschäfte, sondern auch an die der Gefühle gehen."

58. Another film that illustrates this displacement is *Julika [Harvest]* (Bolvary 1936). A true *Heimatfilm* set in Hungary, *Julika* also uses a gypsy band. Although an Austrian film, it was released by Tobis and played all across Germany.

59. Yet another interesting example of this, now mapped back onto the eighteenth century, is *Friedemann Bach* (Müller 1942). See Trumpener (1992, 844) and Schulte-Sasse (1996).

60. Also in 1938, an especially rabid campaign against gypsies was inaugu-rated in the Austrian Burgenland. This is of course interesting for several rea-sons: first, the ethnic content of *Pußta* romanticized in the cinema was not unlike that of Burgenland itself. Secondly, the campaign focused largely on children. "Da in ihren Augen aber alle Zigeunerkinder einer Pest gleichka-men, bot der Erlass in der Praxis die Lösung, nach der sie gesucht hatten: Sie konnten die Zigeunerkinder aus den öffentlichen Schulen entfernen, ohne ihnen die kostspielige Alternative separater Klassen oder Schulen anbieten zu müssen" (Lewy 2000, 109–10).

61. See Maciejewski (1996): "Sinti und Roma werden nicht nur gebraucht, um das Andere als der Moderne zu verkörpern, sie bringen zugleich . . . in den Augen von Nicht-Sinti und Nicht-Roma dieses Andere als das eigene Alte der europäischen Kultur zur Anschauung. Wider Willen werden sie zu Repräsentanten der untergegangenen Welt von gestern."

62. See Baumann (1989, 30–33).

63. "Außerdem versuchte der Komponist [Michael Jary], so viele Zigeuner wie möglich als Musiker in seinem Filmorchester unterzubringen. Das allerdings tat er nicht nur aus edlen Gründen, um die Menschen vor Verfolgung zu schützen, sondern auch aus rein künstlerischen Motiven heraus, denn Sinti und Roma waren erfahrungsgemäß hochmusikalisch. Zwar konnten viele nicht eine einzige Note lesen, aber nachdem man ihnen einen Titel am Klavier nur einmal vorgespielt hatte, beherrschten sie problemlos jeden Takt. Das war kürzlich bei der Aufnahme zu dem Johannes-Heesters-Schlager 'Durch dich wird diese Welt erst schön' besonders deutlich geworden, als Jary einen erst 14-jährigen Zigeunergeiger engagiert hatte."

64. See Currid (2002).

Bibliography

Acton, Thomas. 1974. *Gypsy Politics and Social Change: The Development of Ethnic Ideology and Pressure Politics among British Gypsies from Victorian Reformism to Romany Nationalism*. London: Routledge and Kegan Paul.

Adorno, Theodor W. 1973a. Über den Fetischcharakter in der Musik und die Regression des Hörens. In *Musikalische Schriften*. Frankfurt: Suhrkamp Verlag.

———. 1973b. *Einleitung in die Musiksoziolgie*. Frankfurt am Main: Suhrkamp Verlag.

———. 1984 [1934]. Die Form der Schallplatte. In *Musikalische Schriften*. Frankfurt am Main: Suhrkamp Verlag.

———. 1990 [1941]. On Popular Music. In *On Record: Rock, Pop, and the Written Word*, edited by Simon Frith and Andrew Goodwin. New York: Pantheon Books.

Althusser, Louis. 1971. Ideology and Ideological State Apparatuses. In *Lenin and Philosophy*. New York: Monthly Review Press.

———. 1990. Contradiction and Overdetermination. In *For Marx*. London: Verso.

Altman, Rick. 1987. *The American Film Musical*. Bloomington: Indiana University Press.

Anderson, Benedict. 1983. *Imagined Communities*. New York: Verso.

Anonymous. 1924. Der Rundfunk und sein Publikum: Eine Rundfrage an die deutschen Sendegesellschaften. *Funkalmanach: Offizieller Austellungskatalog zur Grossen Deutschen Funkaustellung*: 84–99.

———. 1927. Hier Charleston auf Welle London! London's Radio Dance Band. *Rundfunk-Rundschau* 2 (17): 331.

———. 1931. Die ganze Welt hört Bayreuth. *Der Deutsche Rundfunk* (35): 12.

———. 1932a. Mein bester Schlager. *Der Deutscher Sender* 3 (17).

———. 1932b. Rundfunk und Bayreuth. *Rundfunk-Jahrbuch*: 99ff.

———. 1933a. Die Kölner Befreiungsfeier. *Rundfunk Jahrbuch*: 124.

————. 1933b. Ein Lied geht um die Welt. *Film Kurier.*

————. 1933c. Tanzlied statt Song und Gassenhauer. *Berliner Illustrirte Zeitung* 42: 1535.

————. 1934. Schöpfer neuer Volkslieder. Was Millionen singen. *Berliner Illustrirte Zeitung* 43 (9): 270.

————. 1938. Von der richtigen 'Einstellung' zum Rundfunkhören. *Die Sendung* 15 (11): 236.

————. 1939a. Mißbrauch klassicher Musik. *Der Deutsche Podium* 7 (26): 30.

————. 1939b. Von der Pußta möcht' ich träumen. *Der Deutsche Podium* 7 (17): 2–3.

————. 1941. Advertisement: Zigeunertraum Solistenverlag. *Das Deutsche Podium: Fachblatt für Unterhaltungsmusik* 9 (48): 4.

————. 1942a. Streifzug durch die Musikgaststätten. *Das Podium der Unterhaltungsmusik* (2925): 260.

————. 1942b. Unterhaltungsmusik im Rundfunk. *Das Podium der Unterhaltungsmusik* 60 (2911): 38.

————. 1942c. Was ist mit den Zigeunern? *Das Podium der Unterhaltungsmusik* (2925): 260.

Antonietto, Alain. 1993. Tziganes. Paris/Berlin/Budapest. 1910–1935. In *Tziganes. Paris/Berlin/Budapest. 1910–1935*. Vincennes: Fremeaux & Associés.

Applegate, Celia. 1990. *A Nation of Provincials: The German Idea of Heimat.* Berkeley: University of California Press.

Arnheim, Rudolf. 1984. Antwort an Martha Maria Gehrke. In *Radio-Kultur in der Weimarer Republik*, edited by I. Schneider. Tübingen: Gunter Narr Verlag.

Aulich, B. 1941. Mozart, Meister der Unterhaltungsmusik. *Reichsrundfunk* 41/42: 115.

————. 1942. Der Musikliebhaber und der Rundfukprogramm. *Reichsrundkfunk* 41/42: 84.

Bade, Klaus. 2000. *Europa in Bewegung: Migration vom späten 18. Jahrhundert bis zur Gegenwart.* Munich: Verlag C. H. Beck.

Bathrick, David. 1997. Making a National Family with the Radio: The Nazi *Wunschkonzert. Modernism/Modernity* 4 (1): 115–27.

Baumann, Max Peter. 1996. The Reflection of the Roma in European Art Music. *World of Music* 38 (1): 95–138.

Baumann, Zygmunt. 1989. *Modernity and the Holocaust.* Ithaca: Cornell University Press.

Bausch, Hans. 1956. *Der Rundfunk im politischen Kräftespiel der Weimarer Republik 1923–1933.* Tübingen: J. C. B. Mohr (Paul Siebeck).

Becher, Johannes R. 1931. Ballade von einem Bauernknecht, der Radio hörte. *Rundfunk Jahrbuch:* 319–20.

Bekker, Paul. 1912. *Beethoven.* Berlin: Schuster und Loeffler.

————. 1916. *Das deutsche Musikleben*. Berlin: Schuster und Loeffler.

Belach, Helga. 1979. . . . als die Traumfabrik kriegswichtig wurde. In *Wir tanzen um die Welt. Deutsche Revuefilme 1933–1945*, edited by H. Belach. Munich: Carl Hanser Verlag.

Benjamin, Walter. 1968. The Work of Art in the Age of Mechanical Reproduction. In *Illuminations: Essays and Reflections*. New York: Schocken Books.

————. 1977a. Paris, die Hauptstadt des XIX. Jahrhunderts. In *Illuminationen*. Frankfurt am Main: Suhrkamp Verlag.

Benz, Wolfgang. 1994. Das Lager Marzahn. Zur nationalsozialistischen Verfolgung der Sinti und Roma und ihre anhaltenden Diskriminierung. In *Die Normalität des Verbrechens. Bilanz und Perspektive der Forschung zu den nationalsozialistischen Gewaltverbrechen*, edited by H. Grabitz. Berlin: Edition Hentrich.

Berlant, Lauren. 1991. *The Anatomy of National Fantasy: Hawthorne, Utopia, and Everyday Life*. Chicago: University of Chicago Press.

————. 1993. National Brands/National Body: Imitation of Life. In *The Phantom Public Sphere*, edited by B. Robbins. Minneapolis: University of Minnesota Press.

————. 1997. *The Queen of America Goes to Washington City: Essays on Sex and Citizenship*. Durham: Duke University Press.

Berlin, Musikverlag CM Roehr. 1942. Wegweiser durch die Unterhaltungsliteratur: Vom Marschlied zur Operette. *Das Podium der Unterhaltungsmusik* 60 (2909): 7.

Berten, W. 1934. Schallplatte, Rundfunk, Tonfilm als Kulturträger. In *Das Atlantisbuch der Musik*, edited by F. Hamel and M. Hürlimann. Berlin: Atlantis Verlag.

Bertram, Otto. 1934. Heimat und Volkstum im deutschen Spielfilm. *Deutsche Film- und Funkwacht* 2 (6): 9–14.

Bhabha, Homi K. 1991. DissemiNation: Time, Narrative, and the Margins of the Modern Nation. In *Nation and Narration*, edited by H. Bhabha. London: Routledge.

Bie, Oskar. 1907. Intime Musik. In *Die Musik*, edited by R. Strauss. Leipzig: C. F. W. Siegel's Musikalienhandlung (R. Linnemann).

————. 1931. Ein Schlager reist um die Welt. *Die Woche* 27 (33): 863–64.

Blanke, Wilhelm. 1935. Hörst du richtig? Von der Kunst des wahren Rundfunkempfangens. *Rufer und Hörer* 4 (10/11): 438.

Blaukopf, Kurt. 1977. *Massenmedium Schallplatte*. Wiesbaden: Breitkopf und Härtel.

Block, Martin. 1997 [1936]. *Die Zigeuner: Ihr Leben und ihre Seele. Dargestellt auf Grund eigener Reisen und Forschungen*. Frankfurt am Main: Peter Lang.

Blume, Eva Maria. 1932. Der Schlager: Ein schädliches Zeitprodukt, das wir bekämpfen. *Volkswart*: 89–90.

———. 1932. Schlagerindustrie—Ein Blick hinter den Kulissen der Schlager-produktion. *Volkswart:* 166–67.

Boberach, Heinz, ed. 1984. *Meldungen aus dem Reich.* Herrsching: Paulak Verlag.

Bohlman, Philip. 1996. *Central European Folk Music. An Annotated Bibliography of Sources in German.* New York: Garland.

Bohlman, Philip, and Brian Currid. 2002. Suturing History, Healing Europe: German National Temporality in *Wolokolamsk Highway. Musical Quarterly* 85 (4).

Bohlman, Philip, and Ronald Radano. 2000. Introduction: Music and Race, Their Past, Their Presence. In *Music and the Racial Imagination*, edited by P. Bohlman and R. Radano. Chicago: University of Chicago Press.

Borchardt, B. 1927. Gemeinde und Radio. *Rundfunk-Rundschau* 2 (3): 42.

Born, Georgina, and David Hesmondhalgh, eds. 2000. *Western Music and Its Others: Difference, Representation, and Appropriation in Music.* Berkeley: University of California Press.

Bourdieu, Pierre. 1984. *Distinction. A Social Critique of the Judgement of Taste.* Translated by R. Nice. Cambridge: Harvard University Press.

Bóvis, Ferene. 1965. Zigeunermusizieren in Ungarn. In *Musik in Geschichte und Gegenwart*, edited by F. Blume. Kassel: Bärenreiter.

Bracher, Karl Dietrich. 1984. *The Age of Ideologies: A History of Political Thought in the Twentieth Century.* New York: St. Martin's Press.

Brachvogel, A. E. 1858. *Friedemann Bach.* Berlin: Globus Verlag.

Brecht, Bertholt. 1967 [1932]. Der Rundfunk als Kommunikationsapparat. In *Gesammelte Werke.* Frankfurt am Main: Suhrkamp Verlag.

Broszat, Martin. 1981. *The Hitler State: The Foundation and Development of the Internal Structure of the Third Reich.* London: Longman.

Brown, Julie. 2000. Bartók, the Gypsies and Hybridity in Music. In *Western Music and Its Others*, edited by G. Born and D. Hesmondhalgh. Berkeley: University of California Press.

Brückner, Hans. 1939. Kurmusik—im alten Gewände. *Der Deutsche Podium* 25: 1–2.

———. 1941. "Beschwingte Musik": Meisterwerke gespielt von Meistern. *Das Deutsche Podium* 9 (47): 2.

Brückner, Peter et al. 1976. Faschistische Öffentlichkeit. Diskussionsbeiträge und Stellungnahmen. *Ästhetik und Kommunkation* 7 (24): 20–51.

Brutz, Fritz 1925. Niedergang des musikalischen Kultur durch Radio. *Allegemeine Musikzeitung:* 635–36.

Buck-Morss, Susan. 1989. *The Dialectics of Seeing: Walter Benjamin and the Arcades Project.* Cambridge: MIT Press.

Burleigh, Michael, and Wolfgang Wipperman. 1991. *The Racial State: Germany 1933–1945.* Cambridge: Cambridge University Press.

Calhoun, Craig, ed. 1992. *Habermas and the Public Sphere*. Cambridge: MIT Press.

Cescotti, Diego. 1999. *Riccardo Zandonai: Catalogo tematico*. Lucca: Libreria Musicale Italiana Editrice.

Christensen, Thomas. 1999. Four-Hand Piano Transcription and Geographies of Nineteenth-Century Musical Reception. *Am Musicological Soc* 52 (2): 255–98.

Connor, Herbert. 1931. Die Schlagerindustrie im Rundfunk. *Die Weltbühne* 27 (21): 764–71.

———. 1931. Diktatur der GEMA. *Weltbühne* 27 (I): 764–71.

———. 1931. Schlagerclique dementiert. Schlagerindustrie im Rundfunk. *Weltbühne* 27 (2): 148–50.

———. 1932. Haben Schlager künstlerischen Wert? *Die Musik* 24: 749–53.

Currid, Brian. 1999. Das Lied einer Nacht: Filmschlager als Organe der Erfahrung. In *Als die Filme singen lernten: Innovation und Tradition im Musikfilm, 1928–1938*, edited by M. Hagener and J. Hans. München: edition text+kritik.

———. 2000. "Ain't I People?": Voicing National Fantasy. In *Music and the Racial Imagination*, edited by P. V. Bohlman and R. Radano. Chicago: University of Chicago Press.

Czada, Peter, and Günter Große. 1993. *Comedian Harmonists: ein Vokalensemble erobert die Welt*. Berlin: Edition Hentrich.

Dahl, Peter. 1978. *Arbeitersender und Volksempfänger: Radio-Bewegung und bürgerlicher Rundfunk bis 1945*. Frankfurt am Main: Syndikat.

Dahlhaus, Carl. 1978. *Die Idee der absoluten Musik*. Kassel: Bärenreiter.

Dahrendorf, Ralf. 1971 [1968]. *Gesellschaft und Demokratie in Deutschland*. Munich: dtv.

Danzi, Michael, and Rainer E. Lotz. 1986. *American Musician in Germany 1924–1939*. Schmitten: Norbert Rücker.

Davis, Simon Weil. 2000. *Living Up to the Ads: Gender Fictions of the 1920s*. Durham: Duke University Press.

Diller, Ansgar. 1980. *Rundfunkpolitik im Dritten Reich*. München: Deutscher Taschenbuch Verlag.

Doane, Mary Anne. 1985. The Voice in the Cinema: The Articulation of Body and Space. In *Film Sound: Theory and Practice*, edited by E. Weis and J. Belton. New York: Columbia University Press.

———. 1987. *The Desire to Desire: The Woman's Film of the 1940s*. Bloomington: Indiana University Press.

Döblin, Alfred. 1961. *Berlin Alexanderplatz*. Solothurn: Walter-Verlag.

Doegen, Wilhelm. 1931. Achtung! Wir senden jetzt Schallplatten. *Rundfunk-Rundschau* 6 (51): 2.

Dollenmayer, David B. 1988. *The Berlin Novels of Alfred Döblin*. Berkeley: University of California Press.

Döring, Hans-Joachim. 1964. *Die Zigeuner im nationalsozialistischen Staat*. Hamburg: Kriminalistik Verlag.

Drechsler, Nanny. 1988. *Die funktion der Musik im deutschen Rundfunk 1933–1945*. Pfaffenweiler: Centaurus-Verlagsgesellschaft.

Dryden, Konrad Claude. 1999. *Riccardo Zandonai: A Biography*. Frankfurt: Peter Lang.

Dümling, Albrecht. 1992. *Die verweigerte Heimat: Leon Jessel—der Komponist des "Schwarzwaldmädel."* Düsseldorf: Der Kleine Verlag.

———, ed. 1993. *Entartete Musik: Dokumentation und Kommentar zur Düsselforfer Ausstellung von 1938*. Düsseldorf: Der Kleine Verlag.

e. 1929. Auf Horchposten. *Rundfunk-Rundschau* 4 (39): 2.

Eley, Geoff. 1986. What Produces Fascism? Pre-Industrial Traditions or a Crisis of the Capitalist State. In *From Unification to Nazism: Reinterpreting the German Past*. Boston: Allen and Unwin.

Elster, A. 1931. Die Lautsprecher-, Rundfunk-, und Tonfilmmusikfrage. *Juristische Wochenschrift* 60: 1866.

Engbring-Romang, Udo. 2001. *Die Verfolgung der Sinti und Roma in Hessen zwischen 1870 und 1950*. Frankfurt: Brandes & Appelt.

Ewens, Franz Josef. 1942. Beschwingte Musik, eine neuer Begriff. *Volksmusik, Ausgabe B* 7 (5): 81.

Ferber, Christian, ed. 1982. *Berliner Illustrirte Zeitung: Zeitbild, Chronik, Moritat für Jedermann 1892–1945*. Berlin: Ullstein Verlag.

Fings, Karola, and Frank Sparing. 1992. 'z. Zt. Zigeunerlager': Die Verfolgung der Düsseldorfer Sinti und Roma im Nationalsozialismus. Cologne: Volksblatt Verlag.

Finkelstein, Norman G. 2000. *The Holocaust Industry: Reflections of the Exploitation of Jewish Suffering*. New York: Verso.

Foucault, Michel. 1972. *The Archaeology of Knowledge and the Discourse on Language*. Translated by A. M. S. Smith. New York: Pantheon.

———. 1984. *The History of Sexuality. An Introduction*. New York: Vintage.

———. 1991. Governmentality. In *The Foucault Effect*, edited by Graham Burchell, Colin Gordon, and Peter Miller. Chicago: University of Chicago Press.

Friedrich, Julius. 1936. Der Jude als Musikfabrikant. *Die Musik* 28 (6): 428–30.

Gehrke, Martha Maria. 1984. Das Ende der privaten Sphäre. In *Radio-Kultur in der Weimarer Republik*, edited by I. Schneider. Tübingen: Gunter Narr Verlag.

Gerigk, Herbert. 1933. Die Unterhaltungsmusik im Rundfunkprogramm. *Die Musik* 26 (1): 13–18.

Gilman, Sander L. 1988. Strauss and the Pervert. In *Reading Opera*. Edited by A. Groos and R. Parker. Princeton: Princeton University Press.

Gledhill, Christine. 1991. Signs of Melodrama. In *Stardom: Industry of Desire*, edited by C. Gledhill. London: Routledge.

Goedecke, Heinz, and Wilhelm Krug. 1941. *Wir beginnen das Wunschkonzert für die Wehrmacht*. Berlin: Niebelungen Verlag.

Goldhagen, Daniel. 1996. *Hitler's Willing Executioners: Ordinary Germans and the Holocaust*. New York: Alfred A. Knopf.

Götzfried, F. 1943. Tanz- und Jazzmusik ist zweierlei. *Das Deutsche Podium, Podium der Unterhaltungsmusik* 60 (42): 393.

Graener, Paul. 1938. Gegen den Schlager. *Die Musik* 31 (2): 112.

Großmann-Vendrey, Susanna. 1997. Rundfunk und etabliertes Musikleben. In *Programmgeschichte des Hörfunks in der Weimarer Republik*, edited by J.-F. Leonhard. Munich: Deutscher Taschenbuch Verlag.

Günther, Felix. 1930. Schlager. *Die Musik* 23 (2):105–7.

Habermas, Jürgen. 1990. *Strukturwandel der Öffentlichheit*. Frankfurt am Main: Suhrkamp.

Hake, Sabine. 1987. Girls and Crisis: The Other Side of Diversion. *New German Critique* 40.

———. 1997. The Melodramatic Imagination of Detlef Sierck: Final Chord and Its Resonances. *Screen* 38 (2): 129–48.

Halefeldt, Horst O. 1990. Das erste Medium für alle? Erwartungen an den Hörfunk in Deutschland Anfang der 20er Jahre. In *Runfunk und Fernsehen 1948–1989*, edited by Hans-Bredow-Institut. Baden-Baden: Nomos Verlagsgesellschaft.

———. 1997. Sendegesellschaften und Rundfunkordnungen. In *Programmgeschichte des Hörfunks in der Weimarer Republik*, edited by J.-F. Leonhard. Munich: Deutscher Taschenbuch Verlag.

Hansen, Miriam. 1991a. Decentric Perspectives: Kracauer's Early Writing on Film and Mass Culture. *New German Critique* 54.

———. 1991b. *Babel and Babylon: Spectatorship in American Film*. Cambridge: Harvard University Press.

Hansen, Miriam Bratu. 1995. America, Paris, the Alps: Kracauer (and Benjamin) on Cinema and Modernity. In *Cinema and the Invention of Modern Life*, edited by L. Charney and V. R. Schwartz. Berkeley: University of California Press.

Hardt, Michael, and Antonio Negri. 2000. *Empire*. Cambridge: Harvard University Press.

Hehemann, Rainer. 1987. *"Die Bekämpfung des Zigeunerunwesens" in Wilhelminischen Deutschland und in der Weimarer Republik*. Frankfurt am Main: Haag und Herchen Verlag.

Heister, Hanns Werner, ed. 1984. *Musik und Musikpolitik im faschistischen Deutschland*. Frankfurt am Main: Fischer Verlag.

Heister, Hanns-Werner. 1983. *Das Konzert. Theorie einer Kulturform*. Wilhelmshaven: Heinrichhofen's Verlag.

Hemetek, Ursula. 1993. Musik als Ausdruck der Identität: Roma and Sinti in

Österreich. In *Musik & Jahrbuch Nr. 1. Der Hochschule für Musik und Darstellende Kunst in Wien*, edited by H. Schwarz. Vienna: Löcker Verlag.

Hille, Willi. 1933. Nationalisierung der deutschen Musik. *Die Musik* 25 (9): 666–69.

Hobsbawm, E. J. 1983. "Mass Producing Traditions: Europe 1870–1914." In *The Invention of Tradition*. Cambridge: Cambridge University Press.

———. 1990. *Nations and Nationalism since 1780*. Cambridge: Cambridge University Press.

Hohmann, Joachim S. 1980. Zigeunermythos und Vorurteil. In *Zigeunerleben: Beiträge zur Sozialgeschichte einer Verfolgung*, edited by Hohmann and R. Schopf. Darmstadt: ms edition.

———. 1981. *Geschichte der Zigeunerverfolgung in Deutschland*. Frankfurt am Main: Campus Verlag.

———. 1990. *Verfolgte ohne Heimat. Geschichte der Zigeuner in Deutschland*. Frankfurt am Main: Peter Lang.

Horkheimer, Maz, and Theodor W. Adorno. 1969. *Dialektik der Aufklärung*. Frankfurt am Main: Fischer Taschenbuch Verlag.

Hull, David Stewart. 1969. *Film in the Third Reich*. Berkeley: University of California Press.

Huyssen, Andreas. 1986. Mass Culture as Woman: Modernism's Other. In *Across the Great Divide: Modernism, Mass Culture, Postmodernism*. Bloomington: Indiana University Press.

Jameson, Frederic. 1981. *The Political Unconscious*. Ithaca: Cornell University Press.

Jary, Micaela. 1993. *Ich weiß, es wird einmal ein Wunder gescheh'n*. Berlin: edition q.

John, Eckhard. 1994. *Musik-Bolschewismus: Die Politisierung der Musik in Deutschland, 1918–1938*. Stuttgart: J. B. Metzler Verlag.

Johnson, James H. 1992. Musical Experience and the Formation of a French Musical Public. *J Modern Hist* 64: 191–26.

———. 1995. *Listening in Paris: A Cultural History*. Berkeley: University of California Press.

Jung, Uli, and Walter Schatzberg, eds. 1992. *Filmkultur zur Zeit der Weimarer Republik*. München: K. G. Saur.

Kater, Michael. 1997. *The Twisted Muse: Musicians and Their Music in the Third Reich*. Oxford: Oxford University Press.

Kater, Michael H. 1992. *Different Drummers: Jazz in the Culture of Nazi Germany*. Oxford: Oxford University Press.

Kayser, Dietrich. 1975. *Schlager: Das Lied als Ware*. Stuttgart: Metzler.

Kershaw, Ian. 1984. *Popular Opinion and Political Dissent in the Third Reich*. Oxford: Oxford University Press.

———. 1985. *The Nazi Dictatorship: Problems and Perspectives of Interpretation.* London: Arnold.

Keun, Irmgard. 1979 [1932]. *Das kunstseidene Mädchen.* Düsseldorf: dtv.

Kirchner, Joachim. 1962. *Das deutsche Zeitschriftenwesen. Seine Geschichte und seine Probleme.* Vol. 2. Wiesbaden: Otto Harrassowitz.

Kittler, Friedrich. 1990. *Discourse Networks 1800/1900.* Translated by Michael Metteer with Chris Cullens. Standford: Stanford University Press.

Klaus, Ulrich. 1996. *Deutsche Tonfilme.* Vol. 7 (1936). Berlin: Klaus Archiv.

Koch, Gertrud. 1988. Von Detlef Sierck zu Douglas Sirk. *Frauen und Film* (44/45).

Koeppen, Wolfgang C. 1934. Rundfunk im Hause—Rundfunk im Heim. *Rufer und Hörer* 4 (3): 103–5.

Kracauer, Siegfried. 1947. *From Caligari to Hitler.* Princeton: Princeton University Press.

———. 1971 [1930]. *Die Angestellten.* Frankfurt am Main: Suhrkamp Verlag.

———. 1974. Unter den Dächern von Paris. In *Kino.* Frankfurt: Suhrkamp Verlag.

———. 1995. Boredom. In *The Mass Ornament.* Cambridge: Harvard University Press.

———. 1995. *The Mass Ornament.* Translated by T. Y. Levin. Cambridge: Harvard University Press.

Kruger, Loren. 1992. *The National Stage: Theatre and Cultural Legitimation in England, France, and America.* Chicago: University of Chicago Press.

Lacey, Kate. 1996. *Feminine Frequencies: Gender, German Radio and the Public Sphere, 1923–1945.* Ann Arbor: University of Michigan Press.

Laclau, Ernesto. 1977. *Politics and Ideology in Marxist Theory: Capitalism, Fascism, Populism.* London: NLB.

———. 1990. *New Reflections on the Revolution of Our Time.* London: Verso.

Laclau, Ernesto, and Chantal Mouffe. 1985. *Hegemony and Socialist Strategy: Towards a Radical Democratic Politics.* London: Verso.

Lange, Horst. 1966. *Jazz in Deutschland: die deutsche Jazz-Chronik 1900–1960.* Berlin: Colloquium Verlag.

Lastra, James. 2000. *Sound Technology and the American Cinema: Perception, Representation, Modernity.* New York: Columbia University Press.

Leander, Zarah. 1973. *Es war so wunderbar!* Hamburg: Hoffman und Campe.

Leiser, Erwin. 1974. *Nazi Cinema.* New York: Collier.

Lerg, Winfried. 1980. Rundfunkpolitik in der Weimarer Republik. In *Rundfunk in Deutschland,* edited by H. Bausch. Munich: Deutscher Taschenbuch Verlag.

Lerg, Winfried B. 1965. *Die Entstehung des Rundfunks in Deutschland: Herkunft und Entwicklung eines publizistischen Mittels.* Frankfurt am Main: Josef Knecht.

Levi, Erik. 1994. *Music in the Third Reich.* New York: St. Martin's Press.

Levin, Thomas Y. 1990. For the Record: Adorno on Music in the Age of Its Technical Reproducibility. *October* 55: 23–47.

Lewy, Gunter. 2000. *The Nazi Persecution of the Gypsies.* Oxford: Oxford University Press.

Liszt, Franz. 1910. *Die Zigeuner und ihre Musik in Ungarn. Gesammelte Schriften, Volume 3.* Leipzig: Breitkopf & Härtel.

Lowry, Stephen. 1991. *Pathos und Politik: Ideologie in Spielfilmen des Nationalsozialismus.* Tübingen: Niemeyer.

Lucassen, Leo. 1996. *Zigeuner. Die Geschichte eines polizeilichen Ordnungsbegriffes in Deutschland, 1700–1945.* Cologne: Böhlau Verlag.

———. 1997. Eternal Vagrants? State Formation, Migration, and Traveling Groups in Western-Europe, 1350–1914. In *Migration, Migration History, History: Old Paradigms and New Perspectives,* edited by J. Lucassen and L. Lucassen. New York: Peter Lang.

Lüdtke, Alf. 1991. Einleitung: Herrschaft als soziale Praxis. In *Herrschaft als soziale Praxis,* edited by A. Lüdtke. Göttingen: Vandenhoeck & Ruprecht.

Lüdtke, Alf, ed. 1992. *Sicherheit, und Wohlfahrt: Polizei, Gesellschaft und Herrschaft im 19. und 20. Jahrhundert.* Frankfurt: Suhrkamp Verlag.

Maciejewski, Franz. 1996. Elemente des Antiziganismus. In *Die gesellschaftliche Konstruktion des Zigeuners,* edited by J. Giere. Frankfurt/New York: Campus Verlag.

Marckwardt, Wilhelm. 1982. *Die Illustrierten der Weimarer Zeit. Publizistische Funktion, ökonomische Entwicklung und inhaltliche Tendenzen.* Munich: Minerva Publikation.

Marßolek, Inge, and Adelheid von Saldern. 1998. Das Radio als historisches und historiographisches Medium. Eine Einführung. In *Zuhören und Gehörtwerden I: Radio im Nationalsozialismus. Zwischen Lenkung und Ablenkung,* edited by I. Marßolek and A. v. Saldern. Tübingen: edition diskord.

———. 1998. *Zuhören und Gehörtwerden I.* Tübingen: edition diskord.

Mason, Tim. 1995. *Nazism, Fascism and the Working Class.* Cambridge: Cambridge University Press.

McCracken, Allison. 2001. Real Men Don't Sing Ballads: The Radio Crooner in Hollywood, 1929–1933. In *Soundtrack Available: Essays on Film and Popular Music,* edited by P. R. Wojcik and A. Knight. Durham: Duke University Press.

Meier, John. 1906. *Kunstlieder im Volksmunde: Materialien und Untersuchungen.* Halle: Max Niemeyer.

Mersmann, Hans. 1931. Schlagerplatte und Persönlichkeit. *Melos* 10 (1): 19.

Mertens, Eberhard. 1995. *Die großen deutsche Filme: Ausgewählte Filmprogramme 1930–1945.* Hildesheim: Olms Presse.

Milton, Sybil. 1994. Antechamber to Birkenau: The Zigeunerlager after 1933.

In *Die Normalität des Verbrechens*, edited by H. Grabitz, K. Bästlein, and J. Tüchel. Berlin: Edition Hentrich.

Mizejewski, Linda. 1992. *Divine Decadence: Fascism, Female Spectacle, and the Making of Sally Bowles*. Princeton: Princeton University Press.

Moll, P. 1937. Vom Niggerjazz z. Zigeunergulasch. *Orchester-Magazin* VIII (6): 4–10.

Mosse, George L. 1975. *The Nationalization of the Masses: Political Symbolism and Mass Movements in Germany from the Napoleonic Wars through the Third Reich*. New York: H. Fertig.

———. 1985. *Nationalism and Sexuality*. Madison: University of Wisconsin Press.

Mühr, Alfred. 1984. *Mephisto ohne Maske. Gustaf Gründgens, Legende und Wahrheit*. Munich: Knaur.

Mungo. 1938. Arisierung der Gefühle. *Musik in Jugend und Volk*.

Nantonek, Hans. 1929. Könige des Schlagers. *Leipziger Illustrirte Zeitung* 172 (4394): 790.

Negt, Oskar, and Alexander Kluge. 1972. *Öffentlichkeit und Erfahrung: Zur Organisationsanalyse von bürgerlicher und proletarischer Öffentlichkeit*. Frankfurt am Main: Suhrkamp Verlag.

———. 1981. *Geschichte und Eigensinn*. Frankfurt: Zweitausendeins.

Niethammer, Lutz, ed. 1983. *Die Jahre weiss man nicht wo man die heute hinsetzen soll*. Vol. 1, *Faschismus Erfahrungen im Ruhrgebiet*. Berlin/Bonn: Dietz.

Novick, Peter. 1999. *The Holocaust in American Life*. New York: Houghton Mifflin Company.

Pater, Monika. 1998. Rundfunkangebote. In *Zuhören und Gehörtwerden I*, edited by I. Marßolek and A. v. Saldern. Tübingen: edition diskord.

Peters, John Durham. 1999. *Speaking into the Air: A History of the Idea of Communication*. Chicago: University of Chicago Press.

Petro, Patrice. 1987. Modernity and Mass Culture in Weimar: Contours of a Discourse on Sexuality in Early Theories of Perception and Representation. *New German Critique* (40): 115–46.

———. 1989. *Joyless Streets: Women and Melodramatic Representation in Weimar Germany*. Princeton: Princeton University Press.

Peukert, Detlev. 1987. Alltag und Barbarei. In *Ist der Nationalsozialismus Geschichte?*, edited by D. Diner. Frankfurt am Main: Fischer Taschenbuch Verlag.

———. 1987. *Inside Nazi Germany: Conformity, Oppostion, and Racism in Everyday Life*. New Haven: Yale University Press.

———. 1989. *The Weimar Republic*. Translated by R. Deveson. New York: Hill and Wang.

Plessner, Helmuth. 1974 [1959]. *Die verspätete Nation*. Frankfurt: Suhrkamp.

Pohle, Heinz. 1955. *Der Rundfunk als Instrument der Politik. Zur Geschichte des deutchen Rundfunks von 1923–1938*. Hamburg: Verlag Hans-Bredow-Institut.

Polster, Bernd, ed. 1989. *"Swing Heil": Jazz im Nationalsozialismus*. Berlin: Transit.

Postone, Moishe. 1993. *Time, Labor, and Social Domination: A Reinterpretation of Marx's Critical Theory*. Cambridge: Cambridge University Press.

Potter, Pamela M. 1998. *Most German of the Arts: Musicology and Society from the Weimar Republic to the End of Hitler's Reich*. New Haven: Yale University Press.

Potter, Pamela M. and Celia Applegate, eds. 2002. *Music and German National Identity*. Chicago: University of Chicago Press.

Poulantzas, Nicos. 1974. *Fascism and Dictatorship*. London: NLB.

———. 1978. *State, Power, Socialism*. Translated by P. Camiller. London: NLB.

Pringsheim, Klaus. 1927. Mehr Rücksicht! *Rundfunk-Rundschau* 2 (15): 288–89.

Prost, Antonine, and Gérard Vincent, eds. 1987. *Histoire de la vie privée: De la Première Guerre mondiale à nous jours*. Paris: Editions du Seuil.

Raabe, Peter. 1942. Neugestaltung des Rundfunkprogramms. *Amtliche Mitteilungen der Reichsmusikkammer* 9 (3): 1.

Radano, Ronald. 2000. Hot Fantasies: American Modernism and the Idea of Black Rhythm. In *Music and the Racial Imagination*, edited by R. Radano and P. Bohlman. Chicago: University of Chicago Press.

———. 1996. Denoting Difference: The Writing of the Slave Spirituals. *Critical Inquiry* 22: 506–44.

Rentschler, Eric. 1996. *The Ministry of Illusion: Nazi Cinema and Its Afterlife*. Cambridge: Harvard University Press.

Resch, Robert Paul. 1992. *Althusser and the Renewal of Marxist Social Theory*. Berkeley: University of California Press.

Ritzel, Fred. 1995. '. . . vom Paradies ein gold'ner Schein'—Schlagerpräsentationen im Tonfilm der Weimarer Republik. In *"Es liegt in der Luft was idiotisches . . ." Populäre Musik zur Zeit der Weimarer Republik*, edited by H. Rösing. Baden-Baden: CODA Musikservice/Arbeitskreis Studium populärer Musik.

Robinson, J. Bradford. 1994. The Jazz Essays of Theodor Adorno: Some Notes on Jazz Reception in Weimar Germany. *Popular Music* 13 (1): 1–25.

s. 1929. Hörer und Hindemith. *Rundfunk-Rundschau* 4 (47): 2.

Saldern, Adelheid von. 1995. *Häuserleben: Zur Geschichte städtischen Arbeiterwohnens vom Kaiserreich bis heute*. Bonn: Verlag J. H. W. Dietz Nachfolger.

Saldern, Adelheid von et al. 1998. Zur politischen und kulturellen Polyvalenz des Radios: Ergebnisse und Ausblicke. In *Zuhören und Gehörtwerden I*, edited by I. Marßolek and A. v. Saldern. Tübingen: edition diskord.

Sárosi, Bálint. 1978. *Gypsy Music*. Budapest: Corvina Press.

Schäfer, Hans Dieter. 1983. Das gespaltene Bewußtsein. Deutsche Kultur und Lebenswirklichkeit 1933–1945. In *Das gespaltene Bewußtsein*. Frankfurt am Main: Ullstein Sachbuch.

Schär, Christian. 1991. *Der Schlager und seine Tänze in Deutschland.* Zürich: Nomos Verlag.

Schenk, Michael. 1994. *Rassismus gegen Sinti und Roma: Zur Kontinuität der Zigeunerverfolgung innerhalb der deutschen Gesellschaft von der Weimarer Republik bis in die Gegenwart.* Frankfurt am Main: Peter Lang.

Schiepe, Hans. 1939. Johann Sebastian Bach als Filmkompanist. *Die Musik* 31 (6).

Schlüter, Hinrich. 1936. Neue Schallplatten: Zu Unterhaltung und Tanz. *Die Musik* 28 (5): 377–80.

Schmidt, Uta C. 1998. Radioaneignung. In *Zuhören und Gehörtwerden II: Radio in der DDR der fünfziger Jahre. Zwischen Lenkung und Ablenkung,* edited by A. v. Saldern and I. Marßolek. Tübingen: edition diskord.

Schoenbaum, David. 1966. *Hitler's Social Revolution: Class and Status in Nazi Germany, 1933–1939.* Garden City, N.Y.: Doubleday.

Schröder, H. 1990. *Tanz und Unterhaltungsmusik in Deutschland 1918–1933.* Bonn: Verlag für systematische Wissenschaft.

Schulte-Sasse, Linda. 1996. *Entertaining the Third Reich.* Durham: Duke University Press.

Schumacher, Renate. 1997. Programmstruktur und Tagesablauf der Hörer. In *Programmgeschichte des Hörfunks in der Weimarer Republik,* edited by J.-F. Leonhard. Munich: Deutscher Taschenbuch Verlag.

———. 1997. Radio als Medium und Faktor des akutellen Geschehens. In *Programmgeschichte des Hörfunks in der Weimarer Republik,* edited by J.-F Leonhard. Munich: Deutscher Taschenbuch Verlag.

Seitler, Dana. 2000. Degenerate America: Biomedicalization and the Technology of Abnormal Personhood in Modern American Culture. Ph.D. diss., English Languages and Literature, University of Chicago, Chicago.

Sennett, Richard. 1976. *The Fall of Public Man.* New York: W. W. Norton and Company.

Silberman, Marc. 1995. *German Cinema: Texts in Context.* Detroit: Wayne State University Press.

Sohn-Rethel, Alfred. 1973. *Ökonomie und Klassenstruktur des deutschen Faschismus.* Frankfurt am Main: Suhrkamp Verlag.

Sonnen, Otto. 1931. Was ist ein Schlager? *Allgemeine Musik-Zeitung* 58 (40).

Soppe, August. 1993. *Rundfunk in Frankfurt am Main 1923–1926: Zur Organisations-, Programm-und Rezeptionsgeschichte eines neuen Mediums.* Munich: K. G. Saur.

Spigel, Lynn. 1992. Make Room for TV: Television and the Family Ideal in Postwar America. Chicago: University of Chicago Press.

Stapper, Michael. 2001. *Unterhaltungsmusik im Rundfunk der Weimarer Republik.* Tutzing: Hans Schneider.

Stein, Gerhard. 1940. Zur Physiologie und Anthropologie der Zigeuner in Deutschland. *Zeitschrift für Ethnologie* 72 (1–3): 74–113.

Stoffels, Ludwig. 1997. Sendeplätze für Kunst und Unterhaltung. In *Programm-geschichte des Hörfunks in der Weimarer Republik*, edited by J.-F. Leonhard. Munich: Deutscher Taschenbuch Verlag.

Streck, Bernhard. 1979. Die 'Bekämpfung des Zigeunerunwesens': Ein Stück moderner Rechtsgeschichte. In *In Auschwitz vergast, bis heute verfolgt. Zur Situation der Roma in Deutschland und Europa*, edited by T. Zülch. Reinbek bei Hamburg: Rowohlt.

Strorek, Henning. 1972. *Dirigierte Öffentlichkeit: Die Zeitung als Herrschafts-mittel in den Anfangsjahren der nationalsozialistischen Regierung*, Opladen: Westdeutscher Verlag.

Tergit, Gabriele. 1978. *Käsebier erobert den Kurfürstendamm*. Berlin: Das Neue Berlin.

Traubner, Richard. 1998. Operette als Stoff und Anregung. Enwicklungen im Musikfilm 1907–1937. In *Musik Spektakel Film: Musiktheater und Tanzkul-tur im deutschen Film 1922–1937*. Munich: edition text + kritik.

Trumpener, Katie. 1992. The Time of the Gypsies: A "People without His-tory" in the Narratives of the West. *Critical Inquiry* 18 (4): 843–84.

———. 1994. Puerto Rico Fever. Douglas Sirk, La Habanera (1937) and the Epistemology of Exoticism. In *Neue Welt/Dritte Welt*, edited by S. Bau-schinger and S. Cocalis. Tübingen: Franche Verlag.

———. 2000. Bela Bartók and the Rise of Comparative Ethnomusicology: Nationalism, Race Purity, and the Legacy of the Austro-Hungarian Empire. In *Music and the Racial Imagination*, edited by R. Radano and P. V. Bohl-man. Chicago: University of Chicago Press.

Vogt, Guntram. 2001. *Die Stadt im Film. Deutsche Spielfilme 1900–2000*. Mar-burg: Schüren Presseverlag.

Wachenfeld. 1939. Aushändigung von Ausweiskarten der Reichsmusikkam-mer an Zigeuner VII 5370/38. *Amtliche Mitteilungen der Reichsmusikkam-mer* 6 (9): 30–31.

Wallerstein, Immanuel. 1991. The Construction of "Peoplehood": Racism, Nationalism, Ethnicity. In *Race, Class, Nation: Ambiguous Identities*, edited by E. Balibar and I. Wallerstein. London: Verso.

Warner, Michael. 1992. The Mass Public and The Mass Subject. In *Haber-mas and the Public Sphere*, edited by C. Calhoun. Cambridge: MIT Press.

Warner, Michael. 2002. *Publics and Counterpublics*. New York: Zone Books.

Weber, William. 1975. *Music and the Middle Class: The Social Structure of Con-cert Life in London, Paris, and Vienna*. New York: Holmes and Meier.

Weidemann, Alfred. 1942. Unterhaltende Musik klassische Meister. *Das Podium der Unterhalutngsmusik* 60 (2909): 2–4.

Weiner, Marc A. 1993. *Undertones of Insurrection: Music, Politics, and the Social Sphere in the Modern German Narrative*. Lincoln: University of Nebraska Press.

wher. 1938. Nie gesehen–und doch bekannt! Der Rundfunk und die Sehnsucht nach der weiten Welt. *Die Sendung* 15 (1): 3–4.

Wicke, Peter. 1987. Das Ende: Populäre Musik im faschistischen Deutschland. In *Ich will aber gerade vom Leben singen* . . . Reinbek bei Hamburg: Rowohlt.

Wippermann, Wolfgang. 1986. *Das Leben in Frankfurt zur NS-Zeit.* Vol. 2. *Die nationalsozialistische Zigeunerverfolgung.* Frankfurt: W. Kramer.

Witte, Karsten. 1995. *Lachende Erben, toller Tag: Filmkomödie im Dritten Reich.* Berlin: Verlag Vorwerk 8.

Worbs, H. C. 1963. Der Schlager. In *Die Musik in Geschichte und Gegenwart,* edited by F. Blume. Kassel: Bärenreiter.

Wulff, A. 1934. 500 Berliner Volksschulkinder erzählen vom Radio. *Rufer und Hörer* 4 (3): 113–25.

Zimmermann, Michael. 1996. *Rassenutopie und Genozid: die nationalsozialistische "Lösung der Zigeunerfrage."* Hamburg: Hans Christians Verlag.

Žižek, Slavoj. 1989. *The Sublime Object of Ideology.* London: Verso.

———. 1994. The Spectre of Ideology. In *Mapping Ideology,* edited by S. Žižek. New York: Verso.

———. 1995. "I Hear You with My Eyes"; or, The Invisible Master. In *Gaze and Voice as Love Objects,* edited by R. Sglecl and S. Žižek. Durham: Duke University Press.

———. 2001. *Did Somebody Say Totalitarianism? Five Interventions in the (Mis)use of a Notion.* London: Verso.

Zweig, Arnold. 1927. Rundfunk und Aesthetik. *Rundfunk-Rundschau* 2 (12): 226.

Index

Brian Currid has published widely in German and English on topics including house music, world beat, and popular music and film. He has taught music and media studies at universities in Germany and the United States and now is a freelance writer and translator in Berlin.